PRAISE FOR *THE GOD ASK*

MW01013138

"Steve Shadrach's *The God Ask* is destined to be one of the classic rock-solid books on raising personal support. Every Christian worker and missions executive needs to include this book in their support raising training curriculum. As Steve says, we are mobilizing people, not money. *The God Ask* will help you adjust your lens of faith so that you can clearly see that God's net worth has not changed since the day of creation, and He is committed to funding His mission."

ELLIS F. GOLDSTEIN – National Director, Ministry Partner Development for Cru, the U.S. ministry of Campus Crusade for Christ

"Full of practical tools and biblical foundations, *The God Ask* turns our focus away from our fears and toward faith in God's abundance. Shadrach inspires us toward excellence, courage, and humility. A must-have resource for anyone engaged in support raising!"

TOM LIN – Vice President and Director of Urbana, InterVarsity Christian Fellowship

"Myself and hundreds of our FCA staff have been impacted by Steve's inspiring ways to raise funds to advance God's kingdom. Unlock the vault for God's blessings for you and your ministry. Read this book!"

COACH LES STECKEL – President/CEO, Fellowship of Christian Athletes

"Asking for support is an aspect of ministry many Christian workers don't look forward to. Steve Shadrach takes the edge off of what may be the tensest moment for a future servant of God. It is biblical and influenced by his many years in ministry."

TOMMY NELSON – Senior Pastor, Denton Bible Church

"After twenty-five years of living on support, I finally got trained by Steve in this material and realized how much I was doing wrong! Steve's practical suggestions and challenging perspectives produce results. I always recommend his Bootcamp for those going into full-time Christian work. Now it's in written form! This is a must-read for every person who seeks to raise their support to serve the King!"

BOB SJOGREN – President, UnveilinGLORY

"Steve Shadrach's *The God Ask* is outstanding and engaging. He builds a sound biblical basis for raising personal support for ministry. Shadrach's own study and experience as a "faith missionary" makes the book captivating. *The God Ask* is integral to the vision of funding and clearly practical in what our part is and how it works. Everyone in ministry needs to read this book. If every Christian read this book, there would be plenty of money to support God's purposes throughout the world."

DENNIS GAYLOR – Former National Director, Chi Alpha Campus Ministries, USA

"A must-read for every missionary. Steve trumpets the clear truth that God will fully fund every bit of your calling you are willing to trust Him for. Then he shows you how. He gives the deep, biblical foundation for realizing God's provision, but also the proven, practical steps to enable anyone — even an introvert like me — to do their part in confidently seeing that provision become a reality."

MIKE D. RIGGINS – Missionary Deployment Coordinator, North American Mission Board, SBC

"*The God Ask* is biblical, practical, and relevant. It will revolutionize your walk and your work in building and sustaining your partnership development team so you can have maximum impact in your life, family, and ministry!"

ADAM DEMARK – Director of Development, New Tribes Mission USA

"I have known Steve Shadrach for more than twenty-five years, and he has always focused on getting the gospel to more and more people around the world. He has a passion and commitment to train workers with excellent God-centered tools for funding their ministry. These tools have benefited Christian workers around the world, including many with Campus Outreach. *The God Ask* is one excellent resource."

MIKE HEARON – Global Resource Team, Campus Outreach

"We send all our church planters to Steve's personal support raising training. In *The God Ask,* Steve equips, empowers, and inspires you. He's thought through every detail of what you need to do. If you're only going to read one book on support raising, *The God Ask* is a must-read!"

DR. BOB ROWLEY – Evangelical Free Church of America

"I have read this book twice already. I can't get enough. You will walk away saying, *Please Lord, allow me the honor of raising support.*"

DR. TODD AHREND – International Director, The Traveling Team

"Every person on earth needs to encounter Jesus Christ and the salvation He alone offers. This means the world needs workers for the harvest who are fully converted, fully trained and fully funded. Steve Shadrach, in *The God Ask,* provides a deeply biblical and powerfully convincing call for those who are sent into mission to never go alone. Called by God and accompanied by Him, we will be fully equipped when we have the prayers and full financial support we need to share the gospel without reserve."

CURTIS MARTIN – Founder & President, FOCUS

The
GOD ASK

STEVE SHADRACH

Published by Via Nations
P.O. Box 3556
Fayetteville, AR 72702
For more support raising resources, visit ViaGenerosity.org

Translations
We desire to make this material available to as many as will use it around the world
in a way that honors everyone involved in the work. If you would like to translate or
adapt this resource to use in your cultural context, we are very open to collaborating
with you. Please contact us at info@vianations.org.

Dedicated to my
friends and co-laborers:

SCOTT MORTON
of The Navigators

ELLIS GOLDSTEIN
of Cru, the U.S. Ministry of Campus Crusade for Christ

DONNA WILSON
of InterVarsity Christian Fellowship

BETTY BARNETT
of Youth With A Mission

MIKE RIGGINS
of North American Mission Board (SBC)

A host of other faithful men and women
who have helped fulfill the Great Commission
by training generations of Christian workers
how to launch their ministries and raise
their personal support.

"O God, for Your glory,
flood the nations with spiritually
healthy, vision-driven, fully funded
Great Commission workers."

The

GOD ASK

*On the day I called,
You answered me;
You made me bold
with strength in my soul.*

Psalm 138:3

Being fully prepared is essential before you begin support raising

 &  **Support Raising Bootcamp™**

The God Ask and Support Raising Bootcamp go hand-in-hand in preparing you for your support raising journey. Our Bootcamps are collaborative training experiences designed to fully equip and prepare you to get to your ministry assignment quickly and fully funded.

 ## Register today.

ViaGenerosity.org/Bootcamp

Table of
CONTENTS

FOREWORD

Steve Shadrach has hit a home run with *The God Ask*!
As I read *The God Ask*, I realized this book is more than a book — it is a life message of a dedicated gospel practitioner! The more I read, the more intrigued I became. Without realizing it, I began thinking of people to ask for support this year — this week! And I was inspired to minister more deeply to my giving partners.

That is a mark of a good book — it stimulates readers not merely to think something or *feel* something, but it promotes doing something!

Steve is a gifted "inspirer." But *The God Ask* will do more than inspire. Whether you are launching out in raising ministry support or whether you are a veteran, this book gives you practical tools to succeed. What is more, TheGodAsk.org/Resources will help you with worksheets on namestorming, action plans, a Bible study, and a resource list if you hit a snag. Steve is not merely a theorist who thinks this stuff *might* work! He has simply written what he has practiced for years.

But one more thing — the biblical basis. Strong biblical roots undergird the tactics Steve suggests. Steve's approaches are directly connected to biblical principles and examples from Jesus, Paul, Nehemiah, and others. Be prepared to encounter Bible leaders who struggled with the same challenges you have.

Thank you, Steve, for *The God Ask*. And God bless you, my Christian worker friend, as you pursue the ministry of fundraising — it is a gospel issue.

Scott Morton
International Funding Coach
The Navigators

The
GOD ASK

↑

Section I

UNLEASHED!

Jesus has paved the way and opened the door. Let's walk through it together.

The
BUTTON

Growing up as the son of a businessman in Dallas, Texas had advantages and disadvantages. Because Dad had lived through the Great Depression years, he instilled his "pull-yourself-up-by-your-bootstraps" perspective into his three sons — of whom I was the middle. Work hard, provide for your family, and retire early were the values he modeled to us. My two industrious brothers majored in business with the goal of becoming millionaires by age thirty. We all assumed I, too, would follow suit into the work world to obtain the "American Dream" and the accompanying financial security. But I came to Christ and felt called into full-time service. After four years as a college minister at a local church, I launched out to start a new campus ministry organization and, of course, raise my support.

Early on, my dad and I both had to overcome the societal norm that asking for support was a disguised form of begging. It didn't help that we had often observed underfunded Christian workers who appeared to us as impoverished nomads. I would have definitely benefited from a book like this to help shape my support raising philosophy in those early days. So, with only a calling from the Lord and a vision for ministry, I took stock of my "possessions": enough money to last us six weeks, a pregnant wife, three young children, plenty of monthly bills, and to put it mildly — a deep, overwhelming sense of urgency.

I wasn't in a panic, but I was definitely a highly motivated man on a mission. I concocted a four-part strategy consisting of:

- Going to every person I knew to meet face-to-face
- Sharing my ministry vision
- Asking them to join our monthly support team
- Closing my mouth and letting them answer

Those four simple steps, in a nutshell, sum up the grand and glorious "secret" to raising your support. If you feel strongly enough about anything, and are prepared to trust God completely, you *will* find a way to accomplish it. Exactly six weeks later we were at full support, ready to launch our ministry — *and* pay all our bills!

✓ Did I pray like crazy? Absolutely.

✓ Did I trust God every step of the way? Yes.

✓ Did I totally rely on His strength and not my own? As far as I know.

✓ Did I give Him honor and glory for the results? No question.

Since 1986, our family has lived and ministered because of the generous, ongoing investments of others who believe in God — and us. And, looking back, we would not want to live any other way! And now I'm excited for you. You are about to enter one of the most stretching periods of your life. Support raising will not limit you or hold you back. It will unleash you! Your life and ministry may never be the same. Whether you're a rookie in support raising, or a veteran coming back for some "refresher training," I hope we can be of help. If you study this material closely, and diligently apply it, there is no reason you can't get to your ministry assignment quickly — and fully funded!

HARD WORK REQUIRED

I was the only male in my family who was not a pole-vaulter or a sprinter — each one in incredible physical shape. I spent my summers during college working at a camp, counseling alongside huge varsity athletes. Yes, I tried to keep up with these guys, but the size and speed genes must have bypassed me. Later, as I began seminary, I dropped any semblance of exercise, desperately attempting to somehow pass my Greek courses. Come late February, I remembered I had promised my camp friend, Spencer, that I would run a marathon with him in Fort Worth.

When 4,000 of us "runners" showed up on that cold and rainy Saturday morning in Texas, I had failed to include one minor detail in my schedule the previous eight months. I had not trained one single day! No need, because I believed myself to be an indestructible twenty-four-year-old warrior, and I certainly wasn't going to break a sweat over a puny little 26.2 mile marathon! With no knowledge of long-distance running, or the concept of "carbing up," I figured keeping a light stomach before the race would be best, so I limited myself to a donut and a cup of coffee!

As the starter's gun went off, I foolishly sprinted out in front of everyone, fantasizing that I was going to be one of the top finishers. I turned to see the crowd of runners behind me and thought, "Come on, if you're going to run a marathon, let's do it!" I didn't last five minutes before reality set in, I slowed way down, and hordes of runners began passing me. I miraculously survived until the twenty-two mile mark when I hit the proverbial "wall." Medics, assigned to spot runners in dire need, three times waded through the crowd, grabbed me by the shoulders, looked me in the eyes, and asked if I could finish the race!

I had many hours of "race time" that day to contemplate my life. With my lungs about to burst and every bone and muscle screaming out in pain, the only thought I had was, "How could I be so foolish, so arrogant, to think that I could complete a marathon without training?" I may have finished the marathon that day… but in reality, it finished me! For weeks I could barely walk, every bone felt disjointed, every muscle ripped to shreds. I was like a little old man hobbling around campus.

FOR THE LONG HAUL: GET TRAINING NOW

Support raising is like a marathon. If you're thinking the Lord may have you in full-time ministry for years to come, you must get training. Be teachable, put together a plan, and seek counsel from those who have raised their full support. Do all this *before* you begin your race! The next three, six, or nine months may feel more like a sprint because your days will be packed with prayers, calls, and appointments morning, noon, and night. But embrace the fact that you're on the front end of a marathon — the tedious and steady building and maintaining of a healthy, long-term support team of ministry partners.

"The will to win is nothing unless you have the will to prepare."

A Boston Marathon winner

If you are going to be successful in support raising, in ministry, yes, even in life… you must do what is necessary. How you approach this training process will affect your life, ministry, marriage, and family. Set the bar high for yourself. There will be tremendous dividends later if you are willing to fully invest yourself now!

YOUR CURRENT EMOTIONAL IQ

How are you feeling about support raising right now? Get in touch with your emotions to determine your current sentiments about this oh-so-scary concept of *asking* others to invest in you and your ministry. Where on this scale best represents your present attitude?[1]

Resist ······ *Oppressive Burden* ······ *Part of Job* ······ *Privilege* ······ *Embrace*

- *Resist* — Do you *detest* the idea of asking others for money? Or at best, it's just a "necessary evil" to you.
- *Oppressive Burden* — You don't hate it, but it feels like a massive weight on your shoulders.
- *Part of Job* — Support raising is not good or bad, it's neutral. The organization is asking you to do it, and so you will.
- *Privilege* — It is a noble and honorable thing to invite and involve others in extending and expanding the kingdom of God. You have a positive attitude.
- *Embrace* — You can't wait to get started. You are fired up!

Regardless of where you placed yourself on this chart, are you open to moving to the right? I will feel successful if I am able to move your emotional IQ just a notch or two!

I have felt each of these emotions just listed. Some days I even have multiple personalities where resistance and embracing are actually battling one another! But don't feel alone. The Lord is with you. Asking God before, during, and after that appointment to work on your behalf will have a profound effect on you — and the person you are meeting with.

THE GOD ASK

Tom Stickney and I were connecting back and forth about support raising. He was processing it from his mission station in Kenya. Stickney has been reaching out to East African college students for years. He began sharing his perspective with me, and I was challenged. He said, "I'm called to be faithful, but it's not my job to get the funds. It's God's. My calling, my ministry, the person I am asking, their assets, everything is all His. So, when I walk into a support appointment I remind myself this is not a 'Tom ask.' No. This is a *God ask.*'" Incredible. I have never been able to shake the phrase "God Ask." In every appointment there are *three* persons present: you, your potential supporter, and God. Here is how it unfolds.

The Support Raiser's Role

Stickney describes the power of the God Ask. "I am simply a mediator seeking to connect His people and His resources with His plan. That takes all the pressure off. The Lord calls some of us to be missionaries in Kenya, and some to be campus workers in America. Others are supposed to wear coats and ties and spend their days investing funds or buying real estate. Once we realize we're *all* in the game, it's a fixed result. We all simply play the role God has assigned us, faithfully fulfilling the Lord's purpose in our lives."

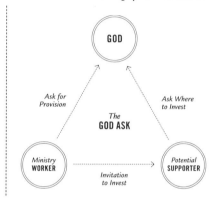

We go to Him for our needs, our funds, our fuel for the ministry. We pray and ask Him before we ask anyone else. We talk to God about His resources before we talk to any man about his. This is vision-driven support raising in a budget-driven world. This is vertical versus horizontal support raising. I don't dare just go to a donor and ask. I always make the God Ask first.

The Potential Donor's Role

1 Chronicles 29:14 confirms where all the resources come from, "But who am I, and who are my people, that we should be able to give as generously as this? Everything comes from you, and we have given you only what comes from your hand" (NIV). This give and receive relationship is not between the supporter and the Christian worker. It is between the supporter and God Himself. The donor doesn't just respond to our request. No, he, too, better make a God Ask to see where the Lord wants him to invest. My friend, Raymond Harris, Dallas businessman and author of *The Heart*

of Business: Solomon's Wisdom for Success in Any Economy, thinks we believers are not stewarding *our* money. A steward handles someone *else's* money. All of us are simply stewarding *His* money.

Consequently, it is the Lord who makes the God Ask of each individual you meet with. This insures the giving is not random or erratic, but out of obedience and stewardship. Harris believes biblical stewardship requires a twofold responsibility. First, we must regularly and sacrificially give. This answers the "How *much* to give?" question everyone seems to focus on. The second responsibility is just as critical. The steward must be strategic as to *where* they invest those funds, seeking to maximize their spiritual return on investment (ROI).

God's Role

My conversation with Tom Stickney moved along those same lines, "It is not *me* asking a person to give," he shared. "It is *God* asking them. If the Lord chooses to rearrange the portions — and move some funds from that person's account over to mine, that is His decision. That is why I need not be nervous before the appointment nor feel depressed or rejected afterwards if the person chooses not to give."[2]

Trusting in the power of God can have a calming effect on us. It is God who is in control of the whole process. It's not just one person asking another person for money. It is about God's sovereign will and choices to transfer His funds around *any way* He chooses. He knows exactly, to the penny, how much money He has stewarded to mankind as a whole and each person individually. Just like an investor would, He, too, is looking for the best ROI possible. The Lord is fully capable of putting just the right amount in our account at just the right time to fund just the right expenses.

THE BUTTON

Sadly, most Christian workers know nothing of these God Ask principles. You would be amazed what some of these good-hearted believers raising support scheme about. They daydream about a long-lost great aunt who suddenly dies and leaves them her millions; or maybe discreetly slipping down to the convenience store to lay down a few bucks hoping to hit the lottery — and presto! — no need to raise support. I dare not even mention casinos or horse racing!

How about you? What is your best-case scenario? If you could push a magic button and be *guaranteed* a full paycheck every single month for the rest of your life, would you push it? That way you could focus *totally* on God and the ministry and not have to expend all this time and money on travel, appointments, newsletters, etc. It seems like a no-brainer; anyone thinking clearly would surely push the button. Right? I have asked this magic button question to thousands of Christian workers and about 95% of them immediately smirk and shoot their hands up. But my prayer is that by the time you finish reading this book, you will actually *choose* not to push that button and join the ranks of the "utterly convinced" who would not want to live and minister any other way.

I feel so deeply about it that I don't want to go *anywhere* without my support team. In fact, I am *afraid* to launch into any ministry endeavor without them! I'm no fool. I need their prayers. I need their encouragement. I need their accountability. I refuse to exchange the raising of my own personal support for any amount of salary or so-called "security." If you, too, are able to come to that conclusion — that *conviction* — I believe you're going to be a lifelong, successful, support raiser.

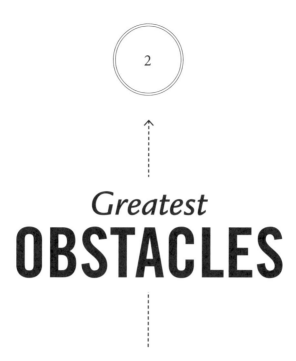

2

Greatest
OBSTACLES

Ever since my wife and I were married, we've had college students living with us. Our strategy has always been to buy or build a big house next to a major campus, then handpick Christian young men or women to live with our family. The motive? We want to pour into these students to raise them up as laborers to help fulfill the Great Commission. When the Son of God visited earth, He cried out with a broken heart: "The harvest is plentiful, but the workers are few" (Matthew 9:37).

We sometimes perceive people as spiritually unresponsive, but this verse claims just the opposite. They are lost and in desperate need of the truth. The solution is more workers: individuals who will take *personal* responsibility reaping this vast harvest and complete the task of world evangelization.

THE GREATEST OBSTACLE

If more laborers are the greatest need, then what is the greatest obstacle to filling that need? In my experience over the years, the most common barrier to raising up full-time Christian workers is finances. Dr. Ralph Winter, founder of the U.S. Center for World Mission, estimated that more than 20,000 Americans each month inquire about staff opportunities with various agencies across the country, yet only a trickle (as little as 1%) of those ever make it into a long-term ministry assignment.[3] Why? My observations over the years are that although they may feel led into ministry, and are all excited about reading the information about that organization, they stop dead in their tracks when they come across a small sentence tucked away someplace in the fine print: "You must raise your own support." Stunned and in shock, they lower their head, turn around, and quietly walk away.

I believe that maybe up to 90% of these 20,000 monthly inquirers respond this way to that short, but terrifying sentence out of fear or ignorance of *how* to raise their support. This is tragic. George Verwer, founder of Operation Mobilization concurs: "I estimate there are over 100,000 young people who have made a commitment to some kind of missionary service, but 95% of them will not make it to that work. We're not able to help them involve their church and parents to raise the necessary finances."[4] We have to solve this problem. We must find a way to unleash these thousands of world changers.

Like me, maybe you, too, have been tempted to walk away from your calling when you found out there was no secret pot of money your organization possessed to pay your salary. Instead, you've taken the road less traveled. You've not only made the momentous decision to follow through on the Lord's leading in your life to pursue full-time ministry, but now you have taken the second, even more extraordinary step of faith, committing yourself to raise your personal support. May God be with you.

YOUR TURN

Scott Morton with the Navigators states: "Unless you specifically identify your obstacles (to reaching 100% of your budget), you'll shortchange what Christ may want to do in your life, and you'll be in danger of developing a shallow financial plan."[5] How about you? Think through some obstacles you have experienced — or fear you might — in getting to 100% of your support. Here are some common things people list:

Personality

"I am a quiet, introverted person. I don't have a salesman personality, and that's why I won't succeed."

Attitude

"I'm just not too sure God is big enough or that we are worthy enough to raise all this money. I feel like a charity case."

Lack of Contacts

"I'm from a small town and church and don't know many people. I think I may fail."

ear

"When I ask someone for money, it's going to totally change my friendship with them. I hate to be rejected."

Weak Training

"The only support training I got was a two-hour session on writing newsletters, and a reporting form to send in every three months. I'm utterly lost!"

Unsupportive Family

"My spouse and parents are embarrassed that I'm asking people for money. They will lose all respect for me."

DON'T FEEL ALONE

Victor Hugo, famous French activist and author of *Les Miserables*, wrote, "The future has many names: The Lazy call it: The Impossible. The Fearful refer to it as: The Unknown. But The Courageous embrace it by saying: 'This is my Challenge.'" There are all kinds of reasons people conjure up to tell themselves and others why raising support will not work.

For instance, take a moment to read this classified ad:

Help Wanted: Pastor for a thriving church in the Midwest. Applicant must be a college graduate and preferably seminary trained. The prospective pastor will be required to solicit salary pledges (as well as moving expenses) from among our church members. This process will take approximately eighteen months, during which the pastor and his family must live "by faith." If interested in this exciting opportunity, write today for our ten-page application form.

If you saw this ad in a Christian magazine, you would laugh out loud and then turn to the cover to make sure it was the annual "April Fools" edition. After mocking this "exciting opportunity," you would declare that no one in their right mind would ever respond to something as outrageous as this. But guess what? You did!

You responded to this seemingly insane and deceptive ad. Replace the word "Pastor" with missionary or campus worker, or whatever your role is, and this describes the path you have chosen. But don't feel alone. Thousands of others have gone before you. Just because you happen to be the first one in your family or church to raise support doesn't mean you're weird.

Our culture might try to push us toward a "real" job or ministry that actually pays you a salary, but this concept of Christian workers receiving a guaranteed monthly paycheck is more of a western, denominational idea over the last one hundred years. The bulk of the world's full-time Christian workers are "faith missionaries." In other words, they don't get the golden, guaranteed payroll check each month. Instead, they live and minister from the ongoing financial gifts of others.

MADE MISTAKES?

If you've done some unwise things in your support raising, don't kick yourself. When a pro golfer makes a bad shot, he tries not to let it ruin his round. Instead, he reflects and learns from his mistake, then shifts all his mental energies toward making the *next* swing the best he can be. I've made so many mistakes. I take comfort in a statement Chuck Swindoll made, "It's *never* too late to start doing what is right."[6] Lamentations 3:23 says that God's loving kindness is new and fresh every morning. I am so thankful He gives us a clean slate each day.

So, whatever blunders or "donor neglect" you've committed, don't despair. You may need to go back to past supporters you did not really appreciate, communicate with, or take the most personal approach with, and simply say: "I'm sorry for not really caring for you the way I should have. Will you forgive me? I've received some training now, and from this point on I will seek to treat you as one of my valuable ministry partners. Are you open to giving me a second chance?" You'll be amazed how forgiving they can be!

PREPARE FOR SPIRITUAL BATTLE

Our battle is not against flesh and blood. Support raising is a spiritual task. It's not about technique, personality, or even experience. The Lord is the only one who can turn a heart and cause it to give. God does it, but He chooses to work through us to accomplish this. If I'm not following the Lord and filled with His Spirit, the last thing I can or will do is pick up the phone to make an appointment. If I'm spiritually empty, there's no way I can sit across from someone and pretend I am an ambassador for Christ. If there is any sin or spiritual stronghold in my life, I must confess and repent.

"The one concern the devil has is to keep Christians from praying. He laughs at our toil, mocks at our wisdom, but trembles when we pray."[7]

Samuel Chadwick, Author and Minister

For me, support raising is stepping into spiritual warfare. It's one of the greatest challenges of my life. Sometimes it feels like a daily, even hourly, battle. Satan will intensify his attacks during this critical and vulnerable period of our lives. "Watch out for your great enemy, the devil. He prowls around like a roaring lion, looking for someone to *devour*" (1 Peter 5:8, NLT, emphasis added). Understand, you have moved up to the top of his "Most Wanted" list. His goal is not just to distract you, but to devour you!

Imagine if the devil could get a wedge into your life at this fragile juncture. What if he could keep you from reaching 100% support and pressing on into ministry? Think of all the lives you would *not* touch for Christ because the enemy was able to "sideline" you. This is why you must "watch over [y]our heart with all diligence, for from it flow the springs of life" (Proverbs 4:23). Unless I keep my mind and heart fixed on the love and power of Christ, I will be a vic*tim* rather than vic*tor*. Don't deceive yourself. The strength of your *public* support raising is directly tied to the strength of your *private* relationship with God.

Andrew Knight, a support trainer for Campus Outreach, confesses, "We will tell ourselves whatever it takes to keep from having to raise support — even if it's a lie. Those lies are from Satan though. John 8:44 teaches 'he is a liar and the father of lies.' Let's thwart that thinking by replacing false information with correct content. Embrace a Romans 12:2 mindset: 'Do not be conformed to this world, but be transformed by the renewal of your mind, so that you may prove what the will of God is, that which is good, pleasing, and perfect.'"[8] In the final analysis, we will either let lies or truth control us and determine our destiny.

You will probably be a spiritual and support raising "casualty" if you choose to attempt to make this voyage alone. In 1792, as William Carey, the famous missionary from England, was about to sail to spend a lifetime in India, he recruited his closest friends in Christ to support him. He shared, "I will descend into the pit, if you will hold tightly to the ropes." Carey was willing to give his life away to reach the lost if his support team would pray, give, and keep him encouraged through correspondence. He did just that, and their partnership lasted for forty impactful years.

It's obvious the need is great. The obstacles are significant. The enemy is lurking. The excuses are everywhere. You'll feel alone and want to quit numerous times during this journey. It will boil down to you… and God, and answering these simple questions:

- Is He the Lord of your life?
- Did He call you into this work?
- Will you draw upon His strength to rise up, persevere, and take hold of this full and healthy support team the Lord wants to entrust to you?

"Greater is He who is in [us] than he who is in the world" (1 John 4:4). To pull this off, you're going to need a God Ask.

3

100% in
100 DAYS

We've conducted an informal survey of the one hundred largest mission agencies. We asked them, "For your staff who *were* able to get to 100% of their budget, what was the average amount of time it took them to raise their full support?"[9] The average range: eighteen to twenty-three months.

When I share that surprising figure around the country, I then ask the question, "How about you? Would *you* like to spend the next eighteen to twenty-three months of *your* life raising support?" The answer is always a resounding "no!" So, who's responsible for creating this drawn-out, self-imposed, support raising affliction? It normally begins when the newly-accepted missionary innocently asks their supervisor: "How long does it usually take someone to raise their support?" Not realizing the newcomer is at such a fragile and impressionable juncture, the seasoned veteran casually responds: "Oh… about eighteen months." With that time frame now firmly cemented in his psyche, the rookie staffer sets out to pace himself, making sure he dare not deviate from the norm!

On the other hand, many of our trainees are shocked when I suggest they could get to 100% support in 100 days. When King Artaxerxes asked Nehemiah how long it would take him to complete his Jerusalem rebuilding project, the trusted servant gave his boss a "definite time" (Nehemiah 2:6). What if Nehemiah had instead given a more *spiritual* answer like, "Oh, it will be finished whenever the Lord leads"? I have a feeling the king would not have been impressed. By the way, Nehemiah pulled it off in just fifty-two days.

But to set a support raising completion date in as little as one hundred days, I must include five requirements. The Christian worker should seek to gain:

- The right training
- The right perspective
- The right approach
- The right accountability
- Be willing to work on it full-time[10]

Mixed with a ton of hard work and the blessings of God, I believe most Christian workers should be able to raise their support in three to six months, hopefully twelve at the very most.

LEADING THE WAY

I don't know the "normal" amount of time it takes for staff in your organization to raise their full support, but can we at least agree to *not* use eighteen to twenty-three months as our standard? What if you were to break the mold in your agency? Set a new pace by passionately pursuing the goal of getting to full support in three, six, or nine months, instead of the twelve to twenty-four that so many groups seem to settle on? God could use you to revolutionize your entire organization, helping blaze a new trail for your ministry!

Do you think God desires Christian workers to get to their assignment quickly — and fully funded? You might be thinking, "Maybe… but 100% in one hundred days?" Don't be shocked. Pastor Steven Furtick claims, "If the size of the vision for your life isn't intimidating to you, there is a good chance it is insulting to God."[11] So my challenge to you to complete the task in one hundred days is no gimmick, but it's no guarantee either! Someone may tell you that 100% in one hundred days is impossible, but with God, nothing is impossible.

Even so, don't hear me say you've failed if you take longer than one hundred days. I share this concept to stretch your faith and provide another standard as you're setting your prayer and support raising goals. You may choose to set a 200 (or even 300) day goal of getting to full support. That's not necessarily bad, because the point is, like Nehemiah, to have a definite starting date and a definite ending date — for your *and* your supporter's sake.[12] Obviously, those who are raising much larger monthly amounts or doing fundraising on a part-time basis might take longer. Just don't let what others say is the "normal" length of time control you. Break the mold. God will go before you.

Believe it or not, I do know someone who got to 100% in just two weeks! How, you ask? He had seventy appointments in fourteen days! In fact, *no one* turned him down! Would you? If you knew of a person so well organized, so dedicated, burdened, and hard working as this, wouldn't you be drawn to invest in him? And don't be fooled: *How* a person goes about raising their support is a huge indicator of how they're going to conduct their ministry.

THE GREATEST PREPARATION FOR MINISTRY

Do you realize the same basic raw materials it takes to go and start a ministry from scratch are the exact ones required to begin and complete a support team? Do you have a:

- Deep faith and calling from God?
- Great love for people?
- Drive to prepare thoroughly?
- Willingness to plan and manage your schedule?
- Strong work ethic?
- Faithful follow-through on all commitments?
- Unbending tenacity of never, ever giving up regardless of the obstacle or setback?

These are some of the essential keys to success in support raising — as well as ministry. The final two are worthy of highlighting. A radical commitment to faithfulness, which is a fruit of the Spirit, really produces results. There are historical and biblical examples of never giving up, even in the midst of insurmountable odds. There are numerous passages exhorting us to diligently persevere with a steady, unwavering faithfulness.

- Proverbs 20:6 (RSV) "Many a man proclaims his own loyalty, but a faithful man who can find?"
- Luke 16:10 "He who is faithful in a very little thing is faithful also in much."

Persevering through this whole fundraising process is going to provide unbelievable training and preparation for your entire life and ministry —

certainly more than any classroom or curriculum could. I don't think the Lord wants us to miss out on the lessons learned. So much so that if a billionaire were to offer to pay all of our staff salaries, I would graciously decline. Yes, I would be open to putting those funds toward ministry projects, but I could not deprive our staff of the incredible spiritual growth they experience when raising personal support. Nor could I rob thousands of our donors of their eternal rewards as a result of our staff personally approaching them to invest in the work of the kingdom.

THE GREATEST PREREQUISITE FOR MINISTRY

Years ago, in the early stages of one of our organizations, we made the decision to begin subsidizing our staff. We rationalized it by saying the economy was so tough, the churches seemed so tapped out, and the new staff were so young. Consequently, we set up a gradual "phase-in" plan where they would raise one-third of their support by year one, two-thirds by year two, and full support by year three. We tried and tweaked here and there, but it never really worked. As soon as the subsidies ran out, so did the staff person — right out the back door! We painfully realized it's simply human nature that a person will only raise what they *have* to raise. This form of "Christian welfare" can create an unhealthy dependency.

It all came to a head one day when a board member declared, "If one of our staff isn't willing or able to go out and raise their full support from scratch, how could we ever expect them to be willing and able to go out and start and establish their ministry from scratch? Raising their full support should be the prerequisite for even coming on our staff!" Wow. We were convicted to the core. Since then, we purposed not to provide any subsidies. Our experience has been that when organizations require their personnel to raise all their own support, it has a way of attracting stronger leaders — and sometimes repelling weaker ones.

How long is it going to take you to get to full support? The answer lies within your own heart. It's usually a self-fulfilling prophecy. If you have allowed yourself to believe it's going to be a one- to two-year process, guess what? That's exactly what will happen! Why lock yourself into that thinking? Get above it, set your sights higher, reach down and challenge yourself like never before. Let the Lord, your family,

"Feelings aren't facts. You don't have to believe everything you tell yourself!"[13]

Rick Warren, Pastor and Author

friends, coworkers, and potential supporters know that you are going to aggressively pursue and accomplish this task in a much, much shorter time. Why? Because you are so burdened to get to your ministry assignment quickly — and fully funded!

Some Christians go into support raising unsure if this is really what God wants, so they begin with, "*If* God wants me to do this, the money will come." Seldom do these people make it to the field because there *will be* a moment in almost everyone's support raising journey that will discourage them, when things aren't working, and they ponder giving up. In those vulnerable moments, never try to decide if God has truly called you. Instead, keep anchored in the sure calling you already have.

One worker made it his goal to raise at least 1% of his total support each day for one hundred days. This so motivated him and his daily appointments that people were sacrificially jumping on his team to help him meet that day's quota. He made it to full support in less than one hundred days! But to have these kinds of results, you are going to need some fresh paradigms. Here's one.

A REAL LIFE STORY: 100% IN 92 DAYS

Kristin was a single woman accepted on our staff. She fully prepared for and attended a two-day support-training session. She secured ten friends to faithfully pray for her during her support raising, recruiting one of them to be her weekly accountability partner. Here are the quick facts:

- After thorough planning, Kristin launched her support raising on June 29th.
- She sent out 180 letters or emails in advance of a phone call.
- She spent 39 hours on the phone asking for and setting up appointments.
- There were 29 people who said no to an appointment. Another 101 said yes and met individually with Kristin.
- Out of 101 appointments, 60 people committed monthly, 22 gave single gifts, and 19 said no.
- She reached 100% budget on October 1st (not just pledges, but with gifts in hand!)

Why can't this be your story too?

4

Fresh
PARADIGMS

No wonder Kate couldn't get to full support. Every time she picked up the phone to call someone for an appointment, a rush of doubts flooded her mind. She was sure the person would reject her request to meet, and she had an extensive list of reasons why. She was too young, too inexperienced, and too shy. She was an administrator instead of a field worker. She had not graduated from college or attended seminary. People knew her parents were wealthy and could pay her way. Her reputation before she came to Christ would surely haunt her at every turn. She had serious questions whether it was even biblical to raise support, and no one had ever taken the time to show her how to do it. She felt totally inadequate.

Like Kate, all of us have some debilitating "support raising blues" songs playing in the back of our minds. They desperately need to be replaced by newer, healthier ones. Whether you are a support raising veteran or you're at that oh-so-tender stage of just considering going into full-time ministry, you might be tempted to click on and listen to the wrong songs. I understand. The decision to launch out and raise support is a huge one. Sometimes it helps to get a fresh paradigm. It's a new pattern, model, or standard to operate from. Commit now to allow the truths of Scripture to form this new paradigm in your mind, rather than other's opinions, your own perceptions, or past experiences. Let's make sure we are humming the right tune.

TAKE THE LEAP OF FAITH

Author and sociologist Tony Campolo surveyed a large group[14] of people aged ninety-five or older and asked them: If you could do life over again, what would you do differently? Almost always one of the top three answers is that they would have taken more risks in life. Reflecting on that, I determined I didn't want to look back on my life someday and regret that I had played it too safe, that I had stayed in the stands watching others give their all — but not me.

Stepping out in faith to raise your support could transform your life forever and will certainly set a precedent from this point forward. John Eldredge in his excellent book *Dare to Desire* shares: "God has rigged the world so that it only works when we embrace risk as the theme of our lives, when we live by faith. All attempts to find a safer life, to live by the expectations of others, just kill the soul in the end."[15] He then asks a penetrating question, "If you had permission to do what you really want to do, what would you do? Don't ask how — that will cut your desire off at the knees. How is never the right question. How is a faithless question; it means 'unless I can see my way clearly I won't venture forth.'"[16]

Remember how Hebrews 11:1 defines faith? "Now faith is the assurance of things *hoped* for, the conviction of things not seen." The dictionary definition of the word "hope" means "a cherished desire with an expectation of fulfillment." No, you cannot literally see a full and healthy monthly support team yet. Yes, it seems like a long way off where you would have forty, sixty, or eighty plus individuals and two, four, or six plus churches partnering with you and regularly investing. But this is where faith and hope come in. Don't let someone douse your determination to quickly raise your entire support by saying something negative like, "Don't get your hopes up." As you and I believe God for what we cannot see or experience now, He develops, in us, the assurance, conviction, and "expectation of fulfillment" that He will do it.

Therefore, we never utter the weak phrase, "*if* I raise my support," but only the strong and faith-filled, "*when* I raise it." I try to never allow my mind to entertain failure. I don't even go there. I have burned all my bridges, all my escape routes, and excuses, and my only option is full speed ahead! So, for instance, it's never that I can't or didn't raise my full support, it's just that I'm at 71% and pressing forward with great vigor! It may feel like you are in the middle of a frenzied one hundred-yard dash right now, but in reality, you are on the front end of a marathon. It is my prayer that you will devote the next ten, twenty, thirty, or forty plus years inviting others to partner with you in ministry through the investing of their finances and prayer.

I am asking God that you would change the way you view yourself. That you would perceive yourself as a "Holy Spirit-Filled Recruiter," committing yourself to spend the rest of your life inviting others to give their time, talent, and treasure to fulfill the Great Commission across the planet. I believe the Holy Spirit is a recruiter. He is spending all His time convicting, challenging, and wooing people to pledge their lives and resources to the person and purposes of Jesus Christ. If we are filled with the Spirit, we will join Him in this eternal, God-honoring, people-involving pursuit.

FOCUS ON JESUS

Hebrews 12 calls us to "[fix] our eyes on Jesus, the author and perfecter of faith" (Hebrews 12:2). This helps get me up in the mornings. It helps me work through challenges and setbacks. Every morning I reflect on a painting in my office that depicts the scene in Revelation 7:9. Christ as the Lamb of God is sitting on the throne in heaven and believers from every tribe, tongue, nation, and people are worshipping Him for all eternity. This is the culmination of all of history, the finish line, the final exam to show what we exchanged our lives for. My goal is not only to be there worshipping the Lamb myself, but to spend my life bringing as many with me as I can!

I'm sure your heart is the same; you have no intention of showing up at the Revelation 7:9 throne all by your lonesome. Those you have led to Christ or discipled will be with you — along with those *they* have led to Christ and discipled. In addition, all those believers who have prayed for you or invested financially in you and your ministry will accompany you. They will be with you around the throne too. They faithfully provided the means by which you could reach others. As it relates to the eternal rewards we receive, don't they get a "fraction of the action" too? They have every right to be there alongside us, eternally basking in the love of Jesus and the incredible fruit He bore in and through *all* of us. It is truly a team effort — a ministry partnership.

We can't accomplish this work alone. That's why the Lord has designed it such that there are three essential persons involved in this kingdom-building endeavor He's called us to. You might be feeling all alone, but the Lord of heaven is by your side, clearing the path for you at every turn. The next person is you. You must be faithful to team up with God and do your part. Then be sure to remember the third teammate — your supporters. You may feel like they're not that interested, but they are. They invest prayer and finances in you and your ministry because they care.

King Solomon stated in Ecclesiastes 4:9 that two are better than one. But then he goes on to say in verse 12 that if two are good, three are even better. "A cord of three strands is not easily broken" (HCSB). I visualize a long, thick rope securely and tightly wound, such that it will never break or fail. In my mind, one of those strong cords represents God Himself. A second cord is you. And the third one? Your remarkable ministry partners. If you choose to forever entwine those three essential persons, that rope will be so strong and so lasting, it will take you clear to eternity! Decide now to focus on the Revelation 7:9 finish line and work backward from there. Join God by spending a lifetime personally inviting others to throw their lot and resources in with you, and you will get to the finish line with a multitude of ministry partners who will forever thank you for including them.

This is where the "God Ask" enters. There may be appointments where it would be appropriate to humbly and respectfully draw this diagram out for a prospective supporter and show them what the roles are for the

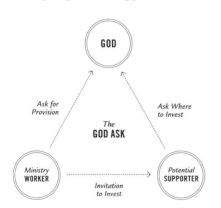

three persons involved in this process. I have friends who like to do that and then transition to the ask by sharing, "I know you pray about where the Lord wants you to give. If investing in us and our ministry fits into your giving goals, we would be honored to have you partner with us somewhere between $100 to $250 a month."

ROOKIE OR VETERAN?

If you are a rookie, and just getting started, you may be struggling with faith… and fear — mainly fear of the unknown. There is a definite newness and excitement to all this, but it's also probably interspersed with bouts of sheer terror!

If you are a ministry veteran and have been out there for a while hacking away, your fear is probably not with the unknown, but with the known! In other words, you know exactly what the challenges are to get to and stay at 100% support, and it has taken its toll on you. Maybe the long-term lack of funds has constricted your ministry or hampered the joy of your marriage. Maybe it has tainted your children's view of ministry and/or support raising. Don't give up!

Years ago, I had a sixty-year-old man start weeping during one of our training sessions. At a break, I asked him if he was okay and if I had said something that upset him. He glanced down, then whispered, "No, I just wish I had received this training thirty years ago. It would have saved our marriage and family so much stress and pain!" One of my primary motives over the years in equipping Christian workers to get to full support is to help strengthen their marriages and families.

Howard Hendricks believes up to 90% of divorces are partly or mainly due to financial pressures.[17] That's sobering, but I believe God wants you to live and minister on support and *not* have to experience the overwhelming financial stress so many couples do. Don't you think the marriages of those in full-time ministry have enough pressures on them without piling on extra financial burdens?

FULL-TIME OR PART-TIME SUPPORT RAISING?

One decision you might need to bring before the Lord is whether to concentrate totally on putting your support team together or do it on a part-time basis along with school or work. Newly-accepted Christian workers who deliberately walk away from their safe and secure regular paychecks in order to raise support full-time, without any visible means to pay the bills, are viewed as foolish, even fanatical, by many coworkers, family, and spiritual leaders. Such workers feel called to ministry, but they are torn between two worlds, not wanting to let go of one source of funds before they see the other definitely coming. As a result, the support efforts of many new staff recruits consist of trying to squeeze in a few appointments each week around their work schedule. This plan may appear to be the most "sensible," but it has tremendous drawbacks. A few are:

Time to Get to Full Support Can Be Doubled or Tripled

A full-time support-raiser can schedule ten to thirty appointments weekly. But someone who continues to devote the best thirty to fifty hours of their week to schoolwork or a secular job will not have the time or energy to make and keep even one-third that many face-to-face appeals. A six-month full-time effort can easily drag out to eighteen or even twenty-four months of part-time focus. I've observed that the rate of "drop outs" — those who give up on their support raising — is considerably higher among the part-timers.

Sense of Urgency Is Lost for You and Your Supporters

Donors hesitate to come on a team until they perceive the newcomer really *needs* their support. Why? Givers want to invest in ministry, not just in support raising efforts or swelling someone's organizational/savings account for some unknown ministry-launching date in the future. Few feel passionately compelled to join a team unless they sense they're supporting a man or woman "on a mission," fully focused and working diligently toward a goal.

One bold concept I've seen some support raisers embrace is to gather a few of your close friends and potential major stakeholders around you and share with them the huge step of faith you are considering taking. Inform them of your desire to leave your job and salary and do support raising *full-time* so you can get to your assignment quickly and with 100% funding. As they see your courage and sacrifice, you will have gained the credibility to ask them to consider partnering with you to provide some significant upfront money. This is to cover all of your ongoing living expenses, thus buying you a three-, six-, or nine-month window of time to focus exclusively on support raising.

I know this may be a terrifying notion because it can appear irrational to let go of a "sure thing" to reach out for something still unseen. If God leads you to do this, it may set you on a course of making or taking bigger and bigger steps of faith in your life and ministry in the years to come. Anthropologist Ralph Blum challenges us: "In each life there comes at least one moment which, if recognized and seized, transforms the course of that life forever. The moment may call you to leap, empty handed, into the void."[18] The times I have taken that kind of exhilarating step of faith, I have seen God come through each and every time.

PROS AND CONS OF A WORKING SPOUSE

Should you raise your *full* support if you have a spouse who is working and earning an income? Your organization may have a policy or the decision may be left to you and your spouse. I fully believe the husband and wife are "worthy of their wages," but be aware there might be potential donors who are hesitant to give if you have a spouse with a good job and salary. They may question if there is a legitimate need to raise another full salary when the couple already has a significant income.

Another factor is you, as the support raiser, might not be as motivated to get to full support, knowing there is a second salary to fall back on. Some donors prefer to give to a couple where *both* husband and wife spend the best hours of their day working together in ministry. This might be the ideal and may aid you in the support raising process, but it's not necessarily the norm.[19]

Remember, in all of this, the freshest and most powerful paradigm you and I can embrace is found in Psalm 138:3: "On the day I called, You answered me; You made me bold with strength in my soul." It is daily, even moment by moment, going to the Lord of the universe and making "The God Ask." He will go before us. He will deliver us. He will show Himself powerful. He will give us all we need.

Go "ALL IN"

The year was 1517, and Hernando Cortez and his three ships of soldiers sailed from Spain to conquer and claim Mexico for his country. When they finally arrived in the Mexican bay, small boats ferried all the soldiers to the shore to prepare for an inland march to the capital city of the Aztec Indian empire to defeat King Montezuma and his forces. Once all the soldiers were on shore, Cortez then motioned for a few men to row back out to the ships. As the soldiers watched, their curiosity turned into horror as the men lit torches and threw them onto the decks of the three ships. The soldiers stood speechless with eyes and mouths wide open as they realized they would *never again* see their home country or families. They had no choice now but to turn, follow Cortez into the heat of the battle, crush the enemy, and win the war. There was no turning back. They either had to go "all in" or not at all.

It's the same for you and me. Satan, the world, even your own flesh will tell you that you *can't* raise your support — or that you *shouldn't* raise your support. Don't believe the lies. They are deceiving you. The word "impossible" is used as an excuse for people to give up or hide out. Now is the time to do away with any escape routes. Set your face like a flint toward the task, and go "all in." Consider these two crucial questions:

1. How long are you planning to be in full-time ministry?
2. How healthy and effective do you want your ministry to be?

Question one is legit. You may be thinking a year or two... or the rest of your life! Regardless of your tenure we *all* want our ministries to be healthy and effective. Why do so few rise to that standard? Because the early decisions we make in the planning stages of our work end up forming the long-term DNA of our ministry. Here are your choices as to which of these two legacies you will leave behind.

A SHORT-TERM, LOW-IMPACT MINISTRY

Picture people carving out towers and moats on the beach, creating a small homemade masterpiece that others stop for a moment to smile, point at... and walk on. Proud of their accomplishment, the castle-builders take a picture, then head back to the hotel, not comprehending that all their efforts will completely vanish when the tide rolls in. Easy come, easy go. But hey, it was fun while it lasted.

A LONG-TERM, HIGH-IMPACT MINISTRY

Now picture a company building a huge skyscraper. I remember one being constructed in downtown Dallas that was to be more than eighty stories high. For twelve months, I heard all kinds of heavy earth-moving equipment busy working, but saw no sign of a skyscraper. Finally, my curiosity got the better of me, and I pulled over to look through a hole in the tall wooden fence around the site. I could tell they had been digging a very deep hole; in fact, it looked eighty stories down! They also had sunk and installed a maze of huge iron columns and poured massive amounts of concrete.

I questioned the need to do all this preliminary work. My rationale? It's underground, invisible to anyone inhabiting or viewing the building. No one is *ever* going to see it or even know it's there. Why spend more time and effort just digging *down* and preparing the foundation than you even do building *up* the actual structure? If I had been the contractor, *and* having no knowledge of construction, I would have scratched my head, looked around to see if the ground was level, turned to the work crew, and said, "Okay boys, let's get started on the first floor!"

"When God wants to make a mushroom, he takes 6 hours. If He wants to make an oak tree, He takes 60 years. Which do you want to be?"[20]

Rick Warren,
Pastor and Author

Proudly completing my edifice of steel and glass, I'm sure the employees working on that eighty-seventh floor wouldn't be too appreciative of my plan the first time a good gust of wind toppled it over!

START WITH THE END IN MIND

Do you want your ministry to be a skyscraper for Christ that will still be standing tall generations from now, or a tiny, short-lived sand castle easily swept aside and forgotten? Thirty years from now, what do you want to look back and observe about your life, your ministry, and your support team? What measures of success will you use? Will there be any regrets? Any wishing you had done something differently? Wisdom would tell us to start with the end in mind.

I believe the Lord gives us tremendous freedom as to what kind of man or woman of God we will become and what the depth and breadth of our ministry impact will someday be. Much of that is inseparably tied to the long-term health and stability of our support team. If this is true, then you should begin on your personal, ministry, and support team excavation project at once! There will *never* be a better time and opportunity to dig deep, lay that hidden groundwork, and undergird a lifetime of service unto God than right now.

However, in regard to developing strong biblical convictions and fundraising stability, if you become impatient and more inclined to the "build now, dig later" approach, unwilling to invest in the costly and time-consuming foundation-laying I am describing, I think you will be sorry. Mark Stephens, FCA state director in Maryland, puts it like this: "Everyone wants to have the exciting 'Friday night lights' ministry experiences and impact. We came on staff to see the Lord use us in powerful ways. It's exhilarating. But, first things first. Before we can go out and publicly minister full-time, we have to first submit ourselves to the behind the scenes hard work, sweat, and tears of 'two-a-days.' We always have to prepare *before* we play."[21] My main goal here is to take your pulse of preparedness. I implore you *not* to commence tomorrow in setting up appointments. Stop, take stock, and spend the next several days or even weeks to do *all* the necessary praying, planning, preparation, and practicing.

A friend of mine would say, "If you will take care of the depth of your life and ministry, God will take care of the breadth. If you will stay focused on the root, He will produce the fruit." Our lives, ministries, and

"How deep a foundation you create will determine how strong and high your structure will be in the years to come."[22]

Mick Ukleja,
American Author

support raising begin and end with the Lord. We have no*where* else to go, no *one* else to go to, but Him… and Him alone. We start by consecrating ourselves to God. Why not plan to slip away for a day or two to pray and express total dependence upon the Father? Like Jesus, this can be like your forty days in the wilderness preparing to do battle with the enemy, or your night at Gethsemane to give up all your rights, abandoning yourself to *His* agenda in your life. The strength of my *public* support raising is directly tied to the strength of my *private* intercession with God.

PRAYER IS WHERE TO BEGIN

"For some days I mourned and fasted and prayed before the God of heaven… 'Lord, let your ear be attentive to the prayer of this your servant and to the prayer of your servants who delight in revering your name. Give your servant success today by granting him favor in the presence of this man.'" (Nehemiah 1:4,11, NIV) Like Nehemiah, the amount of time I spend in prayer can indicate whether I am trusting in God or myself. Sometimes I foolishly think my presence with someone is more powerful and life-changing than *God's* presence. The proof? I can spend two hours with someone in a support appointment and thoroughly enjoy myself. However, if you ask me to spend just two minutes praying for them, it seems like an eternity! That fact alone tells me where the real battle is won or lost. *Whatever* else we do when support raising, we can't neglect prayer.

Psalm 62:11 tells us, "power belongs to God." As much as I'd like to reach into someone's chest and turn their heart toward God, or toward our ministry, *only* the Lord can. Whether it's witnessing or raising support, our persuasiveness and eloquence only goes so far. This is why businessman Tim Howington, who supports many Christian workers, suggests we spend one minute in prayer for every ten minutes we spend with a supporter.[23] "Talk to God about men before you talk to men about God" was author and evangelist Bill Bright's practice.[24]

Isn't it unimaginable that the Father has chosen to do His work in response to our prayers? For us to have the privilege of partnering with God to accomplish His plan is the mother of all mismatches. Just remember who the managing partner is! Recently, I finished making a list of people I want to approach this month. I'm asking some to join our monthly team for the first time, others to restart, and a few regular givers to consider increasing. My plan is all in place, except for one *minor* detail! I haven't "made my requests known to God" as commanded in Philippians 4:5-6. The Lord will go before us and open doors and hearts — but He wants us to make the God Ask first. If you will earnestly and specifically beseech the Lord, you'll end up with a truckload of answered prayers… and a full support team.

CALLING, TESTIMONY, AND VISION

I worked through a spiritual-life timeline with a mentor. It was wonderful to review how God drew me to Himself. I recalled when and how I made the decision to fully follow Jesus Christ. I reflected on the radical changes He has wrought in me over the years. You, too, should do this *before* you dive headlong into your support activities. To make sure you have accurate marching orders from God you should:

Confirm Your Calling

Think back over the weeks and months when the Lord was shaping you and speaking to you about your life, career, pursuits, and passions. Recall the different people, ministries, and experiences used to influence you during those formative times. Were there specific passages or promises in the Word that the Holy Spirit used to lead you or confirm to you He was calling you into ministry? Review, meditate, and pray those back to the Lord. Finally, make a list of the various job or ministry options you were considering and *why* it was you felt so strongly about this particular route.

Think Through Your Testimony

Look closely at your personal testimony of how you came to Christ and the process of responding to an invitation from God to engage in this work full-time. Do you see any correlation between the two? For instance, if you were led to the Lord or impacted during your college years, is that part of the reason why you now want to go on staff with a ministry that reaches out to students? If there is any parallel between when and how you were touched for Christ and the ministry you are about to embark upon, document it. Then, when it comes time to share your story in support appointments, your prospective donors will be able to clearly grasp how your calling and vision is the natural progression and outgrowth of your *own* experience. Simply and visually help them connect those dots. The lights will click on for them as to *why* you feel so passionate about this work.

Map Out Your Vision

In Nehemiah chapter 2, King Artaxerxes had various questions for Nehemiah about when and how he proposed to start and finish his task. From his responses, it was obvious his cupbearer had logged in the necessary prayer and planning time to give the king solid answers. He had thought deeply about every aspect of his work, then transitioned to the even harder work of bathing all the particulars in prayer. What a model for us to work from. Find a private setting, bringing your organization's vision/mission statements and core values, along with your own specific ministry goals, strategy, and job description. Spend a few hours examining, thinking, and praying over every detail. You must fully comprehend and embrace the overall vision, as well as each smaller component. Do you agree with all of it? Is there a full "buy-in" from your heart and mind?

You will *never* convince someone else of the rightness and strategic value of something you still have nagging doubts about! Understanding your own vision is the key to sharing it with others. Maybe you ought to create a FAQ page which lists all the possible questions people might ask of you during your appointments and how to best answer each. Prepare for the basic and simple "softball" inquiries, but also the tougher curveballs thrown at you too.

"Life begins where your comfort zone ends."[25]

*Todd Ahrend,
International Director of
The Traveling Team*

As you put the time and effort into doing these foundation-building exercises, you will walk away with a newfound sense of authority, confidence, and sense of destiny. Artaxerxes observed in his servant a man who was committed to *privately* paying the price in thoroughness, excellence, and integrity. Likewise, your supporters must sense your ministry calling and vision is not some impulsive whim, but a deeply held, thought-out, and prayed-through set of specific marching orders from on high!

And if you are a support raising husband, don't forget this important component of what it means to go "all in." First Timothy 5:8 teaches if a man does not provide for his own family he has "denied the faith and is worse than an unbeliever." In light of that, Ellis Goldstein, National Director for MPD with Cru, has a personal challenge, "Husbands, I want to ask you to make an irrevocable commitment to your wife. Promise her, 'On our wedding day I vowed to take care of you and provide for you. God has called us to serve Him and to raise our support. I renew my resolve to trust the Lord as I lead our family in building a healthy, lifelong support team. I will work morning, noon, and night so our family can serve Him and have all the funds necessary to do so. I will not allow anything to interfere with that. I will not make excuses. I will give it my all.'" Perhaps, you have already made this promise to your wife. If you haven't — do it. God and your wife will be honored.

As you discern God's calling and vision for you, these principles and issues may be helpful, but there will be a host of other questions, fears, struggles, and obstacles you will bring *before* the Lord for extended, uninterrupted times of intercession. If you are married, this prayer retreat should include both husband and wife. Both need to be on the same page with one mind and one heart, unified before the Father. Do this before you jump into the whirlwind of full-time support raising, so you can have solid bearings and handles to hold onto during the challenging, but exciting, journey that awaits you.

Launching out with God-given and fully galvanized bedrock convictions regarding His will for your life and ministry will make a tremendous difference in your support raising. What will give you the freedom and confidence to do the work of God? Only the Word of God. It alone has the power to unleash you. Let's saturate ourselves with the Scriptures to find out what the Lord says about support raising. You'll be glad you did.

The
GOD ASK

Section II
BIG FAITH, BIG ASKS

We're called to acquire biblical wisdom. Let
God, not the world, shape your perspective.

6

God's
OLD TESTAMENT MINISTERS

During one of your support raising appointments, you'll experience one of the most painful and humbling encounters of your life. Maybe it will be with a business executive you are "lucky" enough to snag a meeting with. You spend days preparing for what you *think* is going to be a warm and embracing hour sharing your immaculately-prepared ministry vision. You are believing God that this man will be the sugar daddy you've been praying for, who will sink major dollars into your work.

At the appointed time, you arrive at the top floor and are greeted by the personal assistant who offers you a cold drink and a leather sofa to sit on — and wait. Now, thirty minutes after the meeting was *supposed* to start, the assistant dutifully declares, "Mr. Jones will see you now," and you're finally ushered into the inner sanctum and seated in a small chair in front of a huge desk. While this busy executive finishes his phone call, you glance around the giant office and see his diplomas, awards, luxurious furnishings, and of course, the enormous windows allowing him to look out upon his vast corporate kingdom. When at last he turns and peers

down on you, here are the rapid-fire questions he shoots at you during the
whole two minutes you are "privileged" to have with him:

1. "How did you get my name?"
2. "Now what group are you with?"
3. "Why are you here?"
4. "And what did you say you wanted?"

You hardly get to blurt out a partial answer to each question before he
interrupts with another. Your 120 seconds are up and he rushes out to
his next meeting, but briefly stops to hand you a $50 check marked:
"charitable donation," utters "good luck" — and is gone. Now, sitting alone
in your little chair and cradling your cold drink, you are trying to discern
what just happened here. With your esteem sucked out, you can barely
slither out past the apologetic assistant.

Back in the quiet safety of your bedroom, you lick your wounds and
attempt to somehow resurrect your dashed hopes and dreams. Lifting your
head to look in the mirror, you're positive the word "Loser" must be printed
somewhere on your forehead. Everything around you is screaming for you
to quit putting yourself through this misery, to drop out, and just go get a
job like every other human being on the planet. This is when you may be
tempted to create an exit ramp in your mind and craft an oh-so-spiritual tale
how *the Lord* has led you not to go into ministry, but in a different direction.

CROSSROADS OF YOUR LIFE

It's at this critical juncture when your calling into ministry is tested, where
the battle for control of your life and future will be won or lost. Either you
will give up and walk away or the Lord will use an experience like this to
forever galvanize your deep, abiding confidence that you will never, ever
give up this passion to fulfill God's destiny for your life. What will make
the difference in these excruciating times? The thing that will make you or
break you will be whether or not you have really studied the Scriptures and
gained a rock-solid conviction that continuing to personally ask others to
invest in you and your ministry is good, is right, and is biblical!

Have you put in the time to objectively, inductively, and thoroughly
study the Scriptures on this topic prior to forming your beliefs and
approaches? If not, you need to decide what is going to control you *before*
you embark on this adventure. Will it be fear of rejection or failure? Other
people's opinions? Past experiences? Or the Word of God?

If you're willing to log in the necessary hours to truly understand the Scriptural principles we're about to dive into, they will provide you the hidden "below the surface" foundation that will stand the tests of time and trials. Most Christian workers have strong personal views for or against support raising, but Scott Morton, support trainer for The Navigators, exhorts us, "Until you've spent at least twenty hours in personal Bible study on this topic, how do you know you're not just regurgitating your parents' or church's views, or worse, what the world believes?"[26]

BIBLICAL CONVICTIONS

I pray you have several nerve-racking appointments like the one I described so you will trust God to persevere. Missionaries in India in 1885 who wrote back to the States pleaded for more staff, saying, "Send us more campus workers. Make sure they are trained in success as well as failure, so that we may know they will endure." Don't be afraid of setbacks or so-called "failures." They may very well be your springboard to success! What will keep you in the ministry and support raising saddle five, ten, twenty, thirty plus years from now? Biblical convictions. Convictions are not just what you *believe*, they are what you *do*! Dr. Adrian Rogers claimed the way you build real, lasting convictions is to read, study, and meditate on the same passages over and over again until they finally seep down into your spiritual bloodstream and become part of your DNA.

To create some balance, understand that some of the biblical examples you are about to study are simply a *description* of a past support raising model and not necessarily the *prescription* for what we are commanded to do now. So read, evaluate, pray, and utilize what you believe God wants for you!

GOD'S OLD TESTAMENT MINISTERS

It was the Lord Himself who designed the concept of "full-time ministry workers" and then made sure there was a good system in place to keep them compensated. Looking at the Levites we can learn some timeless principles, and then practically apply them today.

SET APART FOR GOD'S SERVICE (NUMBERS 1:1-3, 47-53)

After the Hebrews had come out of Egypt, the Lord spoke to Moses in Numbers 1:1-3 and told him to assemble every male who was "twenty years old and upward" to prepare them to do battle. This was a greatly anticipated day for hundreds of thousands of these vigorous young men. No forced draft was required because they were eager to obey God by clearing the Promised Land of its idolatrous inhabitants. Strangely enough, there was one particular group left out of this new 600,000 strong army. Numbers 1:47 says, "The Levites, however, were not numbered among them by their fathers' tribe." How could this be? Was this simply an oversight or was it some kind of cruel joke? They were about to be left out of one of the greatest battle plans in all of history.

The Lord revealed why Moses was not to line up the Levites for combat. God had a completely different role for these young men, commanding Moses in Numbers 1:50-54 to "appoint the Levites over the tabernacle of the testimony." I'm sure their assignment to stay behind and do set up/ take down didn't seem nearly as important as defeating the Philistines. Even though everyone was confused, the Lord was firmly in control. Little did the Levites know that this was "Day One" in God's history-long plan to sanctify and set apart certain individuals to represent Him, to serve and lead His people in worship and outreach.

In the same way, if you're going into ministry, don't feel like a second-class citizen. You, too, are part of this legacy of being set apart for His service. To help them, and us, to understand their new ministry assignment, the Lord included a "Support Raising Manual for Levites" in Numbers 18.

WORTHY TO RECEIVE AN INCOME BECAUSE OF THEIR WORK (NUMBERS 18:20-21, 31)

There were approximately 50,000 Levites now milling around wondering exactly what this new ministry role was. Some may have felt this assignment was beneath them. Others probably had doubt and discouragement flooding their hearts. The most immediate question filling their minds may have been, "How in the world are we supposed to support ourselves and earn our keep?" That may be the very question you are asking yourself. But before these Levites could be of any use at all to the *whole* nation of Israel, the Lord had to work overtime to instill the kind of perspectives and practices into these young men that would properly prepare them to fill the role of unselfish servant-priests to the people.

God had to break them down before He could build them up and thus told Aaron and the Levites, "You shall have no inheritance in their land nor own any portion among them; *I* am your portion and your inheritance" (Numbers 18:20, emphasis added). This declaration must have dealt the Levites another blow, realizing their lifelong dream of having their own portion of land in the Promised Land was not to be. Instead, they were to look to God alone for their day-to-day sustenance and long-term security. I'm sure that was a somber moment of counting the cost of what kind of sacrifices were required to be one of God's representatives.

Once that foundation of constant and total reliance upon the Lord was laid, there was no turning back. Knowing their hearts were set upon God's purposes, He could now show them how He was going to fund their lives and ministries. The Lord said, "To the sons of Levi, behold, I have given *all* the *tithe* in Israel for an inheritance, in return for their service which they perform, the service of the tent of meeting" (Numbers 18:21, emphasis added).

God repeats the concept in Numbers 18:31 when He tells them what to do with the offerings the Israelites give them: "You may eat it anywhere, you and your households, for it is your compensation in return for your service in the tent of meeting." They were *worthy* to receive an income strictly because of their *work*. The tithes and offerings the Lord gave them through the Israelites were simply because of their dedicated labor in the ministry. They weren't *demanding* it, but in God's eyes, they were *deserving* of it.

Maybe you've observed an "excuse maker" who says the reason he can't raise his support is because he's not good in front of people, or he doesn't have a ministry video, or he's too young or too old. The way God has set this system up is that you and I deserve to be supported purely "in return for our service" and for no other reason. Not because we're sharp, educated, have outgoing personalities, or slick presentations. The Old and New Testaments teach that we are simply "worthy of our wage."

GIVING AND RECEIVING IS VERTICAL, NOT HORIZONTAL (NUMBERS 18:8, 24)

First semester of Ministry Lessons 101 continued for the Levites as the Lord felt compelled to teach them the difference between the world's economy and His. The world is focused exclusively on buying and selling. Instead, as God's children, we need to be more into giving and receiving. But before the Levites could teach and model this essential principle to the whole nation, they had to first internalize it themselves. Aaron, the chief priest, was to oversee the receiving of the gifts and offerings from the sons of Israel. God assured him, "I have given them to you as a portion and to your sons as a perpetual allotment" (Numbers 18:8). Later in verse 24 the Lord adds, "For the tithe of the sons of Israel, which they offer as an offering to the LORD, I have given to the Levites for an inheritance."

Here's the path of God's provision: The Lord supplied the Israelites with food, animals, and money so they could *vertically* tithe and offer it back up to God. In the same way, the Levites were not to *horizontally* depend on their fellow Israelites for sustenance, but to instead, look up and receive those tithes and offerings — vertically — from God above. Whether they were a "giving Israelite" or a "receiving Levite" the Lord wanted them all to understand that He is the supplier of all their needs. For us, the temptation is great to look to others to meet our needs, but if we are going to raise our support, we, too, must look up, rather than out, for our provision.

THE FIRST AND THE BEST GIFTS BELONGED TO THE LEVITES (NUMBERS 18:12-13)

God wanted to help them understand they were not being demoted to a life of misery and poverty, destined to forever scrounge for leftovers. Quite the opposite. The Lord was determined that *His* representatives would receive "all the best" fresh oil, wine, and grain along with the "first ripe fruits of all that is in their land." And even though it was the Israelites who were making the offerings, the Lord was clear who the *real* source was: "I give them to you," He said. In fact, twelve different times in this chapter alone He declares that it is He who is doing the giving! Ezekiel 44:30 and other passages reinforce the Lord's plan to fully provide for His workers.

I'm grateful God instituted an excellent benefits package for His employees, but something has gone terribly wrong over the centuries, and the Founder's wishes are not being carried out! Even though this concept of giving the first and the best to the Levites was *intended* to be a core value for the nation, it quickly waned — just as it has today. And if your experience has been anything like mine, most religious people expect ministers to be humble — and broke! Consequently, many Christian workers don't receive the first and best, but rather the last and the worst.

If we rightly interpret what was in the mind of God when He designed and implemented this funding plan, we must admit His heart was to thoroughly and excellently cover *all* the needs a Levite and his family had. And just because God's people may not be giving like He desires, it does not change His plan or purpose to completely provide for His full-time servants. Paul touches on the unchanging character of God when he writes: "If we are faithless, He remains faithful, for He cannot deny Himself" (2 Timothy 2:13).

What is the reason many believers don't give the first and best to Christian workers? It may be because we support raisers have conditioned them *not* to! If we don't even ask for or expect the first and the best from God, we will never gain the courage to ask for or expect it from others. And could it be that some donors' small gifts may very well be just them responding to our own low expectations and "poor me" attitudes? Instead, let's set our minds and emotions on our great Provider, Jehovah-Jirah, and believe He wants to *fully* furnish all our needs.

TITHE FROM OFFERINGS RECEIVED (NUMBERS 18:25-26)

One of the final funding lessons God had for these newly minted worship leaders dealt with their own responsibility to give. Now that their questions had been answered as to how they personally would be compensated, the Lord turns to them and basically says, "Your turn now." If they were to effectively teach the nation of Israel the why and how to give sacrificially, the Levites must first be modeling it. The Lord instructed once they received the Israelites' designated gifts, these priests were then to go and "present an offering from it to the LORD, a tithe of the tithe" (Numbers 18:26).

We may get really comfortable always being on the receiving end and forget that God wants us to also participate in this divinely-inspired, circular-giving method He devised. Before we launch out and begin to ask others to substantially invest in us, it is wise to first take stock of our own kingdom giving. I can't believe the Lord is going to move on someone else's heart to give sacrificially to my ministry and me if I'm not even doing that myself. Sometimes we get confused and deceive ourselves into thinking that the giving of our time to God's work is all He expects. No, He desires our time, talent, *and* treasure, and in fact, wants us to set the pace. Leadership principle number one is always: Never ask anyone to do anything that you are not modeling yourself.

> *"If there be any truer measure of a man than by what he does, it must be what he gives."*[27]
>
> *Robert South, English Churchman*

Brad Smith, a missions mobilizer, came up with a profound equation that explains this concept. Here it is: Radical Giving + Radical Asking = Radical Receiving. We support raisers are fervently praying God will consistently provide abundant funds so we can fully fund our family and ministry. Right? But there is a cause and effect to this kind of "radical receiving." Paul talks about this "reap what we sow" principle in 2 Corinthians 9:1-15 as he challenges the Corinthian church to follow through on an earlier financial pledge they made to him and his ministry. Verses 6-8 form the heart of his exhortation:

He who sows sparingly will reap sparingly, and he who sows bountifully will also reap bountifully. Each one must do just as he has purposed in his heart, not grudgingly or under compulsion, for God loves a cheerful giver. And God is able to make all grace abound to you, so that always having all sufficiency in everything, you may have an abundance for every good deed.

We must always start with ourselves. Am I sowing sparingly or bountifully? Can I really describe the amount of giving I do to church and ministries as "radical?" According to the passage, this unleashes God's blessings.

The second essential component to Brad's equation is our need to do "Radical Asking" — both of God and man. I know Christian workers who are willing to make huge financial requests of God, but seem to be afraid or unwilling to personally invite people to invest. Conversely, I know support raisers who boldly challenge others to partner with them, but skip the essential "God Ask" part, arrogantly relying upon their skills, technology, or winsome personality instead.

Can you see how our own radical giving combined with our radical asking (of God and others) can result in the radical receiving of support from God? In fact, verses 10-11 seems to indicate the more you sacrifice, the more you supply seed to the sower, the more God will "multiply your seed" and enrich you "in everything for all liberality…". He is waiting to pour out his financial blessings until we are willing to practice what we preach!

This is what He was trying to get into the minds and hearts of the Levites too. How the Lord provides for these Old Testament representatives gives us amazing insights into the mind of God how He views His workers. The Lord set them apart with honor and dignity, making sure they would be fully provided for. This commandment would be extended through the Old Testament and emerge again when we get to the New Testament. But first, let's discover how God provided for Nehemiah. Here was a man whose big faith produced some big asks.

7

Nehemiah's
VISION

In 586 BC, King Nebuchadnezzar conquered Judah. He brought back the best and the brightest Jews to Babylon to serve in his kingdom. He was profoundly impacted by the faith of Daniel and his young Hebrew companions. Approximately 142 years later (444 BC) the scepter of authority had been passed down to King Artaxerxes. He was not only the most powerful man in all of Persia — but the whole world. It appears he learned from his predecessors, because he, too, brought a capable, young Jewish man into his inner circle, granting him significant responsibility and freedom. Little did the king know just what a man of vision his cupbearer was.

PASSIONATE AND BURDENED ABOUT HIS CAUSE (NEHEMIAH 2:1-3)

In this passage, Nehemiah is grief-stricken weeping, praying, and fasting in response to a report that the people and property of Jerusalem were in great distress. He interceded almost four months before approaching the king with his ministry vision and request for funding. As each day passed, he became more weighed down with the overwhelming devastation back in his homeland. Even though he had never been sad in the presence of the king, this particular day he could no longer conceal his broken heart. "Why is your face sad though you are not sick?" the king asked (Nehemiah 2:2).

Hearing this question instantly paralyzed the young servant with fear because everyone in the kingdom knew the rule. Showing anything but a happy face in the presence of the king brought the death penalty (Esther 4:2). But apparently Nehemiah felt so strongly about his cause, he was willing to die for it. And so he took the risk of a lifetime to tell the king and queen exactly *why* he was so burdened. He began describing the stark realities of desolation back in his beloved Jerusalem. He was speaking with tremendous emotion, not trying to manipulate the king, but just pouring his heart out to a man willing to listen.

How deeply do you feel about the ministry the Lord has called you to? If the desperate needs of those people you are raising support to reach have never caused you to weep, you may want to go back into your prayer closet. If you and I are genuinely moved at the very core of our being, the Lord will use that to profoundly connect with the minds and hearts of our givers. Ellis Goldstein, who directs the support training for all Cru staff, concurs, "God designed us to react and make decisions intellectually and emotionally. In our vision casting, appeal to both."[28]

RECOGNIZE WHO REALLY PROVIDES MONEY AND COURAGE (NEHEMIAH 2:4)

What a relief it must have been to hear the king respond with, "What would you request?" rather than "Off with his head!" Wisely, Nehemiah did not launch right into his carefully crafted plan and proposal, but instead paused to pray to "the God of heaven." And even though the whole first chapter details his private intercessions that the king would be open and receptive, Nehemiah still wanted to briefly acknowledge the "Great Supplier" with one last God Ask before the moment of truth. No, the Scriptures never clearly indicate what tribe Nehemiah was from, but he definitely looked up in the spirit of the Levites and recognized that giving and receiving was a *vertical* transaction, not a *horizontal* one!

Just as Nehemiah understood this appointment was God's sovereign plan, we, too, must openly admit, "Unless the LORD builds the house, they labor in vain who build it" (Psalm 127:1). This is why we bathe in prayer every person, every call, and every appointment we make. Even though our support meetings may not be with rich kings, we still depend wholly on the power of God, rather than twisting arms, or relying on smooth talk, fancy materials, or latest technology.

A HUMBLE APPROACH EARNS RESPECT (NEHEMIAH 2:5)

"If it pleases the king" is how Nehemiah started his dialogue with Artaxerxes. He was not demanding of the king or claiming any special rights because of the years of service he had rendered. He was gentle, kind, and reverent — coming with an attitude of submission. I appreciate that, but *why* did the king suspend the death-penalty rule for his sad-faced servant and replace it with an eager attentiveness to listen and respond? Because Nehemiah had built up a track record of faithfulness over the years. The second phrase out of Nehemiah's mouth was "if your servant has found favor before you." Had he acquired the king's favor? Apparently so, or else he would be dead now!

Artaxerxes knew a good investment when he saw it, realizing that Nehemiah was a man who planned his work… and then worked his plan. Later, we will see how Nehemiah gathered the necessary funds and materials, traveled to Jerusalem, mobilized the people, and rebuilt the walls, gates, and spirits. With obstacles and enemies at every turn, he completed the project in record time — fifty-two days! I'm sure the credibility he built up with the king paved the way for any future request his hard-charging servant wanted to make.

What kind of credibility do you have in the places and with the people you intend to contact to raise support? Are there any kinds of "repairs" that need to be made to reestablish your good name? Years ago, I was counseling a young woman going into ministry. She went back to her hometown to raise her support, but after four months of hard work she was only at 10%. The reason she got so few appointments is she and her family had unpaid bills and debts to people all over town. I told her she might have to go back, get a job, and repay every single dime owed before she could ever restore her credibility and begin to ask others for support. That's exactly what she did.

Let's pray that each of us can develop a strong follow-through with every commitment we make. Nehemiah had demonstrated such hard work and integrity over the years that he had earned the enduring respect of the king. His creed was: Promises made. Promises kept! If you don't have a history like that, maybe now is the time to start building it.

ASK, THEN WAIT FOR A RESPONSE (NEHEMIAH 2:5-9)

Cornell University did a study where they scattered researchers across the nation to sit at the back of classrooms with a stopwatch and notepad. They were trying to determine the average amount of time teachers provided their students to verbally answer the questions they asked. Once the teacher was able to finish asking the question, the average amount of time they paused to allow the students to respond was less than one second! Most of the teachers were so ill-prepared with their question or so afraid of silence they would immediately jump in and repeat, rephrase, or actually answer their own question. Wow. How to kill class participation in one easy step!

It appears Nehemiah was tutored a little differently because he not only walked into his appointment prepared with a series of carefully worded questions, he was fully determined to wait as long as he needed to allow the king to reply. It might be easy to miss, but here was Nehemiah's first ask: "Send me to Judah, to the city of my fathers' tombs, that I may rebuild it" (Nehemiah 2:5). It was to the point. Even more importantly, he was able to put a period at the end of his request! He had prayed and thought *exactly* what to ask the king, and even though he was nervous, he was able to get it out and wait for a response. Granted, it may have been intimidating looking directly at the king and him looking back, but he was determined to make it crystal clear — it was the *king's turn* to talk!

He obviously received a "yes" from Artaxerxes, but he did not know to what extent the king was willing to help. So Nehemiah came with a lineup of specific requests to follow up his initial ask. Chapter 2 verses 7–8 reveal his level of preparation and boldness:

- *Verse 7* — He also asked the king to write letters to foreign officials allowing him to pass through their territories. The answer was yes.
- *Verse 8* — He then asked the king for a letter to the nearby lumberyard, asking them to provide all the materials to rebuild the walls and gates, and even a house for himself. The answer was again, yes.

To be successful in our support raising efforts, we must put in the necessary "prep work" to craft and practice asking several carefully worded questions. When we get face-to-face with our potential ministry partner, we have to exercise the courage and self-control to ask, then *wait* for an answer. If appropriate, make an additional request — then wait again. Ask, wait; ask, wait. Do not be afraid of silence. That is a tangible way to show honor and extend dignity to the person you are meeting with, as well as to make it obvious — it is *their turn* to talk!

OTHER LESSONS FROM NEHEMIAH

Set Specific Start and Finish Dates

"How long will your journey be, and when will you return?" asked the king (Nehemiah 2:6). Nehemiah had prayed and thought out in advance every detail of his plan, so that whatever question the king threw at him, he was ready to respond quickly — and specifically. We don't score any points at all when we step into our contacts' homes to ask them for support, but then give nebulous, even mystical responses to their basic, reasonable questions. Nehemiah had a precise start and finish date to his project that not only relayed a spirit of urgency to Artaxerxes, but also gave the king confidence that his young cupbearer had organizational capabilities way beyond just food and wine tasting.

Be Open to Taking Gifts From Non-Believers

In my studies, I never get the impression Artaxerxes is a follower of the one true God. And just as Daniel and his friends influenced Nebuchadnezzer, the earlier ruler, Nehemiah impressed this king through his godly life and deeds. Support raising can be a great witnessing tool if we can understand we must get close to non-believers if they're ever going to truly see Jesus in us.

Case in point: Chris was a freshman when he applied to go on one of our mission trips to Malaysia. His main obstacles to raising the required $3,500 was that he had no home church, and no Christian family or friends to approach. So, he went to his fraternity and two other chapters, asking them to adopt him as their philanthropic project. All agreed, he raised his funds, and had a powerful ministry among Malaysian students that summer. When he returned, he made a presentation to each of the fraternities showing them picture after picture of young Muslims who had been enslaved to sin, but were now forgiven and set free by Christ.

Chris used his "need" for funds as an excuse to be an incredible spiritual influence in these fraternities. Later, he started Bible studies in each and led several guys to Christ. You never know what the Lord may do, and you might be the only light in their darkness! You might say, "I would never ask a non-believer to be part of my team." Well, sometimes it's not easy to tell who is and isn't a true Christian. I refuse to play Holy Spirit and determine in advance how God may or may not want to use my support raising efforts in people's lives. Can I tell you the criteria I use as to which individuals I include on my "To Contact List?" Every single person I have ever known, or known of, during my entire life!

They all qualify — no matter their religious background. I refuse to reject anyone from the opportunity to invest in God's eternal purposes — and possibly get personally impacted in the process. Just get them on your team. Begin to befriend and pray for them. Expose them to your life and ministry through your various communications. Stand back and watch the Lord work. You may want to adopt the perspective of Billy Sunday, the popular 1920s evangelist. He was willing to accept and utilize gifts from non-believers and would declare, "I'll take the devil's money, I'll wash it in the blood, and I'll spend it on the kingdom!"[29] Use discernment, as there might be someone, who by their reputation or how they earn their income, would tarnish your witness if others knew this person was supporting you.

Ask For Appropriate Amounts

It was obvious Nehemiah thought deeply and planned thoroughly each step of the way — and that impressed the king greatly. Not only did Nehemiah pray big and plan big, he also asked big! After spending extensive time on his knees, he got up and began strategizing, knowing full well this was a God-sized project requiring God-sized resources. He discerned what the king was capable of, and he wanted to make

"Make no small plans. They will not move the hearts of men."[30]

Elton Trueblood, Author and Theologian

sure his "ask" was commensurate with the giver's ability. You don't ask someone who can fund your whole project for just $100 a month! And even though his life was hanging in the balance, the young cupbearer could not help but share the enormous dream brewing within his heart. Then he took an even greater step of faith and asked for a God-sized gift. Why? He was convinced that big visions require big dollars.

Why can't you and I be modern-day Nehemiahs? Why couldn't we follow his example in boldly praying and boldly asking? Is your vision so big, so compelling, so "God-sized," others will be drawn to join you in order to not miss out or be left behind? Nehemiah was a man who dared to dream big dreams and take huge risks, even asking wealthy, influential people to put up the venture capital to make those dreams a reality. Against all odds, this lowly cupbearer, exiled in a far-away land, made a "God Ask" and believed Him for the impossible. How about you? Will you be this generation's Nehemiah?

Jesus and
SUPPORT

Inconceivable. It's hard enough to imagine the Son of God, King of kings and Lord of lords lowering Himself to leave the glories of heaven for thirty-three years to immerse Himself in the trivial pursuits of us mere mortals. Now, are we to also believe the omnipotent and sovereign God purposely *chose* to rely on depraved earthlings for His very sustenance?

He did.

LUKE 8:1-3

"Soon afterwards, He began going around from one city and village to another, proclaiming and preaching the kingdom of God. The twelve were with Him, and also some women who had been healed of evil spirits and sicknesses: Mary who was called Magdalene, from whom seven demons had gone out, and Joanna the wife of Chuza, Herod's steward, and Susanna, and many others *who were contributing to their support out of their private means*" (Luke 8:3, emphasis added).

OTHERS GAVE TO JESUS AND HIS MINISTRY

The people around Him saw His passion, His mission, and His men — and they wanted to invest. They wanted to free Him up to do His work all the time, and everywhere He went. Your potential donors may be the same way, wanting to *see* what you have accomplished in your life and ministry. No need to go into any bragging sessions, but humbly sharing about some of the lives the Lord has allowed you to touch lets them know you are a good "Return On Investment" (ROI). And the best indicator of what you *will* accomplish in the future is what you *have* accomplished in the past.

Jesus and His disciples received ongoing support from individuals. The monetary help they were receiving was not from foundation grants, local synagogue mission budgets, or even major donors. No, the list here names three specific givers, but also "many others who were contributing to their support out of their private means" (Luke 8:3). And these were not one-time gifts, but rather ongoing support. The word "contributing" here in the original language implies continuous action, repeated over and over. This is one verse we point to when we recommend you focus the vast majority of your efforts on asking *individuals* or couples to invest, and that your request is almost always for monthly giving.[31]

THEY CHOSE TO DEPEND ON OTHERS

Jesus could have done it differently and outfitted His followers with moneychangers on each hip — *cha-ching* and out pours gold coins everywhere. That would have drawn a crowd! So *why* would the supreme Lord of the universe, who could snap His fingers and trillions would be at His feet, decide *this* particular method of funding would be the best? Because Jesus was not into *in*dependence, but *inter*dependence. In other words, He wanted to initiate and model a simultaneous reliance upon God *and* those around Him. He was launching the mysterious, interconnected network called the "Body of Christ" where God wants to work in and through us to build up and sustain one another and His work around the world. And even though this concept may fly in the face of us proud, "I don't need help from anybody!" Americans, we must admit that Jesus thought it up, and we had better practice it.

And if Jesus was willing to fund His personal and ministry expenses in this manner, but I am not, what does that say about me? Scott Morton weighs in: "If it were wrong to be supported by the personal gifts of others, Jesus Christ would not have allowed it in His own ministry. If Jesus became vulnerable enough to be supported by others, you and I must be willing as well."[32]

JESUS MINISTERED TO OTHERS FULL-TIME

The Bible never records Jesus going back into carpentry once He launched into His ministry. He didn't attempt to work part-time to support Himself, but instead was 100% focused on His mission, looking to God and others to cover all His personal and ministry expenses. While the apostle Paul does not specify when or where Jesus said this during His public ministry, he recalls Jesus' teaching: "the Lord has commanded that those who preach the gospel should receive their living from the gospel" (1 Corinthians 9:14, NIV). Jesus not only taught, but modeled this principle. Maybe you thought a full-time Christian worker raising support for their ministry was simply an option or personal choice. No. Jesus actually *commanded* us to do so. Our response? Obey!

You may say, "But I'm just an administrator back at the home office. I really don't preach the gospel." Yes you do, not only with your friends and neighbors, but also in and through the ministry you are a part of. Regardless of our particular role, this verse applies to all of us who are part of a ministry seeking to lift up Christ and expand the kingdom of God on earth.

PRINCIPLES FROM CHRIST'S MINISTRY IN LUKE 10

At the beginning of Luke 8, Jesus modeled to His men how He wanted them to raise their support and do their ministry. In fact, everything Jesus ever did was at least partly so His disciples could learn how to do it themselves. Then at the start of Luke 9, He sent the twelve out on their first ministry excursion, briefing them how to fund themselves. Finally, here in Luke 10, Jesus sends out seventy more of His troops on their first short-term missions assignment, and with even greater detail, pulls them together for a mini-support raising training session. Not only did the Savior personally practice what He preached by funding His own personal and ministry expenses via others' giving, but trained and raised up generations who followed His example.

LUKE 10:1-8

"Now after this the Lord appointed seventy others, and sent them in pairs ahead of Him to every city and place where He Himself was going to come. And He was saying to them, 'The harvest is plentiful, but the laborers are few; therefore beseech the Lord of the harvest to send out laborers into His harvest. Go; behold, I send you out as lambs in the midst of wolves. Carry no money belt, no bag, no shoes; and greet no one on the way. Whatever house you enter, first say, "Peace be to this house." If a man of peace is there, your peace will rest on him; but if not, it will return to you. Stay in that house, eating and drinking what they give you; for the laborer is worthy of his wages. Do not keep moving from house to house.'"

DON'T DO IT ALONE

Jesus wisely sent them out in pairs for encouragement and accountability. The master knew they would need each other, and their teamwork would produce far more than what they could each do on their own. This principle is essential in ministry ventures as well as personal support raising. If you're married, get your spouse involved as much as they are willing and able to. They are probably going to be your greatest asset anyway! Whether it's making calls, going on appointments, tracking your gifts, doing the newsletters, or writing thank-you notes, seek to engage your spouse and/or family as much as possible. If you're single, pull in some friends or disciples who can team up with you.

Why do anything alone if you could do it with someone else? Keep in mind Solomon's principle of "two are better than one, for they have a good return for their labor" (Ecclesiastes 4:9). And if you find yourself late one night sitting and folding hundreds of newsletters all by your lonesome, you'll know you haven't quite applied this principle yet!

BE PREPARED FOR REJECTION

Jesus warned His disciples about this, saying, "I send you out as lambs in the midst of wolves" (Luke 10:3). They were to go and search for a hospitable person in that city. When the disciples found that "man of peace" who would provide room and board, then "your peace will rest on him," Jesus said. (Luke 10:6). The Lord even gave the seventy a curse they should call down on the people of a city who rejected their request for support (Luke 10:10-16). Though tempting at times, I don't advise this today!

Do you remember the first time you shared with your family that you were going into full-time ministry *and* you would be raising your financial support? Perhaps you had parents or other family members who were initially so proud of you for doing "God's work," but when they found out you weren't going to be paid a traditional salary, but instead would be forced to "beg" for your income, they did a 180 and stared at you as if you were an alien from another planet — certainly not part of *their* self-respecting family!

Maybe they were skeptical or embarrassed or downright indignant that some sinister group would take advantage of their sweet, innocent daughter or son like that. Shocked that this ministry, like corporations, didn't have a magical pot of profits someplace from which to pay everyone's salaries, they launched into their speech about you needing to *properly* provide for your family, or the ultra-encouraging "don't you dare contact any of our friends at the country club!"

Yes, sometimes the people you think will be excited and supportive of your decision are the very ones who oppose you the most. Whether it's the home-church pastor who's disappointed you chose not to work with his particular denomination or the non-believing sister who's absolutely sure "personal support raising" must be part of a cult initiation, you will probably experience initial push back from a few of those closest to you.

BE WILLING TO GO TO PEOPLE YOU DON'T KNOW

Jesus sent them out in pairs, going door-to-door to people they did *not* know to ask for the food and housing required to carry out their ministry in that city. The Master did not reveal to them which houses to go to or how many doors they would have to knock on before they found a willing host. But He did tell them *what* to say in "whatever house" they entered: "*Peace be to this house*" (Luke 10:5). The disciples were instructed to keep walking, knocking, asking, and waiting to discover which homeowner in that city would be receptive to their request for help. Jesus wanted His followers to have a big faith, and he knew the key to develop that faith was to put them in situations where they needed to make the big asks.

Rick came to Christ late in college and did not have any Christian friends, family, or church. On top of that, he lacked confidence and was socially awkward. Rick wanted to go on a summer mission trip to Indonesia with our ministry, but had no contact base at all to raise his $3,800. So, he put on his geeky glasses and tie and went door-to-door on every floor of almost all the office buildings in town. He would request to see the owner or director, introduce himself and his ministry, and ask for $75, $100, or $150 toward his mission of helping Indonesian college students gain a personal relationship with God. Guess what? He raised 100% of it — all from people he did not know!

Rick got so fired up about reaching Indonesian students that he wanted to do it full-time when he graduated, but now the agency said he must raise $4,600 of support per month to go. He did just that, and again, almost totally from people he hadn't known beforehand. When Rick arrived and began his ministry, he met a young woman who was also a missionary there. They fell in love, got married, and wanted to spend their lives ministering in Asia together. Now, 20 plus years later, and with four kids, Rick and his wife are required to raise over $10,000 a month to cover all personal and ministry expenses. As you might guess, almost all these additional givers were people he had not known previously to his meeting with them and asking.

I was talking recently to a well-known mission leader who worked with Rick for many years. Without solicitation, he stated, "Rick does the best job raising and maintaining his support team of anyone I've known in my thirty years of ministry." I was stunned. I thought to myself, "If Rick, with all his supposed deficiencies and obstacles, can go out, from scratch, and raise his entire support team from people he did not know, then *anyone* ought to be able to do so. No excuses!"

How about you? Are you willing to go anywhere to talk to anyone who will allow you to share about your ministry and opportunity to invest? Are you prepared to strip yourself of any pride or self-importance you may be clinging to in order to embrace the kind of passion, urgency, courage, humility, and plain ol' hard work that Rick did? I pray so.

BUILD LONGER TERM RELATIONSHIPS

"Stay in that house, eating and drinking what they give you... Do not keep moving from house to house" (Luke 10:7). Once the disciples found a "man of peace" who would host them, Jesus commanded them to stay there, accept their hospitality, and to use that home as their base of operations. This concept reinforces the philosophy of support raising we're proposing, whereby each of us should be praying and looking for people who feel strongly enough about us and our ministry that they will want to start giving and stick with us over the long haul.

The disciples were not taught to raise their funds by going to the local synagogue for a love offering, or hold bake sales at the bazaar, or pass out pledge cards at council meetings. Instead, they were to go to people's homes and ask them face-to-face to partner with them. As the ministry expanded and the stay in their host home extended, I'm sure the relationship between the owners and the disciples deepened. I don't think this method of support raising was just a last-minute idea on the part of Jesus. It was a carefully planned strategy designed to multiply passion for the Lord and His work in the hearts of key citizens in each city.

LABORERS DESERVE TO BE SUPPORTED

How could Jesus justify this form of "religious freeloading" on the part of His disciples? Wasn't it a terrible testimony to the townspeople for them to go house-to-house with their hand out rather than just look for work and earn their own keep? Apparently, in the mind of God, "spiritual" work is just as valid and deserving of compensation as any form of physical or mental work. This principle was true for the Levites and repeated here for us. "Stay in that house, eating and drinking what they give you; *for the laborer is worthy of his wages*" (Luke 10:7, emphasis added).

Even though these followers of the Lord may have initially felt timid about living off the support of others, they were reminded of Jesus' modeling to them in Luke 8. They were not to stand on street corners, disheveled, with a hungry look on their face. No. They were working hard representing the Savior, and He wanted them to view themselves and their work as noble, essential, eternal, and just as deserving of full compensation as the farmer, blacksmith, or business owner. They could hold their heads high knowing their mission and its form of funding was right, holy, and biblical. Other New Testament verses that teach this include: Matthew 10:10, 1 Timothy 5:18, and 1 Corinthians 9:14.

God in the flesh came to earth and *chose* to live and minister off the ongoing gifts of individuals. Let's, you and I, *choose* to as well.

9

Paul
THE MOBILIZER

Paul the apostle did more for the early church than anyone. Three trips across Asia, countless converts, disciples, and churches planted. All while enduring persecution. All while living off support. There's a lot we can learn from how Paul went about funding his life and ministry. It seemed everywhere he went he was seeking to raise up people and money to take the gospel where it had not yet gone. Let's see how he operated.

PAUL THE TENTMAKER?

You might have someone respond to your support request by asking, "Why don't you go out and do your ministry the *biblical* way?" They confidently proclaim, "Paul was a tentmaker and didn't raise support. He paid his own way, and you should too!" Before you succumb to that guilt trip, look at the New Testament and understand there are only three places where Paul made tents, with a specific ministry objective in mind each time:

Thessalonica (2 Thessalonians 3:8-9)

Even though Paul spent only two to three weeks with this young church, he immediately recognized them as being lazy and even using their preoccupation with the second coming of Christ as an excuse not to work. As a result, Paul felt the need to model what it meant to work hard.

Ephesus (Acts 20:33-34)

Paul's ministry there caused his converts to quit buying idols of the goddess Diana. Consequently, if he had accepted financial gifts from believers there, he might have been accused of putting the myriad of heathen craftsmen out of business for *personal* gain. He chose to forego support for a brief time in order to protect his testimony and win the lost.

Corinth (Acts 18:4-5)

Paul was temporarily making tents — and thus only able to preach on Sabbaths. But when Silas and Timothy arrived with financial support, he immediately transitioned from *tent*-making to *disciple*-making and began devoting all of his time exclusively to preaching. In 1 Corinthians 9, Paul zealously upheld his right to be supported by the Corinthians, but because of their immaturity (including accusing Paul of preaching for profit), he briefly chose to support himself to be "above reproach."

Yes, Paul did occasionally secure a "regular" job for the sake of the gospel. But, in the final analysis, it's clear the apostle's preferred mode of operation was always *full-time* ministry. He had a conviction, as should we, that he was willing to do anything to get the gospel out — including occasionally stitching a tent or two! This is in no way meant to disparage bi-vocational pastors, or missionaries in closed countries who can only stay if they have valid employment. But even many of them have financial support teams back home.

PAUL BELIEVED HE AND HIS MINISTRY DESERVED SUPPORT

Seldom have I sensed Paul was angry or defensive, but in 1 Corinthians 9:1-18 we seem to get a double-barreled shotgun of both! He was tired of all the false accusations the carnal Corinthian church threw at him. Again, one of the ongoing claims was that the apostle was preaching in order to get rich. Paul spends most of this chapter laying out a biblical and logical foundation of why he — and other Christian workers — *deserve* to be financially supported. First, he raises a series of rhetorical questions exposing the Corinthians' hypocrisy toward him. Then, he sets out to prove his right to live and minister from their gifts, rather than a secular job. In verses 7-10, Paul uses several metaphors to demonstrate his rationale:

- The soldier has the right to have his expenses paid.
- The farmer should get to eat some of the fruit he produces.
- The shepherd should get to drink some of his livestock's milk.

The apostle even pulls out two concepts from the Old Testament to make his point. The ox that is threshing should not be muzzled (1 Corinthians 9:9), implying he should be fed well to allow him to continue to work. The priest who is serving in the temple should get his share of the sacrifice (verse 13), implying the Jews certainly care for their spiritual leaders, shouldn't the Christians take note and do likewise? Ellis Goldstein teaches biblical support raising from both the Old and New Testaments. "It may look different, but the principles are the same," he asserts. For him, the bottom line is, the Bible consistently teaches "the community gives to those called to full-time ministry."[33]

This fascinating mix of questions, illustrations, and verses in 1 Corinthians 9 all lead up to the real kicker in verse 14 where Paul recites Jesus' command for Christian workers to live off the support of others. "In the same way, the Lord has commanded that those who preach the gospel should receive their living from the gospel" (1 Corinthians 9:14, NIV). It surely seems clear that we are required to follow the example of Jesus, and now Paul, to form partnerships with givers as we fulfill our ministry.

PAUL FELT GUILTY FOR *NOT* ASKING

When Paul was challenging the Corinthians (in 2 Corinthians 11) about his right to be supported by them, he was debating with himself as well. "Or did I commit a sin in humbling myself so that you might be exalted, because I preached the gospel of God to you without charge?" (2 Corinthians 11:7). Paul is questioning himself whether he did the right thing by ministering to the Corinthians... but *not* asking them to invest in his work. Interestingly, this is the model that many of us operate by. We raise support from family, friends, and churches and then go to a different location to minister to a group of people who won't or can't support us yet.

It seemed that Paul evaluated situations city-by-city as to how he would choose to fund himself there. In this case, the carnality and confusion of the Corinthians and their false prophets was obvious. At the same time some were railing on Paul because they thought he was preaching to make a profit, others who knew he wasn't taking any compensation for his ministry were busy undermining his credibility because he *wasn't* charging them! In that culture, the Greeks attached value to an orator's message by how much they charged. Paul was constantly trying to walk a fine line between these two groups and their constant accusations.[34]

PAUL USED HIS COMMUNICATION AND TRAVEL TO RAISE SUPPORT

In AD 57 while he was still in Corinth, Paul wrote a long letter to the church at Rome, a city he had never visited. He penned this theological masterpiece for several reasons, including his longstanding pattern of intercession on their behalf (Romans 1:9-10), his desire to give the believers there a detailed explanation of the gospel (Romans 1:15), but also to raise support from them (Romans 15:20-29). In chapter 15, he states he had already preached the gospel in all the regions in his area and now felt led to head west to find new unreached groups, and in verse 24 writes, "whenever I go to Spain — for I hope to see you in passing, and to be helped on my way there by you, when I have first enjoyed your company for a while."

My pastor shared this about Romans. "Paul wrote to the believers in Rome, setting forth the gospel in a clear and compelling manner, in order to prepare them for his visit and gain their support as they traveled to take the gospel to Spain. I have for years thought of Romans as a support raising letter."[35]

PAUL ASKED FOR SUPPORT FOR THE BENEFIT OF THE GIVER

Even though Paul did not appear to own a home or retirement fund, he possessed a supernatural peace and satisfaction very few of us have, declaring, "not that I speak from want, for I have learned to be content" (Philippians 4:11). He was thankful to the believers for their financial support, but he did not ask them to give because he had needs. This is how he put it: "Not that I seek the gift itself, but I seek for the profit which increases to your account" (Philippians 4:17).

Paul understood the power of making the God Ask to supply him, knowing his Father's heavenly bank was full of glorious riches that could fill and refill all that he needed. And, ultimately, Paul didn't *need* anything. His motive in asking was strictly for the givers' benefit. But

Paul's main burden here was to help the Philippians understand vertical giving. They needed to learn to look up to make *their* God Ask, seeking the Lord's direction as to where they should invest. Whether the believers understood it or not, Paul was doing them a huge favor by helping them move some of their earthly treasure to their heavenly bank account. He assured them that as a result of their generosity, God will surely supply all of their future needs from His heavenly bank (Philippians 4:19).

For this reason, I love what Cru's veteran support trainer, Steve Rentz, calls Paul — a "Treasure Transplanter."[36] One of the major callings Paul had in life was not just to mobilize people, but also to raise resources for expanding and extending the kingdom. He was willing to risk relationships as well as his life to ask and challenge people to give — not to him — but to Christ's work through him. He sought to build this same brand of selflessness into his key men, evidenced by his parting exhortation to Titus for him to "help Zenas the lawyer and Apollos on their way so that nothing is lacking for them" (Titus 3:13).

We must commit to spend the rest of our lives being "Treasure Transplanters" in order to help people move from just the temporal, man-made, *horizontal* buying and selling, to the eternal, God-designed, *vertical* giving and receiving. Let's aid believers in transferring huge portions of their earthly gains to their heavenly bank. Let's allow them to enjoy those rewards and multiplying dividends forever. Let's commit to raising up others who have the same sacrificial mindset as you do.

YOU ARE A MOBILIZER

Like the Apostle Paul, you and I should focus on mobilizing people and their resources to the person and purposes of Jesus Christ. We are not as much support raising as we are *supporter* raising! Joe Michie, Creative Director at Via, views his support raising efforts primarily as mobilizing people. As he asks others to partner with him and his ministry through prayer and finances, he seeks to help them:

- See greater meaning in their daily work
- Play a vital role in kingdom work they had not previously envisioned or seen as possible
- Live more strategically by encouraging them to develop goals for their giving
- Partner not only with him, but his ministry
- To pray as well as give

In fact, Joe actually looks for ways to begin discipling his supporters. He prays for opportunities to expand their vision by growing their knowledge of the work God is doing around the world. He encourages his supporters to ask their community group and church to adopt an unreached people group. Joe attempts to help them find practical ways to pray for specific peoples around the world. He shows them opportunities to serve through short-term mission trips. Joe is just trying to draw them into deeper levels of the "World Christian" lifestyle.

How about you? What if you were to start viewing yourself as a mobilizer? Not just moving people's finances from one bank to another, but moving their hearts from a temporal focus to an eternal one. Don't be satisfied with just becoming a treasure transplanter, but stretch out there to mobilize your supporters for kingdom purposes. Embrace the fact that you and I are nothing less than front-line mobilizers. Your fundraising efforts then become getting in the trenches every day, having one-on-one, face-to-face "mobilization appointments" seeking to align God, God's people, and your God-given ministry. You are a spirit-filled *supporter* raiser! For that kind of perspective, that kind of power, those kind of results, you are definitely going to need to regularly make the God Ask!

"You are not raising support, but supporters. Technically, we are 'supporter raising.' We are raising people, not money."[37]

Andrew Knight, Support Trainer for Campus Outreach

A
SUPPORTING
CAST

Sometimes it can feel so un-American to ask. Most of us were brought up where it was considered a weakness to ask for something. We can be so self-sufficient, not needing anything from anybody. This may be American — but it is not Christian. We need to get into our heads that it's not only okay to ask, it is good to ask. It's biblical to ask. I include this concept and others in a final arsenal of passages helping us build our foundation. If you're still wondering, "Does God think it's okay to raise support?" maybe these verses will put those doubts to rest.

GOD REQUIRED THE HEBREWS TO TAKE INITIATIVE

You might be asking the questions: If God is my source, then why do I need to go out and raise funds? Why doesn't it just automatically appear? In the wilderness, the Lord was certainly the One who provided for the Hebrews. But He *required* the people to go out and gather the manna each day. This "us and God" partnership is the way He operates in support raising, as well as ministry… and life!

Through God, Pharoah let Moses and the Hebrews leave the bondage of Egypt behind to go to the wilderness and worship. Exodus 11:2 and 12:35 describe how the Lord knew the Israelites would need raw materials to craft and furnish the ark and tabernacle. God commanded Moses to tell the multitude to ask the Egyptians for clothing and articles of silver and gold as they departed for the Promised Land. In spite of their fear, they obeyed. These non-believing, idol-worshipping, plague-demolished Egyptians gave the Israelites whatever they asked for. Amazing!

THE LORD COMMANDED ELIJAH TO ASK

Someone may come to you with 1 Kings 17:1-7 in hand and say, "You shouldn't be forcing people to give you money. All Elijah did was sit there and God provided everything he needed by sending ravens with food and water for him. Quit pestering people and trusting in your own efforts. Let go and let God!" I'm sure your friend is well intentioned, but he needs to read down the text a bit further. The very next section (1 Kings 17:8-16) recounts how God then told Elijah to finish his meal, get up, go to Sidon, and ask a widow and her son for their last bit of food.

Could you do this? After my big meal, I would feel so guilty about going into town and approaching a poor, emaciated woman with her young, famished son. I can't quite picture these words emerging from my lips, "Excuse me, ma'am. I noticed you and your son are about to eat your last little bit of bread — and die, but I'm wondering if I could have that bread instead of you?" The point is this. Even though the Lord had promised the prophet *and* the widow that He would provide for them, isn't it amazing that God still *required* Elijah to find and approach the woman, and then to *ask* her to give? If he obeyed, God had blessings galore in store for all three of them.

What is God's role, and what is ours? It's hard to discern sometimes. But Mike Congrove, a support raiser and worker in Sudan, believes initiative and hard work on our part are essential; "God does take care of the birds of the air. There are plenty of worms, but they don't just fly into the bird's mouths! The birds are always moving, always looking." As a result, Congrove describes his support raising approach as the "iron triangle" — letters, calls, and appointments. He claims, "There are no shortcuts. The miraculous is found by going through the process."[38] We know the Bible teaches giving because we get to hear many sermons about that. But it teaches taking the initiative to ask also. In fact, 147 times in the

New Testament alone, the word "ask" or "asking" appears. I would call that a theme! James 4:2 is true. We have not because we ask not.

ADVOCATING ON BEHALF OF A THIRD PARTY

John's personal letter to Gaius, a church leader, was to urge him to show hospitality to Demetrius, a traveling preacher, who was also probably the bearer of 3 John. The apostle was writing a referral to Gaius on behalf of his Christian coworker stating, "You will do well to send them on their way in a manner worthy of God" (3 John 6). Thus, John's endorsement of Demetrius' character and ministry was the basis of this appeal: "Therefore we ought to support such men, so that we may be fellow workers with the truth" (3 John 8). This is a classic example of one believer asking another for funds on behalf of a third party in order to help them raise their personal and ministry expenses.

TEACHING GENEROUS GIVING MORE THAN TITHING

What was in the mind of God when He told Israel to "bring the whole tithe into the storehouse, so that there may be food in My house"? This Malachi 3:10 verse is the most common passage pastors rely upon to exhort their congregations to direct their giving toward their church. It is true the Jews were supposed to take 10% of their grain and put it into the storehouse of the temple, but can we legitimately fast-forward that practice thousands of years and make it the obligation of all believers now? I'm sure it was certainly a *description* of their current situation, but are we really properly interpreting Scripture to now require it as the *prescription* for all of our giving today? I am for recognizing "timeless principles" from the Old Testament, but we must not think that all the commands and laws for Israel now apply to the church.

Second Corinthians 9:7 (NIV) summarizes God's heart for our giving today. "Each man should give what he has decided in his heart to give, not reluctantly or under compulsion, for God loves a cheerful giver." Shouldn't our giving under grace exceed anything we would give under the law? In other words, the "want to" should be a greater motivation to give than the "ought to." Consequently, my pastor says if you're fixated with just giving 10% to the church, don't give 10%… give 9% or 11%! He claims God is more interested in our heart and motives than whether or not we own a calculator!

This is why I have been focused on teaching believers to give generously rather than to tithe. Tithing can become a legalistic "check it off" kind of obligation rather than the joyful privilege the Lord intended giving to be. Besides, author Randy Alcorn says 10% should just be the beginning point for believers. He calls it the "training wheels" just to get us started, and that as time goes on our generosity ought to grow way beyond 10%. I agree![39]

A mature, well-studied believer shared with me recently he gives the first 10% of his income to his church and the extra to missionaries. When I asked him where he came up with that formula, he took a long pause and admitted it was simply a "cultural habit" he had formed over the years rather than any biblical command he knew of. This is obviously a hotly-contested issue, but my plea is for us to set aside our "Western Christianity" lens and objectively, honestly, study the Scriptures to see whether this is truly what God is teaching New Testament believers.

OLD VERSUS NEW

Even today, I have a host of commentaries spread out on my desk trying to once again find *any* kind of agreement at all between biblical scholars. The debate rages regarding tithes and offerings in the Old Testament. Were they required? Optional? 23% total? 24.5%? 33%? Even 50%? One of the reasons Jesus came and then gave us the New Testament was so we would stop judging one another based upon rules and regulations.

"We desperately need to explore how much of our understanding of the gospel is American and how much is biblical."[40]

David Platt,
Pastor and Author

Even though some surveys show that most evangelicals believe the Bible does not require tithing, I am committed to teaching others to give much more than just 10%, and to live and give from the heart. My motive in all this is not to decrease the amount of giving to churches, but to *increase* it. But let's also recognize these "sent ones," full-time Christian workers who raise support, are part of the body of Christ too. Giving to them is also giving to the "church."

As a former pastor, I would love to tell you the New Testament clearly teaches tithing to your local church. Peter, Paul, and James are completely silent on the subject, and Jesus Himself only touches on it twice, in Matthew 23:23/Luke 11:42, and then Luke 18:12. In both instances,

He only brings the subject up in order to condemn the religious leaders for putting such a heavy emphasis on tithing! My wife and I give much more than 10% to the Lord's work, and the very first check we write every month is to our local church — but we don't do it because the Bible commands it.

Instead of restrictive formulas or percentages, God gives us numerous empowering principles from the New Testament that we can draw from as we go about our giving. Here are at least four:

1. *To give sacrificially* — like the poor widow did in Luke 21:1-4
2. *To give consistently* — like the Corinthians were told to do in 1 Corinthians 16:2
3. *To give joyously* — like the Ephesians were told to do in Ephesians 5:1-2
4. *To give discretely* — like the disciples were told to do in Matthew 6:1-2

We really do reap what we sow. Matthew 6:33 is true. If we seek God and His kingdom first, "all these things will be added" unto us. My wife and I have experienced the "you can't out-give God" principle over the years. When the economy dipped, we *expected* a drop in support to us. But as our personal giving to our church and others increased, so did the amount donated to us. The Lord keeps showing us that nothing, not even the ups and downs of the U.S. economy, affects Him or the heavenly bank He presides over. From personal experience, if we are faithful to sacrificially invest in the kingdom, God takes great joy to multiply those blessings back to us.

I hope you feel like you know more about what the Bible teaches regarding money, giving, and support raising. This has a way of enlarging your faith, as well as your asks. This firm biblical groundwork must form the basis for having the right perspective to raise your support — in such a way that honors the Lord. All opinions, perceptions, and experiences should submit themselves to the truth of God's Word. Affixing the right lens to how we view God, ministry, ourselves, supporters, money, and asking can make us or break us.

The
GOD ASK

Section III
THE SECRET PRIVILEGE

The highest honor in raising support is partnering with God and your support team.

You Can't.
GOD CAN.

In Mel Gibson's classic movie, *Braveheart,* young William Wallace saw his father, brother, and many other Scots massacred by English soldiers. After seeing the bloody and lifeless bodies, William wanted to immediately rush out and get revenge. But Uncle Argyle, his new caretaker, stopped the boy and shared some wisdom. "First learn to use this," his uncle said, tapping little William on the head. "Then I'll teach you to use this," Argyle added, pointing to his sword.

I've had support raising trainers tell me I wait too long to begin teaching the mechanics and the how-to's of raising personal financial support. But after training thousands of Christian workers, I have come to this conclusion: Christian workers abandon their calling, fail at support raising, or limp along for decades stressed and underfunded due to matters of the heart and mind, much more than poor technique. Our support-training seminars are two nine-hour days, preceded by a required 25-35 hours of preparation. Almost all the prep, and well over half of the on-site training, deal with the head and the heart. In other words, we feel compelled to first help each worker understand the biblical validity of support raising. Based on that, we then labor to give them a healthy perspective of God, their ministry, themselves, and their supporters.

If I can help you gain a biblical conviction and proper attitudes through the reading of this book, the battle is almost won. So please be patient as we hammer away at the basics. Do not skip ahead to the how-to's. Yes, I will get to the tried and tested strategies and best practices. I will also share with you the top mistakes people make in support raising. But trust me, unless you fully grasp the "why?" behind the "how?" you'll never understand, nor experience, the God Ask.

THE POWER OF PERSPECTIVE

If a previous generation's most "frozen moment in time" was the bombing of Pearl Harbor, or the day JFK was assassinated, maybe our most recent "world-altering" snapshot would be 9/11. Even now, some Christian workers still point to that terrorist attack when discussing the success or failure of their support raising efforts. I hear people say, "Ever since 9/11 when the stock market crashed, people became fearful and started hoarding. They didn't want to even meet with me, much less give!"

At the same time, I hear another support raiser share, "God has used that tragedy in some amazing ways. People realize relationships are more important than possessions. They want to give their money and themselves to something that really matters. They are very excited about joining my team." After listening to both sides of the story, I do a double-take, scratch my head, and ask, "Well, *which* is it?" It all depends upon your perspective!

Yes, we can have a "woe is me" attitude about things in life. If we do, we will ultimately determine our own destiny by our constant negativity

"We cannot change our past or how people will act. We cannot change the inevitable. The only thing we can do is play on the one string we have, and that is our attitude. Life is 10% what happens to me and 90% how I react to it."[41]

Chuck Swindoll,
Pastor and Author

and the self-fulfilling prophecies we allow to dominate our thoughts. Are you fixated on any looming challenges or circumstances you perceive as holding you back from getting to your ministry assignment quickly — and fully funded?

We have a choice. We get to decide each day whether we're going to view those so-called "obstacles" as barriers to keep us from our 100% mark or, as an act of our will, *choose* to use them as stepping stones to reach the goal. When Paul exhorted us "to bring every thought captive to the obedience of Christ" he was also referring to all the small-minded, navel-gazing, doomsday attitudes we're sometimes tempted to slip into. My prayer is that God would change your heart so that your view of support raising would move from obligation to opportunity, from a prerequisite to privilege. That you would find a secret joy in getting to partner with God and others in this unique way.

What lens are you viewing support raising through? We have all affixed certain lenses to ourselves that we use to view everything through. Consequently, our perspective will, of course, be colored by the lens we have chosen. All of us have our own dose of "tunnel vision." We view things the way we do because we *think* we are right. I guess if we thought another perspective was a better one, we would adopt it. Right? Not necessarily so, because sometimes it is very painful to change. In fact, to change yourself is virtually impossible. You can't, but God can!

The lens we choose can make us or break us. Years ago, two salesmen were sent to an island to sell shoes and telegraphed back to the home office — one without the right perspective; one with. Salesman One sent a telegram back that stated: "Ten thousand tribal people. None wear shoes. Coming home!" In contrast, Salesman Two had a different perspective. His telegram read: "Ten thousand tribal people. None wear shoes. Send ten thousand pairs!"

When people gain the right perspective on support raising, I have seen them experience such a radical change, they go back to their family, friends, and coworkers completely different. Everything has been transformed, and everyone around them senses it.

When you have such a seismic shift like this, you look at life differently. You look at God and the world differently. You look at your family and friends differently. You look at money and ministry differently. You look at your donors and support raising differently. Allow God to throw away our pitiful man-made lens, and instead let Him hold up His perfect lens for us to peer through. The result? Everything will change!

THE ROAD AHEAD

In the next several chapters, we will address these questions:
- How do you view your God?
- How do you view your ministry?
- How do you view yourself?
- How do you view your supporters?
- How do you view money?
- How do you view asking?

Affixing a *biblical* lens to properly answer each of these questions is essential to developing the right perspective and a healthy support team. The Lord may want to do some surgery on our hearts as we take stock of our various perspectives. Let Him. Start with prayer: *"Oh Lord, please show me if I am off track someplace. I want to be teachable. Open my mind and heart. Give me courage to look within and allow You to make any changes You choose to. If there is something I need to repent of, or recommit to, or study and rethink more deeply, or something that needs to move from beliefs down into convictions, I beseech You, Holy Spirit, to give me the humility and power to do so. In Jesus' name."*

OUR VIEW OF GOD

Where did you get your perception of who God is? From your parents? Sunday school? Maybe from TV or movies? Some view God as a policeman ready to come down hard on any little slip-up. Some view Him as a heavenly Santa Claus, who wants us to sit on His lap each morning and, with a jolly laugh, can't wait to fulfill our wish list. Others casually view Him as the "big man upstairs." The place to always begin when building a healthy perspective is to have the proper view of who this great and sovereign God is. What lens we affix to our God will profoundly affect our relationship with Him, and every area of our life — especially our support raising! To better understand the heart and hand of God, we must believe the following.

He Is Willing

"God our Savior, who desires all men to be saved and to come to the knowledge of the truth" (1 Timothy 2:3-4). Certainly the Lord wants to bring every "lost sheep" into the fold much more than you or I do. We talk a good game, but He has staked His life on it! God yearns to see your life and ministry become fruitful.

He Is Able

"Now to Him who is able to do far more abundantly beyond all that we ask or think, according to the power that works within us" (Ephesians 3:20). Not only is this holy and awesome God willing, He is also able; able to do above and beyond anything we could ever comprehend or even imagine!

This is a key verse you would be wise to memorize during your support raising journey — in order to hold onto as an anchor during some of the dark, stormy days!

From our pulpits we preach a limitless God, but when it comes to funding ministries we think He has a limited budget. Does the Lord have a big money pie in heaven, but it has only so much to go around? He can only dole out a little here to this church, a little there to that ministry, some to this person, but then He sheepishly has to admit, "Sorry my child, my bank is depleted for now. I can't take away from one of these other people. Maybe you can come back tomorrow?" God is not a penny-pinching spendthrift trying to save a buck! This "scarcity mentality," according to Cru's Ellis Goldstein, cripples ministries. His belief? "God's net worth has not changed since the day of creation!"[42]

For those who have learned that God owns everything, He promises to supply all their needs. How? According to His "riches in heaven" (Philippians 4:19). The Lord has an endless source of funds, and He is not greedy or stingy. As Andy Stanley says, "You are invited to tap into the inexhaustible resources of God" and He delights in giving His children what they ask.[43]

MOUNTAINS OR MOLEHILLS?

A couple of classics that have reinforced the shaping of my biblical view of God over the years are J. B. Phillips' *Your God is Too Small* and A. W. Tozer's *Knowledge of the Holy*. Phillips' premise is if our problems and struggles loom large in our minds, it shows we must have an embarrassingly tiny view of our great God. In other words, if having to raise $8,000 a month in ministry support just seems like Mount Everest to you, you may be in desperate need of a "Mindset Makeover."

A. W. Tozer was a prominent pastor and author in Chicago during the twentieth century. As a young man he would go to one of the nearby beaches and, from 4:00 a.m. to 6:00 a.m. each morning, lay facedown in the sand and simply "think about God." His premise: "What comes to our minds when we think about God is probably the most important thing about us."[44]

"I have found that there are three stages in every work of God; first it is impossible, then it is difficult, then it is done."[45]

Hudson Taylor, Founder of China Inland Mission in 1865

We can either honor or dishonor God, dependent upon whether we believe His promises or not. For instance, in Jeremiah 33:3 (NKJV) the Lord claims, "Call to Me, and I will answer you, and show you great and mighty things, which you do not know." Will we pass over this with a cursory nod and move on, or will we stop and literally take Him at His Word? We can pay the Lord the greatest compliment or the greatest insult dependent upon whether we accept what He declares as truth... and then act upon it!

One way to test whether we have a healthy perspective of our God is by taking a look at what we are asking Him. Pull out your prayer list this week and do a little evaluation. Is it filled with dinky little requests? If so, step back for a moment and look at the situation from God's perspective. He appreciates us bringing Him the "small stuff," but don't you know He desires an opportunity to really show Himself strong on our behalf? So prove Him. Test Him. He is waiting. The Lord yearns for us to ask Him for things commensurate with His ability; the kind of prayers that when He does answer them, you and others have to stand back and give the only plausible explanation: "God has done this!" How about you? Are you praying for mountains... or molehills? Truly, the size of our prayers reveals the size of our God.

HONOR OR DISHONOR

My family and I live in Arkansas, home of the Walmart headquarters. Sam Walton, the founder, was the kind of man who drove an old pick-up truck with his dog in the back. What if one foggy morning I was driving to work and noticed an old truck miss the turn at the bridge and instead head down the hill, into the water, and start sinking? I hope I would immediately pull over, race down that hill, and into the water to make the rescue. What if I found the truck already submerged with an elderly man slumped behind the wheel, close to drowning? I dive down and pull him out, swim him to the side, start CPR, and attempt to revive him.

What if the man came to, sat up, and said, "You saved my life! Do you know who I am? I'm Sam Walton, the world's richest man. I want to reward you. I have my checkbook right here. I'll put your name as the payee, sign it, and make it out for *any* amount you tell me to." With pen in hand and waiting for my response he adds, "How much do you want me to give you?" Well, I think to myself, am I a lucky guy or what! I look around, then down at my watch, and say, "Well, Mr. Walton, it's 7:30 a.m. and I am a little hungry. There's a McDonald's right down the street and an Egg

McMuffin sure would taste good right now. How 'bout five bucks?" Astonished and speechless, he finally spits out: "Five dollars? That's it? I've never even written a check that small! But if you say so." He fills in the amount, hands me the check, turns, and walks away.

"The most difficult thing to understand about prayer is why God would place this kind of power in the hands of people like us."[47]

What do you think your family and friends would say to you when you told them that story? Would they congratulate you on your good fortune or ask how the McMuffin was? No! They would scream, "Are you kidding me? The world's richest billionaire was willing to write you a check for *any* amount, and you *only* asked

Ron Dunn, Author and Evangelist

for *five* measly bucks. Have you lost your mind?" In the same way, we dare not "under ask" God.

Legend has it that after a particularly long and brutal battle, the great French Emperor Napoleon and his army finally conquered a highly prized Mediterranean island and its many inhabitants. Afterward, while he and his generals were sitting, drinking, and savoring the victory, a young officer approached Napoleon. When the revered general asked the man what he wanted, he looked straight at Napoleon and said, "Sir, give me this island!" Instantly, all the other generals began to laugh and mock the audacious young man, that is until Napoleon turned and asked one of them for a pen and another for paper. To their amazement, Napoleon wrote out a deed to the island, signed it, and handed it to the lowly, but bold soldier. "How could you do that?" stammered one of his generals, "What made this man worthy to receive this great island after we fought so hard to win it?" "I gave him this island," Napoleon reflected, "because he honored me by the magnitude of his request."[46]

As I think about my own relationship with God and the supplications I lay out before Him, I have to be honest. I do not always honor Him by the magnitude of *my* requests. I desperately want to have the all-believing prayer life resembling the impact and "kick" of a twelve-gauge shotgun, but instead it seems to dribble out more like a BB gun sometimes! My pastor in college, H.D. McCarty, used to say, "When I get to heaven, I don't want to be guilty of asking God — or others — for too little." Me neither. I don't want God to look into my eyes and ask, "Why didn't you ask Me for more? Why didn't you ask others for more?" I want to start now to be able to give Him a good answer then!

THE ULTIMATE PERSPECTIVE

In Mark 10, Jesus was talking with His disciples, and said, "And again He took the twelve aside and began to tell them what was going to happen to Him" (Mark 10:32). This was at least the second, third, or fourth time He had pulled them together to cover this same topic.[48] He must have felt like they *still* didn't get it and needed to go over with them again exactly what was to take place in His final days. In chronological order, the Lord reviews once more the Son of Man's betrayal, trial, condemnation, mockeries, beatings, crucifixion, topped off with "and three days later He will rise again" (Mark 10:34). Apparently, Jesus still didn't get the response He was looking for.

Instead of sympathy or appreciation, James and John approached Jesus and demanded, "Teacher, we want You to do for us whatever we ask of You" (Mark 10:35). It's stunning to me He doesn't rebuke them for being ungrateful. Even in the face of repeated selfishness, the Savior patiently responded in verse 36 with, "What do you want Me to do for you?" This was one of His favorite questions. In verse 51 of the same chapter, Jesus asks it again of a man in a whole different setting.

I believe He is asking you that question right now. Jesus is inviting us to make the God Ask — directly to Him. He has written out a check with your name on it, signed His name to it, and is waiting for you to tell Him *how much* you want Him to fill it out for. I'm *not* talking about money here. I *am* talking about what it is you are asking God for. Are you going to believe Him for big things — or not? Will you stretch out your faith and decide you are going to start asking the Lord proportionate to what He is able to do? You and I have the opportunity of a lifetime at our fingertips: Simply and humbly, we can choose to honor Him by the magnitude of our requests.

How you view your God will determine your success in support raising. You and I cannot have a personal relationship with God unless we have proper perspective of who He is. This relationship is at the core of every single area of life. The only place I find any sustaining vision, passion, or daily motivation to accomplish anything is from Him. In John 15, Jesus said, "Apart from Me, you can do nothing." Zero. I'm a fool for even entertaining the thought of relying on my own intelligence, gifts, or skills. Full funding, impressive ministry results, all the trappings of a successful life add up to emptiness without the Lord. Attempting to do our support raising apart from His power is absolute insanity. Don't do it.

(12)

↑

Choosing
PASSION

My wife and I have had the joy of working with thousands of college students and have engaged in countless conversations with them about what they're going to do as they approach graduation. Up to that point, they had felt safe and secure knowing they were simply coming back to campus for another year of school. But now that they were being kicked out of the nest, they felt a strong need to pray, get counsel, pursue options, and make decisions. As I chat with these twenty-one to twenty-five-year olds, I love to pose an unusual question. "If you could do *anything* with your life, what would you want to do? Just for a moment, free your mind from school loans or parents' wishes or boyfriend pressure. Put no constraints or parameters on it. Write down what *you* would love to do with your life if *you* got to choose."

Most have never allowed their mind or heart to think that broadly or freely. They've been conditioned to operate under some set of exterior expectations or self-imposed limitations. A few have sat there so long staring at that blank sheet, I thought they might pass out! They finally get an inspirational thought, and begin enthusiastically scribbling something. They finish with a smile, pass it over

There are many things in life that will catch your eye, but only a few will catch your heart. Pursue those!

to me, and I take a look. Nine out of ten times I pass it back to them, look deep into their eyes and quietly say, "Go do this."

There is a reason they feel so excited about the specific direction, cause, or vocation they wrote down. It's because *God* is the One who put it in their heart. "Delight yourself in the LORD; and He will give you the desires of your heart" (Psalm 37:4). "Are you delighting yourself in the Lord?" I ask the graduating senior. "I am certainly seeking to," they reply. "Well then," I respond, "you've just written down the desires of your heart. So, go for it." Too simplistic or idealistic? I probably do have a more "wide-open" view of helping a person discover God's direction for their life, but I believe this exercise strikes at the core of understanding what each of us were designed to do.

"STAGE TWO" GREAT COMMISSION LIVING

The place to begin and end is always with the Lord Jesus. Having established this, we can build on this foundation by gaining a radical but wise view of the work God has called us to. You have taken huge steps of faith. It is He who is putting all the pieces together, but the Lord is using you to do it. Filling out your staff application and interviewing for your ministry position was the easy part. Now comes stage two. When you and I take this enormous second step of raising your full support, it will set the course for the rest of our lives and ministries. What a milestone. A stake driven into the ground. A breakthrough for our faith and fears for each of us. Walking toward and conquering this challenge will prepare you for the giants you meet along the way. It will transform your ministry.

For example, what if, in the face of incredible odds, you went out, trusted God, and from scratch, raised your *entire* support? Now you get to report to your assignment and begin planning out your ministry. Someone

"Risk more than others think is safe. Care more than others think is wise. Dream more than others think is practical. Expect more than others think is possible."

A West Point Cadet

suggests you put together a weekly meeting where you'll be teaching biblical leadership principles to the coaches of all the high schools in your city. Whispering in your other ear, though, are key people telling you why it won't work — but all you can think about is how *God* worked mightily through you to raise your full support and conquer the fears you encountered. You pray and decide to take a big step of faith again, and start by going to the biggest high school in the city to have a one-on-one with the head coach. You ask if he and his staff will be the first to commit.

Why not make a decision that this kind of attitude and action will become "the norm" for all of your future personal, family, financial, and ministry decisions? Choosing to pursue this kind of passion in support raising has a way of carrying over into all areas of your life and will help you major on the majors in your ministry. The Great Commission needs to be central to your passion and the most significant cause you have. If there was a greater one, I would go after it, and I would be disappointed if you didn't do the same! This is why I have committed myself to provide support training for Great Commission ministries only. These are groups involved in one or more of these biblical "kingdom expanding" activities:

- *Evangelism* — winning people to Christ
- *Establishing* — building them up in the faith
- *Equipping* — training them to win and build up others
- *Exporting* — sending them out to reproduce the process

This building up of the body of Christ on earth is why God has placed you and me in the ministry.

CALLED BY GOD

When Robbie Knievel, son of the infamous daredevil Evil Knievel, made a 228-foot motorcycle jump across a portion of the Grand Canyon, he was interviewed by a reporter and asked how he happened to choose this particular profession. He simply responded, "Everybody has a calling. This is mine." Yes, Robbie, everyone has a calling — but it doesn't have to be a death wish! The calling we received from the Lord is not a leap into the dark, but into the light. Some believe you aren't qualified to enter into full-time ministry unless you first see a light from heaven, with trumpets blowing, tears flowing, goose bumps popping, topped off with a final act of surrender accompanied by a powerful middle-of-the-night "liver quiver."

Whether you had an emotional "Damascus Road" experience or you just made a logical decision to give all of your time and energies to the Lord's work, you still must possess a deep, abiding confidence from God Himself that *this* ministry is what He wants you to do. It needs to be a package deal where support raising is as much a part of your calling as the actual ministry. Author and ministry leader Chuck Colson communicates the seriousness of our task, "We are not engaged in some vague philanthropic exercise. We are dealing with life and death. And we had better get on with this business of proclaiming the gospel."[49]

SOLD ON THE VISION

Sometime during your life, you might have someone come to you with an investment opportunity, confidently promising you will double your money if only you'll put in $50,000 along with ten other investors into this "can't lose" deal. Your first question directed to him should be, "How much of *your* own money are you putting in?" If it is not a substantial amount, he is not truly sold on the vision. How naïve of him to think he could ever sincerely convince you or anyone else to put money into this project if he is not willing to do the same. This concept applies to your ministry as well. Unless you're sold on it, you'll never sell it to others. We must set the pace for the people we are leading or seeking to influence. In other words, if I want my supporters to feel strongly about my ministry, I'm going to have to feel *super* strong about it. Helen Keller believed that "The greatest tragedy to befall a person is to have sight, but lack vision."[50]

If the ministry you are headed into is just something that sounds interesting or fun to you, or a way to help some needy people for a couple of years before you get into your "real career," I'm afraid you will face an uphill battle in soliciting committed financial supporters. Unless you believe, deep in your soul, that your vision is from God and is the most strategic thing you could do with your life, you will not experience much receptiveness from the potential donors you meet with. Oh, people may make a "charitable donation," but few will be moved to significantly invest and become a ministry partner with you.

EMBRACE YOUR DESTINY

The Word of God is the will of God and the Lord has given us much more freedom than we realize to discern and implement His marching orders for us. He places in each of us a special "bent," a passion, that if we can uncover and pursue, we will experience fulfillment and blessing in our lives and ministries. You will have built-in motivation, and the likelihood of being successful shoots straight up if you are doing what you want to do more than anything else in the world. And if it requires raising your support to pull it off, you'll probably see some remarkable receptivity as donors get a taste of your authentic excitement, purpose, and sense of destiny. When I'm discipling someone who wants to go into full-time ministry, I sometimes set up a couple of interviews for them with very well-paying jobs in their majors, with companies run by various friends of mine. I don't want them to go into ministry out of "default," but because they believe deeply God has called them to do so. Giving them the opportunity to say "no" and walk away from incredible job opportunities and salaries has a way of solidifying that conviction. I'm not sure I have ever met someone who regretted choosing passion over prosperity.

GETTING ADMINISTRATORS FUNDED

At this stage, you may be saying, "You don't understand. In our organization, I'm just an administrator. How in the world am I going to raise my support? I'm not in a foreign country or on a college campus. I'm stuck behind a desk here at our headquarters working on projects." Again, it's a matter of perspective. You can meet your goals or destroy your chances of getting to full support based upon how you view your ministry.

"If you cannot do great things, do small things in a great way."[51]

Don't believe the rumor going around that administrative or IT people can't raise their support and must always be paid salaries. We have a thirty-eight-year-old, quiet, reserved techie type we recently brought on staff. He went through our support raising training, then went home and asked six couples to invest some front-end launching funds to allow him to quit his job and focus on support raising. He jumped right in, traveling to different cities, setting up appointments, humbly asking people face-to-face to join his team. Eighty days later he surpassed 100% with a huge buffer and was getting ready to sell his home and move to our headquarters.

*Napoleon Hill,
American Author*

A story is told of the reporter who asked this short question to three bricklayers constructing a cathedral. "What are you doing?" The first worker smirked, "I'm laying bricks." The second smiled at the question and replied, "I'm building a church." But the third stood up, raised his hands to the sky and proclaimed, "I am bringing glory to God!" All three men doing the exact same thing, but with radically different perspectives. Similarly, I have talked to many administrative staff over the years whose job titles may be the same, but who are worlds apart in how they view their roles. Here's how three administrators who have the same exact job description view their role.

Staffer #1: "I just answer emails and talk on the phone all day."
Staffer #2: "I provide administrative support for all our staff."
Staffer #3: "I'm a vital link between our 200 plus missionaries in Central Asia and our home office here as we seek to plant 5,000 churches among the lost by the year 2025. As a resource coordinator, I provide all the tools and information they need to do their very strategic grass-roots evangelism and disciple-making among unreached people groups where most have never even heard of Jesus! It would be an honor to have you partnering with us in this critical ministry."

Three different individuals. All with the exact same title and role. Only one has had her ministry lens transformed and views her calling through God's eyes, not her own. Only one viewed support raising as a secret privilege. Only one is fully funded. Administrative staffers are worth their weight in gold and essential to the functioning of the ministry. Some ministry leaders don't value them as they should. Consequently, these administrators don't put much stock in themselves. As a result, when they look a potential donor in the eye, it's hard for them to truly believe their role is that critical.

Don't let family, staff, friends, or donors determine the significance of the ministry you fulfill. Destroy the "poor me" voices that play in the back of your mind. Look up to catch a heavenly vision for the grand and glorious work the Great Commander has called you to. It may appear you are "behind-the-lines," but do not be deceived, you are just as vital as any member of God's army. You are working hard to fulfill your heavenly assignment, and biblically, you deserve to be supported.

If you believe you are in the most strategic position you could be and God has called you to do it, those convictions will be revealed during your support appointments. What your actual job description happens to be isn't as important as having a deeply imbedded vision and passion to fulfill it. A lot is tied to how you view yourself. A short self-examination may be in order. It may be a little painful, but oh so helpful.

13

Worthy of the
WAGE

Matthew was good-looking, well educated, a strong speaker, gifted leader, and discipler who wanted to join our staff. As he and his equally impressive wife launched out to raise their support, they got stuck at the halfway mark on their fundraising. Believing they were a great investment and a couple we wanted to get behind, I told him my family wanted to come on their monthly team. "No," he protested, "there are a lot of other people you're involved with who are headed into ministry who need support." I assured him that was true, but we felt strongly about coming onto *their* monthly team, already deciding the amount. Deflecting me again, he added, "There are other great workers you need to be investing in." In frustration, I declared, "We have the first check right here. We *are* coming on your team!" A third time he repelled our intentions, so I looked at him and asked, "Matthew, are you a good investment?" He paused and looked away. He took a deep breath. He finally whispered, "I don't know if I am or not." If he didn't even see *himself* as a good investment, how could he *ever* convince anyone else he was? No wonder my friend Matthew was struggling to get to full support. He did not truly believe what Jesus said about him in Luke 10:7, "for the laborer is worthy of his wages."

HOW DOES GOD VIEW YOU?

Look up for a moment and imagine looking into the face of God.

- What does He think about YOU... right now?
- How does He perceive and view you at this very moment?
- Does He love you completely and unconditionally... or is it on some kind of a performance basis?
- Has the Lord paid for and forgiven all of your past, present, and future sins — or not?
- Has He made you His child and a member of His "forever family" — or not?
- Does He have a specific plan for your life that's full of abundance and blessing — or not?

If I don't have an assurance God totally loves and forgives me, how can I possibly love or forgive myself — or others? Neil Anderson has written a number of great books,[52] all geared to help us view ourselves the way God does. Anderson exhorts us to meditate on and fully comprehend our position in Christ. He claims, "Understanding your identity in Christ is absolutely essential to your success at living the victorious Christian life."[53] He points out that the Bible calls us sinners just a handful of times, while we're referred to as saints or holy ones hundreds of times! We have a decision to make. We can choose to view ourselves as defiled, degraded, defeated sinners, or we can look at ourselves the way God does in Ephesians 1:4: Saints who are "holy and blameless."

A proper self-image is not thinking more highly or more lowly of ourselves than we ought. It's simply looking at ourselves the way God does. If we can do this, we will possess the healthiest and most balanced self-image of all — a biblical self-esteem. This has everything to do with your success or failure in support raising — and every other area of life. One of the greatest questions anyone can answer about himself is also the simplest — "Who am I?" Before you can present yourself or your ministry to anyone else, you must have settled exactly who *you* are in your heart. Jesus believes you are worthy of your wage. Do you believe that?

HOW DO YOU VIEW YOURSELF?

We project to others what we think of ourselves. If I don't have confidence or respect for myself, others pick up on it and will not have much confidence or respect for me either. We definitely teach others how to treat us, and if you think poorly of your personality, appearance, gifts, skills, or experience, it becomes painfully obvious to the person you are meeting with. Studies indicate up to 93% of our communication with others is not the actual words we speak, but the nonverbal signals we send. Our expressions, demeanor, eyes, shoulders, hands, level of enthusiasm, intensity, and animation reveal what's really going on inside of us.[54] After all, Proverbs 23:7 does teach, "As a man thinks within himself, so he is."

One of the great biblical examples of this is in Numbers 13. The twelve spies went into the Promised Land to scout it out before the Hebrew nation was to enter and claim what God had given them. Joshua and Caleb came back ready to invade. The other ten spies were terrified of the giants in the land. They later confessed, "we became like grasshoppers in our own sight, and so we were in their sight" in Numbers 13:33. Why did the giants view the ten spies as little "grasshoppers?" Because those spies viewed *themselves* as little "grasshoppers." Instead of trusting God, believing His promise, and moving out with courage, fear paralyzed them.

How are you going to handle sitting in the office of a modern-day version of a "giant" — maybe like that intimidating businessman at the top of the skyscraper who graces you with five minutes of his precious time? If he senses you possess a "grasshopper mentality" of yourself or your ministry, he will immediately pick up on it. He may shoo you out after saying in essence, "out of my office, little grasshopper!" This is not about becoming cocky or arrogant, walking into people's homes or offices with the swagger of a gunslinger. But with God's help, you must kill the negative self-perception that tends to cripple us. The key is filling our minds with Scripture and taking what God has said about us and our calling as truth.

What do you think? After being sentenced to forty years of wandering around the desert as the consequence for their unbelief, I wonder if the ten spies and the whole nation wished they could go back and face the giants when the Lord first told them to?[55]

ARE YOU A GOOD INVESTMENT?

Once Matthew, our new staffer, deflected a third time my attempt to come onto his support team, I realized we needed to have a talk. Our next two hours were full of heartfelt honesty. Though he had every reason to feel confident about himself and his ministry, he did not feel worthy. He was letting the dreaded "grasshopper mentality" control his thinking. This will determine whether we ask people for $50, $100, $200, $300, or more per month. Christian workers who do not view themselves as worthy of significant investment will ask for low amounts — or no amounts at all!

Americans certainly understand the concept of investing. Over half of U.S. citizens are investing in the stock market. If you were to send off for brochures from various mutual funds, you would quickly get back some slick and colorful booklets touting the fund's success and above-market returns. Their earnings chart always points upward — luring you into sending them a monthly check to invest in one of their risk-free, "growth and income" funds. Their whole goal is to prove to you they will have a good "ROI" — Return on Investment.

Similar to your friends looking for the right stock to invest in to give them a good ROI, they also are running you through a similar grid as you sit across from them at Starbucks. They are subconsciously evaluating your appearance, attitude, vision, passion, presentation materials, trying to discern what comfort level they have in adding you as a new investment in their "giving portfolio." As you lay out your ministry mission, goals, and projected impact, you're trying to assure your friend if he will direct some strategic giving dollars toward you and your ministry, they will yield some excellent heavenly returns. Just as in the business world a person would put together a business plan and go to a bank to secure funding, we are putting together a "ministry business" plan where we are starting our ministry from scratch and presenting it to potential investors.

"The moment you alter your perception of yourself and your future, both you and your future begin to change."[56]

Marilee Zdenek, Founder of Right-Brain Resources

Some may think, "This all sounds so worldly to me. Shouldn't they just give because God tells them to, regardless if I was late for our meeting, had typos in my presentation, or was stuttering badly?" As much as I would like to tell you every appointment you have will be with a committed believer who has a biblical understanding of vertical giving, this is simply not the case. The majority of people who come on your team will initially be giving from a horizontal motivation. They were impressed with how *you* looked, what *you* said, how *you* came across, and they want to invest. To a large degree, how they view you will be based on how you view yourself. And how you view yourself will be based upon how you perceive God views you.

WALK TOWARD YOUR FEARS

Timothy, the young pastor in Ephesus, was struggling when he received a letter from Paul, his mentor of seventeen years. The apostle was near death, but wanted to encourage his long-time disciple one last time. He wrote, "For God has not given us a spirit of [fear], but of power and love and discipline" (2 Timothy 1:7). Timothy was struggling with timidity and being ashamed of the Lord, the gospel, and even Paul himself. Timothy felt isolated and was letting all the obstacles and opposition from believers and non-believers cause him to shrink back. In essence, the theme of Paul's final exhortation to Timothy was: walk toward your fears.

We all have fears. Your greatest adversary can be yourself. The Bible says God is for you. Satan or others have no power over a child of God. The only one who can ruin you is you! Larry Crabb in his book *Encouragement* writes, "All of us have layers of fear around the 'real us.' They are defense mechanisms."[57] We gravitate toward what is safe and comfortable, and run away from or avoid things that are scary or intimidating. Even though that's human nature, this seems to be a pitiful way to operate. In support raising, as well as life, we have a decision virtually every single day. Will I let fear dominate me, or will I walk toward my fears and do what I am afraid to do?

A survey was taken of one hundred men awarded the Medal of Honor, the highest tribute to bravery a soldier can receive. The interviewer asked each one, "What is courage?" I would expect these men to answer, "Not being afraid." No. All of them had been afraid, deathly afraid. They confessed their hearts were racing as they walked through the jungles of Vietnam, knowing at any moment they could be attacked and killed. Consequently, their definition of courage was not the *absence* of fear. To them, the definition of courage was going ahead and "*doing* what you are afraid to do." They were purposely making life-threatening decisions to walk *toward* their fears and not away from them.

I've observed Christian workers can be bold when preaching a sermon, sharing Christ on an airplane, or passing out tracts on the sidewalk. Yet when it comes to meeting *face-to-face* with a prospective donor to present their ministry vision, they shrivel up. I have seen grown men become paralyzed with fear during support appointments. Why is that? Why does the idea of sitting across a table from another human being and asking them to invest in us and our ministries send chills up our spine? My estimation is that 99% of Christian workers experience fear of asking for money. The other 1% are liars!

THE GOLDEN QUESTION

Ministries do personal support raising just like they do their personal witnessing. Consider the necessary steps in both activities:

1. Creating the need.
2. Sharing the solution.
3. Asking for a decision.

Even though rejection is possible, the bottom line for both endeavors is: Are you willing to ask the "golden question?" After presenting the gospel to someone, the most difficult sequence of words is the part where you ask them to make a decision. For some, actually mouthing these words can be a terrifying experience. "Would you like to receive Jesus Christ into your life as *your* Lord and Savior — right now?" Keeping my eyes on theirs, zipping the lip, and waiting for their response is so difficult. Why? Because they *might* say "no," and I hate to be rejected! So I can let this fear factor shape my theology by rationalizing away the need to ask people to receive Christ. I then claim God is surely big enough to save someone without my little questions.

The fears we face in evangelism are like the ones we experience in support raising. As a result, many Christian workers will only use group meetings, appeal letters, pledge cards, blogs with "donate here" buttons to do their asking for them. And even those who actually meet with donors one-on-one sometimes can't bring themselves to verbalize the golden question. "Mr. Smith, it would be such an honor to have you and your family investing in us and our ministry. I am wondering if you would consider supporting us for $100 or even $150 a month? What do you think?" In support raising, like evangelism, we need to make the God Ask first, but then have the courage to invite them to respond — and let them answer!

Why do many Christian workers choose *not* to directly ask in person? They come up with all kinds of theological or philosophical reasons, but I believe, deep down, it is a fear of rejection. Personally, I don't enjoy making people feel uncomfortable, so I ask my golden questions as casually and relationally as possible — but I still ask.

Think about it. As a Christian worker, if I can't even ask the simple golden question in evangelism, how am I *ever* going to be able to ask it in support raising? Furthermore, do I even have the right to? If you are struggling mustering up the courage to ask people face-to-face to join your personal support teams, you might evaluate how you're doing in personally asking individuals to believe and receive Christ. If you can break through the fear and faith barriers in witnessing, it will shoot adrenaline into your soul and help give you the courage to walk toward your fears in support raising. Once you've asked enough people the golden question in evangelism, asking others the question in support raising is easy!

Note: Have you noticed there's a direct correlation between the number of people you *ask* to receive Christ into their lives, and the number that actually do so? The more you ask, the more response you are likely to get! Guess what? The same correlation exists with inviting people to invest in you and your work.

EVERYTHING WITH EXCELLENCE

When stopped along an interstate, it's usually because highway department workers are repairing the road. I normally see five or six men standing around, leaning on their shovels, talking — while one person digs. Then they shift and the next guy in line works some while the others carry on with their discussion. I get the impression they're trading jokes and sports stories rather than comparing engineering solutions to their repair project. I don't get the sense they consider themselves "professionals," doing their work with a high standard of excellence.

I have also observed a few Navy SEALS. They may or may not have had the same kind of family upbringing or educational background as those construction workers, but SEALS carry themselves in a *completely* different manner. They demand of themselves and those around them an incredible level of professionalism and excellence. As I evaluate my own life and the Christian workers I've been around over the years, I have to ask, "Are we operating more like the highway department guys or Navy SEALS?"

Have we set the bar extremely high in order to bring glory to God, be a testimony to the world, and accomplish our goals? Do we possess a willingness to do *whatever* is necessary to complete the task the Lord assigned us? Or are we just clocking in each day, putting in our hours, and getting by? If we understand we are children of the King, generals in God's army, and trained for combat in the spiritual battle, we must think, speak, and act like it! Why? In everything we do and everywhere we go, we represent Jesus, our family, our ministry, and ourselves. Pastor Bill Hybels in his book *Honest to God?* shares, "Christian workers should epitomize character qualities like self-discipline, perseverance, and initiative. They should be self-motivated, prompt, organized, and industrious. Their efforts should result in work of the very highest quality."[58]

Author Robert Lewis was speaking to a group of Christian leaders and declared, "Why should we let the world outdo us in *anything*?"[59] The group was baffled. What did he just say? We reasoned that certainly the world is going to outdo us in the quality of their materials, technology, and programs. They have all the money and expertise, and we don't. Right? Lewis challenged our thinking and helped us understand believers should have a profoundly higher standard than secular corporations and we should not make any excuses for inferiority or compromise in what we create and present to a watching world. Wow, did I need to rearrange my thinking!

TELL ME ABOUT YOUR WORK ETHIC

This kind of pursuit of excellence motivates us to get up each morning and sacrifice the very best of our time and energies to "work heartily as for the Lord" (Colossians 3:23). It seems Christian workers have some of the worst reputations and many view us as lazy freeloaders. Where did they get this impression? We, who are on support, can foster this concept. We tend to view ourselves as "independent contractors" — setting our own goals, agenda, and schedule — with very little accountability to others. I'm certainly not advocating becoming workaholics, but should we not be working as hard or harder than the very people who are knocking out eight-, ten-, twelve-hour workdays in order to make enough money to send in their $100 or $200 a month to free us up to do ministry?

If your supporters could look at the hours you keep and the ministry you accomplish on a daily and weekly basis, would they feel good about their investment in you? Or would they privately wonder if you are taking advantage of their sacrifice and generosity? Don't ever give them any reason to think you are not worthy of your wage. A good exercise for you would be to take your goals, agenda, and schedule and lay it out before a few of your businessmen/women supporters, asking them to be brutally honest about what they *really* think about your work ethic. It may be difficult to hear!

POOR TALK CAN BE TOXIC

Many Christian ministries are infected with people who are constantly complaining about how *much* things cost, what they *don't* have, or how tight their budget is. They're drowning in an ocean of discontent and they don't realize it. This pity party called "poor talk" usually surfaces in the forms of:

- *Sarcastic Jokes* — "The next time my husband takes me out to dinner, it will probably be the Marriage Feast of the Lamb in heaven! Haha."
- *Hinting* — "We're hoping to get the air conditioner fixed when our support increases."
- *Comparing* — "Sure would be nice to send our kids to a Christian school like the Newtons do."

I cringe when I hear a poor talker respond to compliments with their brand of disclaimers. They feel compelled to inform us their new coat was on sale, their new camera was bought with tax refunds, and their vacation was discounted with a coupon they spent hours on the Internet searching for. Instead of using their ministry newsletter to communicate vision and changed lives, they subtly manipulate the sympathies of their donors by sneaking poor talk into the "Prayer Requests" section. They usually look something like, "Pray that God would provide for our kids' dental needs." "Pray someone would give us a computer." "Pray our mission funds come in by December 1st."

Most people want to impress others by how *much* they spend for things, but Christian workers seem to boast about how *little* they pay! Listen in on a conversation at a ministry gathering:

Staff person #1: "That's a nice shirt."
Staff person #2: "Yeah, I got it on sale for $9.95 at Walmart."
Staff person #1: "That's nothing. I got mine at Goodwill for only $3.00!"
Staff person #3: "You wasteful, ungodly, lazy sloths! I found mine in a dumpster behind our house!"

This "poor-me" attitude robs us of the dignity of our position and casts us as beggars in our supporters' eyes. Instead of going out and giving others the opportunity to invest in our ministry and us, we rationalize, blame our circumstances, and slip into denial. This is usually when the credit cards come out, and we start down the slippery slope of living off of borrowed money. Other toxic consequences of poor talk may include the following:

Poisoned Ministry Morale

When people are more concerned about *their* money, *their* needs, *their* struggles, they will gradually lose sight of the vision. And if we (or our families) are more focused on clipping coupons and saving pennies than winning the world to Christ, we have gotten off track.

Twisted View of Spirituality

This "poverty theology" is why some Christian workers are still driving that broken-down twenty-year-old van — and bragging about it! Poor talk is a strange strain of the disease called "self-righteousness."

Weakened Staff Recruitment

The fastest way to drive off potential staff candidates is for them to get a small but lethal dose of our poor talk. People want to join a team that is strong spiritually, socially, emotionally, and of course, financially.

How you view yourself will determine your success in support raising. If, deep down, we believe raising support is a form of begging, we will view ourselves as beggars. Our attitudes and self-image will come through loud and clear to everyone around us. No wonder they see us as beggars. We taught them to! If potential donors don't see you working hard with excellence, or if they hear or see any poor talk, or if they perceive you are focused on *your* needs rather than vision, they will not want to invest. But if they discern you are a man or woman on a mission from God, willing to make any sacrifice in order to complete the Great Commission, they will want to rise to your expectations and jump on your team for significant amounts. If they sense you view support raising not as a burden, but as a secret privilege, they, too, will give out of the "want to" rather than the "ought to."

I know there are stresses and pressures in living on support, but the solution is to set a healthy budget and raise at least 100%… and then do away with *all* poor talk. We've been discussing how our supporters may view us. Now, let's see how God wants us to view them!

14

Treasure
TRANSPLANTING

Mother Teresa was often asked what she believed was the greatest source of suffering. Her answer: loneliness. She was right. Even in the middle of millions of wall-to-wall people, we live in a lonely world. You might walk into someone's office who appears to have it all together with a successful life, but more times than not, they are lonely. Many of them would like to personally connect with someone who has real meaning and direction in their life, someone with vision and passion who would include them in their endeavors.

Believe it or not, many of your supporters envy you. At some juncture, they may have realized making and selling a billion widgets just didn't give them the kick in life they thought it would. Success does not always equal significance. Their net worth could be a hundred times yours, but they may harbor regrets about their life, secretly wishing they possessed the personal and spiritual drive, zeal, and sense of eternal purpose you do.

Just because they may have prestige or power in the world's eyes, never view yourself as inferior or less valuable than the people you meet with. You won't feel nearly as intimidated by any of your high-powered appointments if you choose to view them as friends, teammates, and ministry partners. Decide in your heart that this process is not *fund*raising, but primarily *friend* raising! It is a ministry of relationships.

This concept is what YWAM's Betty Barnett so effectively communicates in her excellent book on raising support, *Friend Raising*. This great truth sparks four thoughts in my mind:

1) GET OTHERS INVOLVED IN THE GREAT COMMISSION

It's a privilege God wants to extend to every believer. If you don't ask them, they may *never* get asked to participate. We learned how Paul viewed himself as a treasure transplanter, asking others to give, not because he had need, but because their gifts would be "credited to their account" in heaven (Philippians 4:17 NIV). You and I are asking others to give for *their* sake, not ours! Praise God, I am at 100% of my budget, and with a full buffer. So why do I continue to set up support appointments with others? I don't want to withhold from *anyone* the chance to give and participate in the establishing of His church everywhere. If your supporters are true children of God, they already have a heavenly account that is open and active. Now you and I get to help them build it up, and experience the compounding interest for all eternity! In fact, if I know someone — and I have never invited them to participate in this eternal investment plan — I feel guilty. I haven't been a true friend to them.

> *"We must view support raising as such a reward that to withhold it from potential partners is doing them a great disservice."[60]*
>
> *Andrew Knight, Support Trainer for Campus Outreach*

In Matthew 6:20 Jesus commanded us to "store up for yourselves treasure in heaven." We each then have *two* bank accounts — an earthly one and a heavenly one. Our job as support raisers is to be their personal, private investment banker, showing the potential client the benefits of funneling hard-earned income from their local bank to their eternal one. They may not thank you now for your persistent phone calls pressing them for an appointment or the audacious risk you took in asking them in person for a giving commitment. But *someday* I believe they will *forever* be grateful for your "never-give-up" attitude by working hard to include them on your team.

I am purely speculating here, but could it be, in heaven, part of your joy and rewards are other believers who seek you out to thank you because you were the only one who ever met with them and asked them to invest in the things of God? If so, they might point to their heavenly bank and say, "I was so foolish and short-sighted on earth. The eternal treasure I have here in heaven would have been so much smaller if you had not taken the risk to come challenge me to give. Thank you, thank you!"

2) PEOPLE DON'T GIVE TO NEEDS, THEY GIVE TO DREAMS

The one thing you have those you meet with probably don't is a ministry vision and strategy. So in your appointment don't pull out your budget. Pull out your vision! Wouldn't you be surprised if you laid out your budget and they said, "I just happened to have my budget with me too," and now you are comparing figures. Whoever has the higher income, that's who has to support the other. That scenario would be a classic case of horizontal thinking at best and a form of Christian socialism at worst!

This is also why you will fail if you broadcast some kind of financial crisis to your supporters. They might respond once to your "We're going under unless you help!" plea, but not again. If you *ever* hint of an emergency appeal again, they'll privately conclude either you should learn how to manage your money better or you need to get up off the couch and go raise more funds. Personally, any kind of immediate "need" I might have I privately take to God, and if appropriate, prayerfully approach a close supporter or two who know my motives and track record well enough to "bail me out" if required. If a veteran staffer does have a legitimate crisis, it might be acceptable for their supervisor to send a one-time appeal to the staffer's supporters.

Your supporters will be interested in your ministry, but they subconsciously and primarily are giving to you. I put it this way: people give to people — justified by a cause. As fired up as you are about your ministry, be careful not to do overkill in the explanation of it. Yes, you could spend hours expanding each and every little aspect of your outreach goals and strategies, but don't torture your supporters! They will grant you *some* time to listen to the visionary highlights of what you're doing, but the bottom line is: most of them are giving because of *you*. They appreciate your dedication to reaching homeless people for the Lord, but almost all who come on your team would still do so if you had chosen prison ministry or orphan care instead.

As long as your cause is a biblical one and others can readily see the connection between your work and lives being changed, you are on fairly safe ground. Be prepared to drill down deeper if someone has a question during a support appointment, but otherwise keep your ministry presentation simple, powerful, graphically pleasing, centered on changed lives, and hitting just a few of the visionary and exciting "mountain-top" facets of your work.

3) BECOME A "BLESSINGS BROKER"

Many Christian workers spend an inordinate amount of time and energy trying to reduce personal and ministry expenditures. Consequently, $100 may sound like a lot of money to you. My plea: don't project what *you* make or spend upon others! Most Christian workers have some sort of a poverty mentality that is different than the normal American. One hundred dollars is what their family spent at the movies last night. It's what they spent to fill up their SUV, a month of cable, or a green fee for a round of golf. Most of the people you approach will not *perceive* themselves as wealthy, but if you compare them to the rest of the world, they are very rich.

For you who are raising support in the States, the following statistics should be encouraging. The USA Giving Foundation produces an annual report on how much Americans give away each year. The total is now well over $300 billion and approaching $400 billion in coming years. Out of those hundreds of billions given annually, the largest recipient of those contributions (over 33%) is to religious causes, far exceeding donations to education, health, and other areas.[61]

In other words, there is a lot of treasure out there to transplant! We are the wealthiest, most generous nation in all of history. We Americans designate the lion share of our charity to religious organizations. That means there's never been a better time or place to raise financial support than right here and right now. When I step back and ponder the breadth of that uncomfortable little truth, it has a way of shutting down my excuses as to *why* I can't get to full support.

One of the main themes of the Bible is we have been "blessed to be a blessing." If there was *ever* a blessed nation in all of history it would have to be ours. God has poured out His bountiful abundance upon us for a reason — not to hoard it for ourselves, but to pass it on to a lost and needy world. Going to various people here in the States to ask them to give is simply you helping them fulfill the biblical mandate to pass on their blessings. You're just the messenger; the middleman; or what one support raiser calls a "Blessings Broker."

4) DON'T FORGET THE WIVES

In my typically male, laser-focused, one-track mind I've been going about my fundraising for twenty-five plus years as if the only two people who really mattered were me and the man I was asking for support. How foolish and small thinking I was to totally neglect the wives!

Many times the wife is more spiritual than the husband, with a more receptive heart toward God — and to you and your work. Regardless of the spiritual level of each spouse, usually the husband, at least shares (or even fully delegates) to the wife decisions regarding where the giving dollars go. She may very well be the "Treasure Secretary" for that family, not just accounting for their giving, but actually saying yea or nay to each funding request. In addition, she may be into relationships and communication more than her husband. In other words, do I *really* believe that as soon as I email a newsletter to the husband, he immediately prints it off and rushes home to show his wife and family? No!

I know you'll be approaching a number of single people in your fundraising, but the majority of people you meet with will probably have a job, a salary, and a spouse. Here are some changes my wife and I have made to make sure we're fully including the husband *and* the wife:

- Carol directly contacts each wife and has her fill out a "Get to Know You" sheet. She puts them in a notebook with contact info, children's names, prayer needs, etc. so we can wish them a happy birthday, anniversary, and pray for them.
- We are now emailing a copy of our newsletter to the wife's email address too.
- Carol calls or texts occasionally to get personal prayer requests from the wives.
- Along with my sending an occasional note or small gift to the husbands, she is doing the same for the wives.
- Each month, Carol and I take a half-day of prayer, and part of our time is lifting up our supporters. We then let them know we prayed for them.
- When a supporter has a newborn, Carol embroiders the baby's name on an outfit and sends it to the mother.
- She is using various social media to connect with the wives, so that we can be a part of each other's lives and families.
- For those wives with young children, Carol sends them mission education resources to help them build world vision into their kids' lives.

Whether you are single or married, our list may not fit you. Brainstorm with your spouse and/or others on your staff and come up with fun, creative ways to make sure you're really connecting with *both* the husbands and wives on your team. Remember "where your treasure is, there your heart will be also" (Luke 12:34). You're already transplanting some of their earthly treasure to their heavenly bank. And God uses that to open up their heart to you and your ministry. If you then prayerfully and lovingly touch the heart of that husband (and especially that wife) you may have gained a lifelong supporter.

Just know that how you view your supporters can make or break you. Affix a lens to your perspective that will help you view your donors as teammates and friends. I love the way Campus Crusade for Christ and other ministries refer to their donors as "Ministry Partners." That's a perfect way to describe these precious people. You can call them donors, supporters, or givers, just don't treat them like an ATM card you swipe each month, expecting them to spit out money on command. That kind of "gimme, gimme" attitude is a recipe for disaster. Remember, they are our ministry *partners*. So, handle with care!

15

Vision-Driven
FUNDRAISING

Jesus talked about money more than any other topic. More than heaven. More than hell. Not only do two thirds of the parables deal with money, but money is discussed more than 2,300 times in the Bible. How we view and handle money is one of the main barometers of our spiritual lives. Two of the greatest human resources the Lord lends to us during our short stay on earth are time and money. If someone were to look at *your* schedule and expenditures, what would they conclude about your values and priorities?

Whether you're shopping for groceries, looking for a car, planning a trip, buying a laptop, or just trying on some new jeans, what is the question that everyone, especially Christian workers, asks multiple times a day?

"How much does it cost?"

Is that the filter you and your spouse and children have affixed to every family or ministry opportunity, and all goods and services? Are you tired of having that question dominate every single decision? It's a form of slavery and bondage I believe God never intended for us. I'm not preaching a "wealth = the blessings of God" prosperity gospel. The other extreme is the "poverty = spirituality" ditch where it's more pious to drive a twenty-year-old car with 300,000 miles than a late model Honda. Let's stay on the road and find a balanced and biblical way to live and minister.

WHAT'S PULLING YOUR TRAIN?

Money is not good or bad. It is neutral, but it does have the "innate power to attract or deceive," according to Scott Morton. Love of it can be the root of all kinds of evil, but it can also be used for the glory of God and the advancement of the kingdom. I think God wants three things. For us to:

1. Be freed from bondage to money.
2. Not be bound by *any* temporal limitation.
3. View money simply as a tool to accomplish His purposes.

Over the years, the U.S. has been embroiled in various wars. I can almost imagine our Secretary of Defense gathered around a table with our top generals strategizing how to fight the battle. I can't quite picture one of our military leaders complaining, "Man, these planes are expensive. Over 50 million bucks apiece! Are there any cheaper generic brands we can pick up at a local wholesaler?"

Their objective is not to save money; it is to win the war — at *any* cost. It seems obvious they are willing to spend *whatever* they need to in order to achieve victory. In contrast, you and I have been enlisted in a much bigger battle than any country has ever fought. As good soldiers of Christ Jesus, we have embraced the great conflict of the ages, the clash between God and Satan, the eternal struggle over the souls of every man and woman on earth. This invisible, behind-the-scenes spiritual war has immanently more far-reaching consequences than any man-made one.

How about you? Are you *fully* engaged and running to the front lines to do battle with the enemy? Is your goal to be, and do, and spend whatever it takes to win this war? Enrolling in His army means Jesus Christ is our commanding officer, and "make disciples of all nations" our marching orders. It means we will let vision pull our train, *not* budget, and trust God to supply everything we could possibly need to get the job done.

When Bill Bright, founder of Campus Crusade for Christ, was alive, he would annually gather his key leaders from around the world. Each one brought their proposed ministry strategy for the upcoming year so the whole team could discuss, evaluate, and pray over the plans together. The only rule was no one was allowed to mention *anything* about money or costs until after the presentations were finished. *Then* they would put a price tag next to each part of the finalized plan, total it up, pray, then matter-of-factly state, "To pull off what we believe God wants to do this next year we need to go out and raise $289 million dollars. Let's go!" Can you see why hundreds of people over the years committed multimillion dollar gifts to Dr. Bright and his ministry? These donors never sensed budgets were pulling his train. Only vision.

If people you meet with sense the extent of your vision is just to raise your *own* support, you will struggle putting your team together. Deep down, if getting to 100% is dominating your thinking, instead of your ministry vision, they won't want to invest. But, if they sense you getting to full budget is just a small stepping-stone toward fulfilling your bigger and greater vision, they will jump on your team — substantially! Check your heart. Is getting to 100% simply a *means* to the end — or the end itself?

SAVING SOULS OR SAVING PENNIES

Christian workers are notorious for focusing on a single tree and missing the entire forest, aren't we? We get confused into thinking we need to somehow *save* God money by spending inordinate amounts of time and energy clipping coupons, collecting pennies, and scavenging every garage sale and thrift store within fifty miles! I know many believers who seem to be more interested in saving a buck than they are saving a soul. They get more excited about finding a bargain than they do making a disciple!

I don't want to get to the end of my life, meet God face-to-face, only to proudly say to Him: "I sure saved you a lot of money, Lord!" I have a feeling God would be astonished, shake His head, and respond, "Save *Me* money? You gotta be kidding! Why didn't you just focus on the things I commanded you to? My heavenly bank was nice and full. Why did you exchange so much of your valuable and irreplaceable time on earth for something as temporal and replenishable as money?" Rick Warren puts it like this, "Time is more important than money. You can always get more money, but your time is fixed. Use money to save time."[62]

"Money can become an idol for us if we become so focused on being frugal that it becomes our god."[63]

Alan Smith, Life Coach

I know it's hard to fathom, but there is something even more important than thriftiness. It's *strategicness*! Living our lives and doing our ministry for the glory of God is infinitely more significant than any trivial pursuit we may dabble in. I think we men are especially guilty of pushing our wives and children into this endless quest and vicious cycle of pinching pennies, cutting corners, desperately trying to scrape by on bare basics. We even spiritualize this survival mentality by claiming we are living a strategic "wartime lifestyle" when, in fact, we have blinded ourselves and family and are missing the real war altogether! The solution? Lifting our eyes off our so-called "needs," gazing intently upon the Lord, and raising our *full* support; not just to meet our budget, but to fulfill our vision!

I fully agree with InterVarsity's Donna Wilson, when she admonishes us not to "buy into a culture of materialism and consumerism."[64] I respect believers who purposely live below their means so they can redirect more resources to the kingdom. But many Christian workers *think* they are committed to a wartime lifestyle, when in reality they are living a "simple lifestyle." I'm sure you have observed people or magazines heavily emphasizing living *simply*, sometimes calling themselves "minimalists." I admire them for trying to cut out the excess and clutter from their lives, but some believe they are serving God in some way by doing that.

I would like to ask those people to take it to the next level, move from the temporal to the eternal, and try to determine the real motive behind their simplicity. Here are some differences between a support raiser who has embraced a Simple Lifestyle rather than a Wartime Lifestyle.

Simple Lifestyle	Wartime Lifestyle
Budget pulls their train	Vision pulls their train
Constantly asks, "How much does it cost?"	Constantly asks, "What is God's will?"
Driving force: Meeting their needs	Driving force: Expanding God's kingdom
Priority on saving money	Priority on saving souls
Goal: How LITTLE can I spend?	Goal: How MUCH do I need to spend to win the battle?
Setting support raising budget as low as possible so they don't have to raise much support	Setting support raising budget as much as possible to maximize fruitfulness of family and ministry
Values money over time	Values time over money
Their small vision attracts small dollars	Their big vision attracts big dollars
Supporters feel sorry for the Christian worker	Supporters admire and want to emulate them
They feel limited in their family and ministry by lack of funds	They feel freedom in their family and ministry by abundant funds
View of support raising: necessary evil	View of support raising: incredible opportunity
Man-centered	God-centered
Conclusion: God's resources are limited	Conclusion: God's resources are unlimited

How you view yourself, money, and support raising will determine how you come across to your potential supporters. Are you a beggar or a believer, believing *God* to fund your ministry and meet all your needs? If you will trust and seek Him first He promises to take care of your needs and "all these things will be added to you" (Matthew 6:33). Many Christian workers have that turned around, though.

A PASTOR'S PERCEPTION

Charlie Loften lived and ministered on support for eight years before entering seminary and the pastorate. Now he and his church are approached for support by a variety of workers. He thinks it's obvious what perspective and attitude support raisers bring to the appointment. He describes the two options you can use to motivate others to join your support team:

Through Guilt and Pressure

You come to your potential supporters desperate, worn down, and discouraged. You talk about how hard support raising is and how much more you have to do. You tell stories that imply you are impoverished and barely making it. You *think* you are communicating to people you are nobly suffering for the cause and making "sacrifices" others won't make. In reality, all you are doing is appealing to people's guilt. The potential supporter thinks, "These poor missionaries are starving and getting into debt, and I could do something about it."

The upside to this strategy is that it's typically effective. People do respond to guilt, and quickly. The downside — and it's a big one — is that it is a very shallow and short-term motivator. People begin to resent things they have done through guilt. They are also only compelled to give when you are desperate. If you do get on track financially, they are off the hook. They're not really investing in your ministry, but in helping you survive.

Through Casting Vision

Why do you do what you do? What has God laid on your heart? What do you hope to see the Lord do in and through you? What real difference will your ministry make in the lives of the people you are reaching — and ultimately in the big picture of reaching the whole world for Christ? If you have compelling answers to these questions, you can stir the hearts and imagination of the potential supporter. People respond to vision. There's certainly no lack of causes or people they *could* be financially supporting. However, what they may lack is feeling that what they are doing is truly making a difference in the world. Can you supply them with that? This is harder, and takes more time, but if you can show them what God is doing through you and the difference you and your ministry are making, their personal (and financial!) investment in you will continually grow.

Some Christian workers are paralyzed with fear and perceive support raising like a ball and chain attached to their ankles. They have fixed in their minds, "If we just had more money, *then* we could really do our ministry the way we need, and properly provide for our families." I am *not* recommending an expensive, luxurious existence with comforts and conveniences everywhere. I am simply trying to help every Christian worker, every missionary, every person who raises their support to ask themselves the why question. *Why* am I living the way I live? Am I trying to save money so I won't have to raise more funds, or am I doing it to fulfill God's purposes on earth? Let's stay in the battle and not get sidetracked. Seek to apply Paul's exhortation to young Timothy: "No soldier in active service entangles himself in the affairs of everyday life, so that he may please the one who enlisted him as a soldier" (2 Timothy 2:4).

So, what is your role in this eternal, worldwide battle God has us engaged in? Do you view yourself as a leader in God's army, seeking to raise whatever amounts of resources required to triumph over Satan and his ploys? *How* you perceive yourself and your role will determine whether you're satisfied in just living a small, quiet, "simple" lifestyle or whether you choose to lift your eyes, expand your vision, and move up to embrace an aggressive, all-out, "wartime" lifestyle.

HOW MUCH SHOULD WE RAISE?

This question was posed to Scott Morton during one of our training sessions. His answer was short, but profound. "Raise enough to maximize the fruitfulness of your family and ministry." To maximize fruitfulness will be different for everyone. It may mean sending your children to a private school, or purchasing a high-powered computer, or taking a week-long family vacation each year to refresh and recharge. Whatever it means, we should not judge others by our/their personal choices. Should we drive that old broken-down car or the brand-new SUV? Probably neither, but let God — not the expectations or standards of others — help you decide.

Most organizations have set amounts or at least ranges their staff is required to raise. Usually there is some degree of flexibility built in. This gives you the freedom to raise funds for ministry expenses, travel, number of children, cost-of-living adjustments, and pension.[65] Some groups even allow down payments for a house, future education funds, or adoption expenses to be raised. As you fill out your budget, don't start with a figure in mind, then try to unrealistically squeeze all your expenses into that. Instead, take Bill Bright's approach and prayerfully write down every single item you will need to maximize the fruitfulness of *your* family and ministry. Then attach price tags to everything, total it up, and that becomes your "holy number" — the 100% figure you will keep praying for and raising until you get to at least that amount.

We must develop a new mindset whereby our possessions and money merely become tools to bring glory to God and strategically extend His kingdom. Move from a simple to a wartime lifestyle in order to raise as much funds as needed to win this battle. Leave behind your budget-driven days and adopt a vision-driven future!

Power of
ASKING

Making paradigm shifts is hard. Once an unhealthy philosophy of support raising has been cemented in your mind, it can't just be remixed. Only a sledgehammer will do. It's time to pull it out! At the end of this chapter, we're going to ask you to make a final, once-and-for-all commitment to plan your whole support raising strategy around one central theme. You will focus on:

Asking individuals face-to-face
to join your monthly support team
and waiting for them to respond.

MARRIAGE PROPOSALS

Before we get started, let's take a survey. This one is for engaged or married women — but I think you all will enjoy it. Ladies, try to remember back to *how* your husband proposed to you (in this culture, I am assuming it is the man who does the proposing). There are several different modes of communication available to the male that he could utilize in asking a female to be his wife. As you look over these options please recall the particular method he chose to employ in your situation:

- *Fax machine* — maybe you were married in the 80s and your man wanted to impress you with his latest technology and faxed you a proposal, maybe even with a "cover sheet" full of hearts.
- *Letter* — maybe your husband was an English major and wanted to woo you with some passionate prose and mailed you a letter of proposal — doused with cologne, of course.
- *Email* — maybe you got engaged in the 90s and your partner thought he would wow you with his new laptop and send you an email proposal, adding some yellow, bouncing smiley-faces at the end … to seal the deal!
- *Phone* — maybe your spouse was very busy and couldn't find the time to meet personally, so he called to "sweet talk" you into marrying him, whispering tender words of affection. Or better yet, maybe he wanted to try out the newly downloaded "Marriage Proposal" App on his smartphone!
- *Text* — maybe your beloved just mastered the art of driving and texting at the same time and punched out "Want u 2 B my wife. Wil u mry me?" Or he thought it might be cool to write on your profile "wall" a romantic proposal, so all your friends would see it and go, "Awwww… how sweet!"

So, which of these five alternatives did your husband or fiancé choose? Oops. Wait a minute, I left one out. Sorry.

- *Face-to-face* — I know this one is a little outdated, but maybe you have an old-fashioned man who wanted to propose in person. I doubt it, but I wanted to throw this one in just in case.

Okay, ladies, which one is it? *Of course,* it's the last one — face-to-face. In fact, if your husband had chosen any other method to propose, you probably would have said, "No!"

Women love to describe the proposal — how their boyfriend planned the one-on-one evening. At just the right moment, he looked lovingly into her eyes, popped the carefully crafted question, and then zipped the lip to await her answer. If these exact *same* guys would apply these exact *same* methods in support raising, we would have a stadium full of Christian workers at 100% support!

Whether it's a marriage proposal, the need to confront a rebellious teenager, or sharing the gospel — if it's important — you do it face-to-face. When we choose this more personal and direct approach with people, it communicates two critical things to them: 1) *You* are very important to me, and 2) What I have to *say* to you is very important.

In support raising, we can most definitely opt for other quicker, easier options. But if we do, it will send a clear message: The person we supposedly are asking to be a ministry partner does not mean much to us. Secondly, what we have to say — our message — does not possess much value. Why is it that we take shortcuts and choose to substitute in a letter, call, banquet, blog, or card to do the asking for us? It's no wonder the potential supporter doesn't feel honored. Shortcuts will always cut short your support.

THE APPROACH YOU CHOOSE

You may think you are too busy to use this personal approach. Or you may consider yourself a great speaker able to convince large groups of people to join your team. If so, make note of this sobering survey Scott Morton took of one hundred Navigator staffers who made 7,800 financial appeals. Here are the four different methods they utilized:

- Spoke and asked in a group — The result? Only 9% of those appealed to in a group supported the staffer.
- Sent letter to individuals — The study showed 14% gave.
- Sent individual letter, then followed with call — 27% ended up giving.
- Face-to-face — 46% of the people they met with in an individual appointment financially partnered with them. My experience and that of many we have trained is that about half of the people you meet with in person will join your team.[66]

There is a very important caveat this study doesn't necessarily reveal. The 9%, 14%, and 27% listed above are normally very weak and shallow commitments, whereas the 46% who came on board in face-to-face appointment are much stronger and deeper. Here's the missing factor: *How* you go about securing your new donor will say everything about:

- The *amount* of their gift
- The *consistency* of their giving
- The *longevity* of their giving

If we choose a less personal route, they *may* come on our team, but many times it will end up being a superficial, short-term commitment, for a smaller amount, on an inconsistent basis. If you commit to the more loving and customized approach, similar to the marriage proposal, that person will *always* remember the respect, sensitivity, courage, and care you showed. Many will not be able to pull their checkbooks out fast enough in order to commit larger amounts — and for the long haul. There's something about a face-to-face encounter (that includes a verbal commitment) that creates an "expectations exchange" they will *never forget*.

Especially with all the technology available to us, it is tempting to use one of the quicker, painless options. Even the apostle John struggled with this and resolved in his heart that the *personal* approach with his disciples was indispensable. He shared, "Though I have many things to write to you, I do not want to do so with paper and ink; but I hope to come to you and speak face to face, so that your joy may be made full" (2 John 1:12).

The majority of people I met with face-to-face when I first began are still on my monthly team. They continue to give like clockwork, and even increase every few years. I'm not just looking for supporters. I'm looking for supporters for life! Like proposing, *how* you ask someone can make all the difference. Please, honor them by doing it face-to-face.

And if the economy happens to turn downward and your ministry partner is forced to scale back their overall giving, they may decrease some of their charitable or organizational donations. But the *last* commitment they'll usually drop is yours. Why? Because they met with you eyeball-to-eyeball and a crystal-clear expectations exchange took place. Making the ask in person with your ministry partners is the absolute best way to help recession-proof your support team through the ups and downs our fragile economy seems to experience.

ASKING IS THE KEY

Why individuals give to a *particular* person or cause almost always points to one main reason: they were asked. The simple power of asking was brought home to me as I was talking with a supporter. He was a successful sales manager, making more than $250,000 a year from selling surgical equipment to doctors and hospitals. That week he was interviewing eighteen individuals for three open sales positions. We talked on the phone again the next week, and I asked him if he was able to select which three of the eighteen he wanted to offer a job.

He matter-of-factly stated, "Didn't offer *any* of them a job."

"What?" I said, "Not a single one of them was qualified to be a sales person?"

"Oh no," he replied. "Some of them were *over*qualified — like presidents of companies wanting to come interview with me because of the large salary."

Confused, I asked, "Well, if there were a number who were qualified — or even overqualified — *why* didn't you hire them?"

He calmly said, "None of them *asked* me for the job. Oh, they droned on during the forty-five minute interview, about the position, income, perks, even vacation. But not a single person said, 'I respect this company and the products. I can be successful selling them for you. Will you hire me?'"

My friend concluded, "If a person can't even *ask* for the job in a simple interview, how could I ever expect them to meet with doctors and hospital administrators and *ask* for the order?"

I was stunned.

This applies to support raising too. Do you *want* the person sitting across from you in an appointment to become a ministry partner with you? Do you *want* them to invest in you and your ministry? If so, you need to *ask* for their commitment.

A wealthy Catholic woman was gradually dying of cancer. In her final months, her beloved priest visited every day at the hospital. He did this out of concern for her, but also believing the childless woman would leave her fortune to the local parish. After her passing and the funeral, the priest attended the reading of the will and to his utter amazement, this faithful lifelong member did not give anything to her own Catholic church. Instead she left it all to some local evangelistic association. The bewildered priest tracked down the leader of the organization and fired questions at him. "Who are you?" and "How did you know my parishioner?" and "Why did she leave all of her fortune to you rather than us?" "Well," the man admitted, "I really didn't know her at all. I saw an article in the paper about her and visited her in the hospital one day. I asked if she would consider giving to our ministry so her life and legacy could live on through touching others for Christ. That's all I did." Speechless, the priest walked away in shock and regret — blindly presuming his daily praying and caring for the woman would surely result in her leaving her wealth to the parish she loved. He painfully realized his one big mistake — he had chosen to *assume* rather than ask.

This story also illustrates our motives, focus, and eyes ought to be "fixed… on Jesus, the author and perfecter of our faith" (Hebrews 12:2, NIV)… rather than on others. I know of some Christian workers who have a warped and unbiblical concept of giving and asking. Sometimes the support-raiser feels the need to barter for, or "earn" the gift, or to somehow pay the supporter back for their generosity. Paul addresses this horizontal thinking in Galatians 1:10: "For am I now seeking the favor of men, or of God?" It's what drives a Christian worker to offer, "We appreciate so much you coming on our team. Let us know whenever you need a babysitter or someone to mow your yard. That's the least we could do!" Please… they are investing so you can give your *entire* self to impact the world for Christ — not so you can be their personal pastor or do favors for them.

ASKING FOR TOO LITTLE CAN OFFEND

I don't come on anyone's support team unless they are willing to make the time and effort to meet with me face-to-face and *ask* me. Ronnie came to my home and did a superb job laying out his vision to reach students and see his campus become a launching pad to touch the world with the gospel. I was thoroughly impressed and ready to sign on. When it came to the close, he looked me in the eye, and solemnly asked, "In order to help us impact this campus for Christ and see hundreds of students sent out as laborers to reach the world, I want to ask you and your wife if you will partner with us by investing $35 a month." In textbook fashion, he finished his question, zipped the lip, and waited for my answer.

I was desperately trying to keep a straight face. My mind was swirling with all kinds of thoughts and emotions. I was totally embarrassed for Ronnie. I thought, "That's *all* you are asking for? That's *all* you think your vision is worth?" Not only was I grappling with those questions, I was feeling a little offended. He must have thought I was too poor and not able to give more, or too greedy, not willing to give more. We joined for the exact $35 he requested, but we would have given more. This good-hearted, but undiscerning, campus worker thought he would offend me. In reality, he did. By asking too little. If you ask big it lets your supporter know you believe they have resources and are generous enough to share them.

In contrast, a girl asked me for a support appointment during a mealtime at a conference. The ministry presentation was okay, nothing profound, certainly not near as much vision or passion as Ronnie showed. When it came time for the ask, she, too, looked me in the eye, and said, "Steve, it would be such an honor to have you and your wife on my monthly support team. Would you consider investing $200 a month in me and my ministry?" She also waited for me to respond, but this time a *whole* different set of thoughts and emotions were rambling through my brain. I thought, "That's significant. You must really believe you and your ministry are *worth* $200 per month. Plus, you must think I possess enough resources and generosity to accommodate your request!"

I will never forget the respect and esteem she showed me by meeting with me personally and asking for a significant amount. If she does a good job appreciating and communicating with us, and occasionally asking for an increase, we might someday fulfill her original expectation and make it up to that $200 a month level!

Are you afraid of asking for too much? If you happened to do so, know that you can *always* come down into a more comfortable range for the donor. Think deeply for a moment: Just how much *are* you and your ministry worth? $100? $200? $300? $500 or more a month? I pray you will choose to ask big — of God and others. If you'll do it in a humble, prayerful, sensitive way, you won't offend them. In fact, you'll probably affirm and honor them by the *magnitude* of your request.

PERSONAL APPOINTMENT SURVEY

It seems like once a week I hear, "I don't know about you, but *everyone* in my town, my church, my circles is all tapped out. Everyone is asking for money." I beg to differ. The general public may be getting a steady stream of direct-mail appeals, email bombardments, fundraising banquet invites, and random phone calls. I would bet, however, the majority of your prospective ministry partners have *never* experienced the approach I'm recommending. Introducing Exhibit A:

Think back over the course of your *whole* life and try to remember if you personally have *ever* had this experience:

1. Someone called you up for a support appointment;
2. They met with you individually;
3. They laid out their ministry vision for you;
4. They asked you to come on their monthly team for a specific amount or range;
5. They waited for you to respond.

I have given thousands of adult believers this survey. About 90% admit they have never had this experience — not even once! Now you may be part of this esteemed 10% who *have* had a personalized support appointment and understand the power of it. But more than likely, you are part of the "uninitiated" 90% and may very well have negative thoughts playing in your mind creating excuses why people *won't* give or *can't* give. It's a crime a seventy-year-old man or woman who's been a believer in

Christ for fifty plus years would go through their entire life and never ever have the simple, but potent experience I describe above. It's a tragedy to deprive them of this once-in-a-lifetime opportunity. You inviting them to invest may be the *only* chance they'll ever have to be challenged to look up, make the God Ask, and seek wisdom how they should direct their giving dollars. Do it!

COMMITMENT TIME

Centuries ago there was an army preparing for war. Their ranks were full of thousands of able-bodied men capable of crushing *any* opponent. Their leaders provided them the very best weapons and spent years drilling each regiment for hand-to-hand "fight to the death" warfare. The tribe of Ephraim believed themselves to be especially brave. But when the day finally came that their enemy appeared on the hill, and it was time to rush forward to engage them, these soldiers' hearts melted within them. Instead of boldly moving ahead, and lifting their weapons to shoot, they spun around and ran away in fear. This is how Psalm 78:9 (NIV) describes these young Israelites: "The men of Ephraim, though armed with bows, turned back on the day of battle."

These men were well trained and equipped, but when the moment of truth arrived, they gave up. As for us, we dare not go any further in spending all this time praying and planning, budgeting and organizing, developing and practicing tools, listing and prioritizing myriads of names, unless you are willing to commit yourself, right now, to approaching individuals face-to-face, asking for monthly support, and giving them the opportunity to respond.

I don't want you to deceive yourself like the men of Ephraim did or waste your or anyone else's time. This secret privilege of support raising we speak of contains five nonnegotiables you need to sign off on:

1. Will you commit to making the God Ask *before* you invite others to invest?
2. Will you commit to approach *individuals* or couples for support?
3. Will you commit to actually *asking* these individuals to financially partner with you?
4. Will you commit to doing the asking *face-to-face*?
5. Will you commit to being quiet and letting *them* respond to your ask?

Will you put your "yes" on the table?

The
GOD ASK

Section IV

PREPARE FOR IMPACT

The will to succeed is nothing without the will to plan.

Maximizing Your
FRUITFULNESS

Our wake-up call came at 10 p.m. on a warm spring night in 1988. My wife and I were riding a motorbike along a backstreet in a small Mexican town. A car ran a stop sign at an intersection and broadsided us, throwing Carol off and causing a number of severe injuries. I scooped her up, flagged a taxi, and carried her to what I *thought* was a hospital. It turned out to be a filthy, non-equipped outdoor clinic with a young, inexperienced "doctor" who spoke no English. After he saw two bones sticking out of my wife's ankle, he was shocked. When he turned to me, hands out, shrugging his shoulders, I knew we were in serious trouble. Making several late-night calls to my physician friends in America, they informed me unless I got Carol to a trauma hospital quickly she would lose her leg from gangrene. I secured a Miami-based, medically-equipped jet to transport us back to Houston for surgeries on her ankle, broken collarbone, and collapsed lung.

The operations were successful, but our troubles were just beginning. This tragedy launched an eye-opening journey of just how fragile, unprepared, and foolish we were regarding our personal finances. Receiving the $7,300 bill for that uninsured jet ride, along with the growing pile of hospital and medical bills was a shock. Added to this we had a home where we housed and fed five college students. We also had four young children ages three, two, one, and three months who were dependent upon a mommy now laid up in bed, unable to move.

With no savings, investments, or emergency funds, we persuaded the credit card companies to give us more time and smaller payments. After maxing out our credit card from getting cash advances and charging groceries, we decided we had to quit giving. Then things *really* spiraled downward. We cried out to God. We bought a book on Christian financial concepts to help us find and understand from the Scriptures how the Lord wanted us to handle our funds and get out of this disastrous financial rut. How did we do it?

STEP BY STEP

We Reestablished Our Giving

We committed at least the *first* 10% of all of our income to kingdom work. This would be the very first checks written each month. No exceptions. No compromise.

We Determined to Kill Our Credit Card Debt

We promised the Lord that if He would help us erase our massive bill by Christmas, we would never again pay a single penny of credit card interest. God delivered through several unexpected sources, and by His grace, we've never allowed a balance to be carried forward on any card since then.

We Began A Monthly Savings Plan

We set aside another 10% of our income for other emergencies and large expenditures.

We launched a small investment strategy, whereby we could prepare for our future and our kid's college.

We Created A Budget

This was the first time in our marriage to draw up a detailed monthly financial plan. We determined exactly where, when, and how we would steward our resources.

We are no experts, but if your financial house is not in order, then you too may need a wake-up call. I just hope it's not as catastrophic as ours! If you do find yourself in a rut right now, either of your *own* digging or "broadsided" like we were, take note of the four steps of faith I just listed. Also, as you begin, remember:

DANGERS OF DEBT

Some explain their situation by saying, "There are good debts and bad debts." Yes and no. Traditionally, buying and financing a house is a wise decision because your investment supposedly will appreciate. Many Christian workers have secured home loans to be good stewards and build up long-term equity. Some have been hurt by those mortgages. Maybe their eyes were bigger than their bank account and sought too lofty a house with too shallow financial resources. To protect yourself against financial bondage, keep in mind Proverbs 22:7: "The rich rules over the poor, and the borrower becomes the lender's slave."

Another form of debt is school loans. More and more graduates are finishing up their studies with substantial amounts to pay back. Even though it's usually a reasonable monthly amount with a small interest rate it still appears daunting. Some who feel drawn into ministry delay fulfilling their calling until they can first pay off all their school loans. This may sound noble, but it's not clear thinking. You're choosing *not* to follow God's call on your life for the next five years for a measly $529 a month at 5% interest? My advice to anyone who has school loans is to build it right into your support raising total and *never* look back. If someone happens to ask to see your budget during a support appointment, and they notice you have a monthly school loan payment included, they won't criticize you — they will compliment you. They'll be impressed you put yourself through college and are now being faithful to pay it back.

Personally, I clearly distinguish between school loans and consumer debt. If you have college loans I would counsel you *not* to let it hold you back one single day from entering into ministry and raising your support. On the other hand, if you carry a credit card balance I strongly advise you to *not* yet ask others to support you. First *kill* that consumer debt by getting a second or third job if necessary. Be willing to go to extreme measures to aggressively destroy it. Pray about making a vow before the Lord to never pay another penny of credit card interest again.

CLEAR CONSCIENCE ABOUT YOUR STANDARD OF LIVING

How much should a Christian worker make, and what should our standard of living be? The unwritten rules of the game seem to say it's okay for church staffers, especially of larger churches, to live at a higher level than missionaries who live on support. Maybe this is the case because, deep down, many believers view support raising as begging. And, of course, beggars should barely get by. I wish I knew who made up these double standards! There is something I definitely admire about those who *choose* to operate within a thrifty and austere budget, and I love to save a buck as much as the next guy. But, again, I believe vision-driven Christians ought to rise above the man-made "simple" lifestyle to embrace the God-ordained "wartime" lifestyle. In order to win the worldwide spiritual battle the Lord has drafted us for, we shouldn't be scrounging around focused on how *little* we can spend, but rather lift our eyes toward our Great Commander and Heavenly Provider, asking "How *much* do *You* want me to spend to win this war?" This will prove we really believe that time is *always* worth more than money.

I remember one conversation I had with a Christian worker who was raising support in Dallas. He mentioned he was going to meet with a potential supporter in Charlotte. His plan was to take a Greyhound bus up to see him that would take two days up and two days back. Matter-of-factly I asked, "Why don't you just fly? I think it's only a two-hour flight." His answer: "I'm going to save some money." Privately, I was dumbfounded, speechless, and embarrassed for him. I wanted to scream: "You're going to trade four whole days of your life as well as delay fulfilling God's ministry calling in order to *save* some money?" Unbelievable!

I want to challenge you to truly prepare for impact. As you begin to create a financial plan, make sure *vision* is your North Star, not your budget. One way to help you do this is to always use Morton's principle as your decision-making grid: Raise enough funds to maximize the fruitfulness of your family and ministry. Go before the Lord and ask Him what that means for your life, your family, your ministry. It will look different for every person. Prayerfully finish putting together the final financial figure that reflects your honest, heart-felt convictions as to what "maximizing fruitfulness" means for you. Have a clear conscience about it. Don't let people shame you or guilt you into adopting *their* standards.[67]

Keep in mind you must balance this perspective with the organization you've joined. They may have an exact amount you are required to raise. If so, you may want to humbly and respectfully go to your supervisor and appeal to them, showing why certain increases are essential if you're going to *truly* steward your family or ministry. Most groups do build in some flexibility, providing their staff with a "range" whereby they can raise more if they choose or need to. This is true especially if there is a variance in the cost of living in the different cities or countries staff reside.

RAISE MORE THAN JUST 100%

Don't use "maximizing fruitfulness" as a smoke screen for luxurious living. At the same time, don't set the bare minimum as your goal, where you are crawling to the finish line, collapsing at the 100% mark, and thanking God the torture is finally over! That pitiful approach will be obvious to all and severely hamper you *ever* getting fully funded.

In my experience, you would be very wise to raise more than 100%, and keep it in your account as a buffer. Why?

- You're going to have attrition where occasionally someone drops off your team.
- You're going to have supporters who miss months.
- You're going to have unexpected emergencies or "divine ministry opportunities" that arise.
- You may want to transfer some "excess" funds from your account to another needy staffer or an organizational project you feel strongly about.
- Your ministry vision is going to grow each year and it will require more "vision dollars."

PREPARING YOUR BUDGET

Get out your calculator, bills, family and ministry goals and plans. Be aware that husbands and wives usually approach this financial-planning assignment differently. Understand God has created women with a nurturing, nesting instinct where they need and desire stability and security. Financial guru Dave Ramsey asks husbands, "Has your wife's 'financial security gland' been met?" Have you raised enough to calm her fears and stresses? We men, on the other hand, seem to gravitate toward the bare essentials. This contrast is real, so be prepared for some deep discussions and compromises as the two become one in the budget.

Consequently, include *all* the essentials, even saving and investing, not downplaying those as optional or "unspiritual." The Scriptures are full of verses encouraging us to save for our future, our children, and emergencies as well as key passages on the importance of investing. Examples:

- *Saving* — Go to the ant, O sluggard, observe her ways and be wise, which, having no chief, officer or ruler, prepares her food in the summer and gathers her provision in the harvest. (Proverbs 6:6-8)
- *Investing* — A good man leaves an inheritance to his children's children, and the wealth of the sinner is stored up for the righteous. (Proverbs 13:22)

Here's a sobering example of why we should save and invest. Recently released figures show what college will likely cost by 2030 based on inflation rates. At that time, the average sticker price for a private university will be around $130,428 per year and a public university at least $41,228 annually. The implication? If you want to someday send your children to college, you better start saving now![68]

You want to have a clear conscience about your budget and not pad or inflate it beyond what is wise or necessary. Paul addresses this aspect of financial integrity: "We want to avoid any criticism of the way we administer this liberal [generous] gift. For we are taking pains to do what is right, not only in the eyes of the Lord but also in the eyes of men" (2 Corinthians 8:20-21, NIV). We must take pains as well.

Take a moment to peruse the budget work sheet at TheGodAsk.org/ Resources. Why all the exhaustive line items of expenses? Why include categories like vitamins, pet care, entertainment, and school supplies? Because that is life! Those are *real* expenditures you will be making and you better budget for them. There are a myriad of other essentials you'd do well not to overlook. Here are two:

1) Support Raising War Chest

How much time and money do you think it's going to take to get you to 100% of your funding? As you put together your personal and ministry expense budget, don't forget to create a separate document listing all the estimated travel, meals, phone, postage, printing expenses, *any* and *all* miscellaneous items that will be required for you to do your full and complete support raising in an excellent and thorough way. Once you have the breakdown and total figure, pray and approach a few individuals. Ask them to consider taking all or some of that budget as a way of "frontloading" your ministry, helping your support team get firmly established for the long haul.

2) Ministry Launching Fund

There will also be expenses related to moving to your new assignment and getting started in your work. Transporting your household to your new location, office setup, equipment, supplies, first month's rent and utilities, business cards, cell phone, ministry materials, the list goes on. Whether you're a young single worker who just needs $2,500 to get you started or a family heading overseas long-term with a $75,000 moving expense, don't neglect to budget. Some people you approach won't commit to you monthly or annually, but are willing to help you launch. A few will choose to become a regular giver *and* contribute toward this startup fund — *if* you ask them.

INDIVIDUAL FUNDING PROJECTS

Understand there are great ways for people to partner with you and your ministry besides just monthly or annual giving. As you are thinking through your budget, consider breaking out certain items you think specific supporters might be interested in taking on. Why not prayerfully craft "Ministry Projects" to present to key donors? In contrast to the one-size-fits-all mentality, here's how to creatively help some of your ministry supporters feel more appreciated and affirmed — to have more ownership and a true feeling of partnership with you and your work:

List One: Think exhaustively about all of your personal and ministry needs, expenditures, and potential opportunities. Break out ones that could be logical stand-alone funding projects you could legitimately present to an individual, couple, church, or company.

List Two: Produce a comprehensive printout of all your past, current, and potential supporters. Lay it next to List One. Take each project and look through your List Two names, asking God to give you wisdom as to *who* might be interested in funding that particular opportunity. Try to match up items with people who have a background or connection associated with that project. Identify a few able to donate "gifts in kind" like medical services, building materials, or computer equipment as a way of supporting you. Write, call, or better yet, set up an appointment to lay the proposal in front of them.

MY PROJECT ASKS

I needed a dependable late-model ministry car. I could have borrowed the money or pulled it out of savings, but why waste a splendid opportunity to involve a supporter or two who might jump at the chance to meet an important need like this? I prayed, thought, then called a long-time giver who just "happened" to have sold some stock that morning, and was wondering what to do with the profit. He not only sent the entire amount needed to buy me a vehicle, he added more to pay off our other car too!

Years ago, I started on a graduate degree where annually I would fly to Denver, rent a car and hotel room, pay for meals, tuition, and books; then fly home. It was $3,000 total each trip/class. It hit me just how expensive this whole program would be. I prayed through my list of regular and periodic givers, thinking through who might have an interest in me getting this kind of training. Right there in the airport I selected three names, wrote out and mailed a letter to each detailing the "what, why, and how much" of my classes/trips and asking each man if he would be my sponsor. I called each one to answer questions and get a decision. The very first man responded, "Tell me when and where to send each check." He paid for every single penny over an eight-year period. I had to contact the other two and promise them I would think of other projects they could take on soon!

Instead of directly approaching *individuals* with requests like this, I could have chosen the quicker, easier, less risky route of posting in my newsletters: "If anyone wants to help with my seminary expenses please send money!" or "Join the Shadrach Car Fund Today!" or the "hint-hint" method of slipping these appeals into the "Prayer Requests" section. I might have received a few paltry charitable donations as a result, but the bigger damage would have been done. My pleas would have permanently put me on par with the local beggar in most people's minds. Also, those two supporters who *did* respond to my customized "asks" (car, seminary expenses) would have *never* given if they had just seen my appeals in a general newsletter or email.

If you opt to resort to this broader, impersonal "cattle call" approach to support raising, just know it makes your friends and donors feel like they are just nameless, faceless people in a huge herd of others you are uncaringly attempting to corral. You don't want that, do you?

PARTNER WITH BUSINESS PEOPLE

There is a powerful work of the Spirit sweeping our nation and beyond known as "Business as Mission" or BAM. The world has become flat as it relates to lay people wanting to *directly* touch the nations for Christ. These men and women have become spiritual "revolutionaries."[69] They are no longer satisfied just sitting in church, giving to the building program, and being a greeter at the door. They want to do more and believe they personally have resources, ideas, and experience they can offer to a lost world. These BAM'ers can have immediate and life-changing impact. They want their *own* finger prints to be all over this evangelizing-the-world assignment Jesus gave *all* of us — not just vocational Christian workers.[70]

Many business owners are looking for a ministry or missionary to partner with. They desire to bring *their* expertise and profits to the table and help open doors for the gospel. Think through the business-related people you know in your contact base and note which ones already have a BAM-type vision. Go to these, and others you think would be open to the concept, with a proposal on how they could practically and financially adopt you and your organization as their ministry partner. We have several individuals who are blessing us (as they are being blessed) by giving a percentage of their company's ongoing profits. One business owner actually approached me recently with a partnership proposal!

God wants you, your family, and ministry to be fruitful. Let vision determine your budget rather than allow your budget to limit your vision. A careful, prayerful crafting of your financial strategy, including identifying projects and people for specialized funding, can be a creative and fun way to present investment opportunities. Don't miss out on getting your friends, family, *everyone* involved. Start now to stretch your mind to think of the hundreds of people who need to be on your contact list. It's time to namestorm!

(18)

NAMESTORMING

Jake was the life of the party and seemed to know everyone from
everywhere. Yes, he was young, but very networked. As he felt called
into ministry, we started discussing support raising. He needed to begin
brainstorming potential contacts — what some call "namestorming." To my
astonishment he could hardly think of anyone! I sent him to his hometown
to drive down every street listing names of people he remembered. He
came back with forty, including his little league coach, the mayor, and
the butcher he once worked for. I took him into his fraternity house,
and we perused the photo composites from his years there. We recorded
another forty names. We went through the alumni list of the particular
fraternity chapter he was part of and found another fifty. My prodding
helped stimulate his mind, thus opening a floodgate of concentric circles
of friends and contacts he had made over the years — that he didn't realize.

I often interact with full-time ministry staff who can think of very
few people to put on their contact list. I would like to say to them, "You're
telling me you're forty-three years old, been in Christian work for sixteen
years, and can only come up with seventy-six possible support contacts? I
think you love the ministry, it's just people that you dislike!"

Before we get into the how-to's, here is a marriage and networking
thought: If you've been married in the last three years, you're still on your

honeymoon! Right? Regardless of who attended, that list becomes like solid gold as the invitees like to help the young couple get off on the right foot. Many will meet with you and come on your team. And a tip for you singles: If possible, have as large a wedding as possible. You'll never know when it will come in handy!

RECORD AND RETAIN

Now, it's your turn. Once you and your supervisor feel good about your budget, it's time to really get down to business for extensive namestorming. You have a lot of work to do, so clear the schedule for a while. Ask the Lord for energy, endurance, creativity, and a strong memory — to retrace every stage of your *entire* life. Attempt to remember every single name from your past.

Secure an excellent computer database program to allow you to quickly and efficiently enter and track all your contact's pertinent information, preferably one developed to aid Christian workers raising support.[71] Find one in which you can enter and maintain all your contacts' information, track all your giving, produce graphs and reports, mail merge, see when someone's missed a month, be alerted to send a thank-you note or birthday card, and schedule your tasks. TheGodAsk.org/Resources has several great options.

MAKE OLD FRIENDS NEW SUPPORTERS

Take half a day to create a complete timeline of your life. Go back and think through *every* year from childhood up to the present. Reconstruct and write down *all* the activities, clubs, teams, churches, jobs, neighborhoods, and school classes you were *ever* part of. After making an exhaustive list of all those categories, go back and start writing as many names as you possibly can connect to each of those groups. Pull out all the annuals and group pictures of you in your growing-up years to jog your memory. Don't leave someone out because you weren't close to them, or they weren't a Christian, or you haven't seen them for a while. Just get their names on the list. Make no excuses or exceptions for them as to *why* they wouldn't want to hear from you.

Brainstorming: No bad ideas

Namestorming: No bad names

You must be thinking, "You gotta be kidding. There's *no way* I'm gonna go back to my eighth grade biology-lab partner to ask her for support. I haven't talked to her in sixteen years! Even if I knew *how* to track her down, as soon as I contact her, she'll immediately know all I care about is her money." I fully understand your concerns. I've had Christian workers tell me their solution to this quandary is to *first* invite their old friend out for coffee or golf or something and try to rebuild the rapport *before* they do the ask. In my opinion, that is the *worst* thing you could do! Even if it's a whole year later with five lunches and golf rounds that you finally broach the funding subject, their initial skepticism of your motives will be confirmed. They'll immediately realize, "Ahhh, *now* I know why you called me."

When I am attempting to reconnect with those from my past, I like to compose a personalized pre-call letter or email to each. I briefly catch them up on my life, conversion to Christ, family, job, and how God has now led me into this strategic ministry. Then I would include something like:

> I have the responsibility and privilege to raise all my personal and operational expenses before I can launch my ministry. I've been praying and thinking of key individuals who have had a part in my life over the years. So, at this exciting but scary juncture, I'm going back to the very roots of my life and asking old friends like you to allow me to share with them the ministry vision and financial goals the Lord has laid before me. I know it's been forever since we have seen each other, but at one time in our lives you meant something to me and I meant something to you. You may or may not be able to join me and invest in this new venture, but it would be an honor to share my story with you — and to catch up after all these years! I would like to give you a call next week and see if there might be a time to meet. I look forward to reconnecting.

Is that so frightening? What's the worst that could happen once you call? And the best? An old friend just might become a new supporter![72]

A few of you can't even come up with seventy-six people to put on your list. My ballpark estimate of the average number of friends and acquaintances you have is probably around 1,000. Out of those 1,000 people you've met or known during your life, I estimate the average number you've actually kept up with is around sixty. I'm sure you included the sixty on your namestorm contact list, but I bet you left off the majority of the 940 others you don't keep in touch with. So what if you *do* go back and try to reconnect with people from the 940 list, but someone responds,

"Sorry, not interested in seeing you" — what have you lost? Absolutely nothing! Yes, you can get your feelings hurt if you want to and go home and get depressed, or you can simply put that name right back into the "lost touch" file — where they had been residing for nineteen years anyway — and move on to the next one!

YOU WILL LOSE A FRIEND

Go ahead and resolve in your heart now, that in all likelihood you *will* lose a friend during support raising. Is that okay with you? Just like witnessing, there will be someone upset when you approach them. Everyone has strong opinions about asking for money, and you are bound to run into a person or two in your support raising travels who gets offended by what you're doing, and doesn't want to be your friend any more. Think about it. Were they really your friend in the first place? But I know people who will devise their entire support raising philosophy and approach terrified someone *might* be offended or reject them. Write it down. Someone will!

SOCIAL MEDIA: THE SUPPORT RAISER'S NEW BEST FRIEND

Another way to generate lots of new names is accessing social networks via the Internet. Whereas it used to be weird to go back and contact someone who was part of your previous life, it's now okay, even cool to track down your fourth grade spelling bee runner-up, your ninth grade math teacher, your college friend from the chemistry club, or your former neighbor from three moves ago. Joining various social media groups and "friending" people can create a natural crack in the door to reestablish your relationship, update on life and family, share memories and pics, or alert them when you're coming through town. Many times this can easily segue into sharing about your ministry and support goals.

Right now, my teenage daughter is going through every one of my social media "friends" and creating a spreadsheet of names, hometowns, and email addresses to send a personalized email to each. I will see if they might want to receive our periodic email ministry newsletter update.

TRACK DOWN CONTACT INFO

With the advent of the Internet, it's amazing how much detailed information we can gather on various potential supporters. All kinds of technology is being developed to help us find and connect with each other more easily.

Discover it, learn it, use it.

An unlikely success story came my way a few years ago when I decided to track down an old college friend. I had lost touch for more than seven years. I did a name search on the web and found him in a Minneapolis suburb. His specific address or phone wasn't listed — but his neighbor's info was. I called this neighbor, asked if a new couple had moved onto their block recently, confirmed with them it was my friend, and asked the neighbor to take a note over to my friend. We were able to talk on the phone the next week. They came on our team for $150 a month, and a few years ago they bumped up to $300 a month. Not only that, but our renewed friendship, and now partnership, is sweeter than ever.

RECRUIT TEAMMATES TO JOIN YOU

Get your parents, your longtime friends, and your spouse to look at your timeline and help you fill in gaps. They will remind you of other groups or activities you were part of and be able to add other names of people you or they were associated with. If married, go through the same extensive timeline, groupings, and namestorming exercise with your spouse. Search through your old school annuals, past and present church directories, even photo albums to prod your memory, helping you list hundreds of names from old youth groups, company gatherings, Sunday school retreats, high school graduation, mission trips, and neighborhood associations. When it comes to namestorming, don't become an isolated lone ranger. Figure out creative ways to incorporate others. Here are two other ways to multiply your efforts beyond just what *you* can do:

1) Steering Committees

I have a close friend who created a Steering Committee where he and his wife recruited twelve supporters to meet together once a month during the support raising period. The purpose was to pray for the support raising couple, namestorm for new contacts, set up appointments for them, and encourage and hold them accountable. Some even set up a second committee in another city where they are concentrating their efforts, too. Whatever you choose to call it, try starting this group, keep it going to help you every month until you reach 100%. Give them a good job description and appreciate them, and they'll stick with you.

2) Key Men or Women

As you are preparing for impact, you can include other brothers and sisters in Christ to join you. Look for one or two key men or women who will stand shoulder-to-shoulder with you. Help them to view and grasp the broad scope of the financial and ministry challenge ahead. They must be willing to do what is necessary to get you to your assignment — quickly and fully funded. One former staffer of ours found just the right person to be his "key man" and this person ended up networking and funneling *180* new contacts to him. You never know if someone might be the solution to an incredible breakthrough for you — until you ask!

ACCOUNTABILITY IS ESSENTIAL

There is one more critical name you must come up with—your accountability partner. Let me first give you the rationale. Why do many organizations have perpetually underfunded staff? Well, often the leaders of the ministry either don't raise support or are below budget themselves. There is also frequently no enforced policy requiring underfunded personnel to suspend their ministry to focus exclusively on support. And finally, there's often no one-to-one accountability structure to make sure staff get to full budget—and stay there! Let's solve number three right now. This week you can pray and carefully select the right accountability partner and commit yourself to that person.

I'm not referring to a coach or trouble shooter, but a durable and discerning believer who will faithfully walk with you every single week until you get to the top of your support raising mountain. Don't let it be a friend or someone else who is currently raising support, who might be tempted to go easy on you. It actually may be an advantage if they know nothing about support raising. Make sure they possess plenty of confidence and "tough love" though. If you don't know a former drill sergeant, find a business person (who understands hiring/firing, goal setting, deadlines, quotas, etc.) who will be the kind of hard core, black and white partner you need—someone who will firmly question you if you don't reach the number of calls and face-to-face asks you agreed to each week!

You might be saying, "Gosh, Steve, that sounds so legalistic to me." Friends, I threw legalism out the window eons ago. Desperate men do desperate things and if you are truly serious about getting fully funded quickly, you will not just agree to accountability, you will aggressively embrace it! Solomon understood this when he shared, "Two are better than one because they have a good return for their labor. For if either of them falls, the one will lift up his companion. But woe to the one who falls when there is not another to lift him up" (Ecclesiastes 4:9, 10).

Go to TheGodAsk.org/Resources and download the Support Raising Accountability Covenant that you can make to your accountability partner, and the commitment they can make back to you. Review it line by line with your partner, then both of you pray together and sign it. You will also find the Support Raising Weekly Accountability Sheet online. Send a copy (completely filled out!) to your partner every week at the same time. Then you take responsibility to call your partner promptly afterwards, and let them ask you any question about anything! You will experience the benefits of honesty, transparency, encouragement, and teamwork.

FINAL TIPS

It's good to invite different local churches to join your personal support team. You may have someone oppose you enlisting their church or friends to give toward your far-off ministry. They may say: "How can you raise money from one group of people in order to go to another group in a different location to do your ministry? Aren't the people you minister to supposed to support you?" Yes, ideally that is true. But there are numerous biblical exceptions. Paul received money from other outside churches to go do ministry in Corinth, Thessalonica, and Ephesus (See Acts 18:1, 2 Corinthians 11:7-8, 1 Thessalonians 2:9, 2 Thessalonians 3:8, Acts 20:34).[73]

People often ask me, "How many names should I have on my contact list?" As many as possible, but certainly several hundred — at least. I knew one twenty-five-year-old who had been hired by a stock-brokerage firm. They required him to bring *1,000 names* and contact info with him on his first day of work. This would be the beginning point to build his clientele. These were not names he had copied from the phone book. No, they were people he had known or met somehow, someway, during his short twenty-five years of life. Talk about namestorming! This guy paid a price to put the list together. I hope we are more committed to reaching the world for Christ than others are to selling stocks and bonds.

It all depends how serious you are about getting to full support. It all rests how much you are willing to bathe this whole process in prayer, making big God Asks all day, every day. How dedicated would you say you are to long, laborious hours of timelining, namestorming, and Internet searching? How much of the prerequisite "do-what-is-necessary" attitude do you possess to build a broad, extensive contact base to draw from? How about it? Are you still willing to do what is necessary?

19

Dollars and
SENSE

Bart was a prominent athlete in college. He assumed he could exempt himself from the laborious process we must all go through in reaching full support. We brought this young leader and his wife on our staff and provided them with great support training. But Bart had other plans. He determined the hundreds of hours on the phone, traveling, and meeting face-to-face with supporters was unnecessary. He believed God was telling him to instead select his top one hundred contacts from across the state to approach. All in one single day he sent off a letter to the entire one hundred, asking for the same monthly amount, and including a self-addressed envelope to mail back their first check. Confident all the money would come rolling in in just a matter of a few days, he sat back, prayed, and checked the mail. I begged him not to follow this plan. He proclaimed, "No, God has told me." I wanted to say, "No He hasn't," but that would have been unspiritual!

I got a knock on my office door about three months later. Normally supremely self-assured, Bart entered quiet and eyes downcast. He seemed to be a little more teachable as he revealed to me only *two* of the "Top One Hundred" had even responded. Those two were simply "one-time" gifts. He was shocked and dejected, but now ready for help. I exhorted him to go back to each of the one hundred and set up individual face-to-face appointments.

He tried but felt embarrassed in light of the letter he had previously sent. Consequently he never really put together a solid team. After financially limping along for three years, he and his disillusioned wife finally departed for a "real" job and paycheck. I was deeply saddened. If there was anyone who could have easily put his team together, it was Bart. Instead he chose shortcuts and a one-size-fits-all approach. It doomed him.

We can't afford to cut any corners in preparation. "Failing to plan is planning to fail" is the wise old saying. So before you begin, "Commit your works to the LORD and your plans will be established" (Proverbs 16:3). By this stage of the process, you and your family, friends, and key supporters should have logged numerous days and weeks scouring over every fragment of your lives, every sliver of activity you've ever participated in, every place you've ever lived, worked, studied, played, and worshipped in your entire life. You can now humbly stand back with a sense of satisfaction, confident you have done a complete exhaustive — and exhausting — job of namestorming. If so, you are off to a good start.

PRIORITIZE NAMES

Now that you have this landslide of names gathered, how do you organize them? Who do you approach first, second, third? How are you supposed to know what to ask? The place to begin is to segment your huge list into high-, medium-, and low-priority people.

High Priority

These are people you are fairly confident will want to partner with you, probably individuals with whom you have natural God-given connections. They care about you *personally*, or have a passion for your *cause*, or have been influenced by your *organization* in the past.

Medium Priority

These contacts are ones you are not sure will give. It's 50/50. They could go either way. If you pray diligently, choose the personal route to approach them, do an excellent job presenting and asking, God may impress them to join your team.

Low Priority

These contacts are people you're pretty sure won't want to give, but you are going to keep their name on the list anyway. You *never* know. You may get to 100% without approaching any from this list. A few of you, though, may be required to work through all three lists — as well as big batches of referrals before you hit full funding.

DISCERN AMOUNTS TO ASK FOR

Determining a dollar amount or a range to ask for will not be a mystical experience where the figure appears next to each name as you make the call. Start with your high priority people and pray over each person. Ask God for wisdom. Consider putting together a list of factors that will come into play as you evaluate each person. Here are suggestions:

Your Relationship With Them

This is huge. How well do you know them? How well do they know you?

Their Passion for Your Cause

How deeply do they feel about what you do? I knew of one young man who hated to raise support, but because he was planning to help orphans in Africa, he raised his support in record time. Everyone wanted to participate!

Their Past Giving

Has this contact given substantially to you or some other person or group you know of? If so, this is an indicator of what they can or will give in the future.

Their Professions

You probably are not going to ask your hairdresser for as much as you do your orthopedic surgeon friend. For example, never ask an hourly-waged worker for less than $75 a month though. You can always come down lower, but never start at less than $75.

Their Lifestyles

This could be the most deceptive of all. They may live in a mansion and drive a Lexus, but they also may be deeply in debt!

Their Christian Maturity and Understanding of Giving

I am more likely to increase the amount I am asking someone to invest if they walk with Christ and have embraced the biblical concepts of giving. In other words, they view it as a "vertical privilege" instead of a "horizontal duty."

There may be other factors you want to include. Remember to repeat this prayer/evaluation process again with each of your medium-priority people, and if need be with your low priority. You may get to full support with your high-and medium-priority contacts. I pray so!

If you need to raise $6,000 in monthly support, and if half of your face-to-face appointments result in new donors, what amounts will you need to be asking for?

Average Gift	Actual Donors	# of F/F Appts
$40/mo.	150	300
$50/mo.	120	240
$60/mo.	100	200
$75/mo.	80	160
$100/mo.	60	120
$125/mo.	48	96
$150/mo.	40	80
$200/mo.	30	60

Note: If you want to be working on getting to full support for the rest of your life, just keep asking for small amounts!

Never ask a professional or a double-income couple for less than $100 a month. You might be thinking "$100! You must be kidding! That's a lot of money. No one in my church or town can afford that!" I beg to differ. You may be living a Spartan existence right now and know fifty-eight ways to fix hot dogs, but open your eyes to current realities. I know the financial "hand wringers" broadcast their dire economic forecasts on cable news each night, but let's admit it: Over the last 200 years Americans have *made* more — and *given* more than any group of people on earth — ever. I study annual charts of what different professions earn annually and how often they get pay raises. No matter what part of the U.S. you live in, certainly compared to the rest of the world, you are surrounded by people with vast resources. Please don't attach what $100 may mean to you to the rest of the country!

COMMON PROBLEMS IN ASKING

Telling Yourself Certain People Can't or Won't Give

For instance, what about approaching recent college grads? You can't do that, can you? They just finished school! That is actually the *exact* time to ask them. Not only will they have cash for the first time in life, you will be helping them to establish their giving patterns. In fact, we have a young staff couple who approached a number of their friends still in college. I was astounded to learn how sacrificially these students gave. It made me realize that everyone is a candidate to join your support team.

Asking Everyone for the Same Amount

"Bart," in the opening story, naively thought he could quickly raise his support by asking one hundred people to each give $25. But people like to be treated individually. They appreciate you thinking and praying for them and customizing your ask. We must bathe this whole process and each potential ministry partner in prayer, seeking God's wisdom to ask at just the right level or range.

Asking Too Low

Someone could look at your giving records and tell a lot about how you've gone about raising your support. Your financial reports contain the facts. When I see numerous small gifts on someone's report, I ask the Christian worker how much monthly support they asked for in each appointment. They usually bow their head and whisper, "Everyone for $50," or they might confess, "I didn't ask them for an amount at all." Oops. Bad move! I've observed support raisers usually get what they ask for. If you decide you are going to ask people for $50 a month — your average gift size for your whole team will be $40 or so. If you ask everyone for $100 a month, the average will be about $85/$90. If you're asking $150, the average is $130, and so on.

Not Asking At All

Potential donors are not mindreaders. You have to give them *some* idea of what it is you are asking them to do! They watch a religious TV program where the speaker asks everyone for $19.95. They switch the channel and the next speaker wants you to send in a $500 seed gift. Only twice in the hundreds of support appointments I've had over the years did someone stop me before my specific ask and say, "Don't suggest an amount. Let us just pray about it and let you know." The rest greatly appreciated me giving them guidance on what I was requesting.

I may notice one of our staff has a donor who gives sporadically, seeming to miss a month or two here and there. I gently ask the staffer, "Did you meet with this person face-to-face?" A little embarrassed, they usually admit they only called them or sent them a letter/email, or had solicited them in a group setting. Almost without exception, a face-to-face individual appointment is going to yield a larger, more consistent, more lasting monthly commitment than *any* alternative approach.

THE OCCASIONAL EXCEPTION

Okay, what if the person you want to ask really *does* live at a distance — a long distance? You might be thinking, "Are you telling me I'm supposed to buy a plane ticket, rent a car, get a hotel room in a city 2,000 miles away in order to take my old high school teammate out for an appointment where he may or may not come on my team for $75 a month?" No, probably not.

We go into greater detail on this at the end of Chapter 25, but if a friend of yours is so far removed from where you live, or any of the cities where you are planning support trips, you might be wise to do your ask via letter or email. Then follow up with a phone or video call to answer questions, catch up on their life, and to get their decision. But if less than 90% of your total asks are not done face-to-face, I would guess you are probably cutting corners, taking the easy way out, or conjuring up excuses why you can't travel to meet with them in person.

Occasionally there is the individual living at a far distance who, if you will take the time and money to go see them, *will* come on your team for a very substantial amount. Years ago, my flying 2,000 miles to see a friend and share about our ministry communicated to him that both he and my message were very important. Consequently, he's become our largest financial stakeholder. I can assure you, he is not the kind of person who would have made that kind of commitment with just a phone call or email! Again, when making your support raising travel decisions always let vision pull your train, never the budget.

It's hard work praying and thinking through every single person on your list as to when, and how, and what to ask for. Making the God Ask means you are diligently seeking wisdom from Him each step of the way. Always choose the most personal approach possible when inviting someone to join your team. The Lord will guide you to ask the right people for the right amount in the right way. I promise.

20

Outfitting Your
TOOL BELT

Tonya was one sharp girl. Her people skills were off the charts — and she knew it. Before she decided to enter full-time ministry, her profession of choice had been telemarketing. She was good at it. She went through the required support raising training, but she wasn't really listening or taking notes. She assumed with her background and talents, she could skip over a lot of the laborious "grunt work," as she called it, and just begin meeting with people. Who needed scripts, brochures, or laptop presentation when God had given her such a winsome personality, she reasoned? Instead of taking the days and days of painstaking preparation and the extensive role-playing of the various support raising tools she had been asked to develop, she decided to go for it on her own. To her it was a grand adventure of confidence and faith. To others it was foolish, even arrogant.

If you are preparing today, chances are you won't be repairing tomorrow.

Once on the trail, in a different city, she ran into obstacles. Confused looks and unanswerable questions were everywhere. Her rosy predictions of instant success turned into a nightmare. People were not showing up for appointments because she had not confirmed ahead of time. Some were not impressed by her rambling, shoot-from-the-hip style of explaining her ministry. Others doubted the credibility of her organization and plans because she had not prepared any professional-looking materials.

Now humbled, Tonya went back to the drawing board. She huddled with her supervisor to debrief and plan, then hid out in her apartment for the next ten days — doing nothing but the four P's: praying, planning, preparing, and practicing. Our lesson: commit to lay the proper groundwork *before* you make that first phone call or have your initial appointment. In this chapter, we will provide you just an initial overview and rationale for the basic tools you will need to launch. As you prepare for impact, here are the three major parts to the process.

TOOL #1: YOUR PHONE SCRIPT

Work hard on this. Craft it and recraft it. Practice it with others. Get their feedback. How does it sound? Too short? Too long? Personal? You can really hurt yourself by preparing improperly. As elementary as it may seem, have that script in front of you during your first forty to fifty conversations, until you get so familiar, so comfortable with what you want to communicate that you no longer need the help. As you create your phone script, understand you can say too much about money on the initial phone call, and you can also say too little about it:

- *Too much* — "The reason I am calling you is because I want to ask you to meet with me. During our appointment I am going to be asking you to commit to my personal financial support team for $100-$150 a month."
- *Too little* — "I, uhhh, just wanted to stop by and have, ummm, some fellowship, and share about our ministry, and, uhhh, maybe some of our needs, but mainly just to catch up and ask for prayer."
- *Just right* — "I would love to get the chance to sit down with you and share a bit about our ministry vision and financial goals. I'm going to be downtown later this week. I'm wondering if there might be a mid-morning or mid-afternoon slot somewhere in your schedule on Thursday or Friday that I could fit into?"

Beware: The more you say about money the more likely they are to want to answer you right there on the phone — *instead* of meeting with you. The total purpose of the phone call is to get the appointment! At the same time you don't want to sacrifice integrity. Not mentioning finances can be deceptive and may come off as a "bait and switch." This will hurt your credibility.

TOOL #2: YOUR MINISTRY PRESENTATION

You may want to incorporate all of your ministry info into a portfolio: a small folder, binder, or notebook with each page slipped into a clear sheet protector. Hire someone with graphic design skills to craft powerful, visually-pleasing documents. Ideas to include in your Portfolio: cover page, ministry vision and mission statement, history and overview of organization, needs or problems your ministry meets, story of a life impacted by your ministry, your personal or spiritual story, ministry action photos, your role and goals, levels of giving chart, commitment/ response page, and referrals sheet. It's important to have an appendix section to refer to if needed. It should include a statement of faith, your budget, and endorsements.

Using technology in your presentation is good, but don't overdo it. Some support raisers get so enamored with their extensive computer-based presentations with all the bells and whistles, it can be very distracting. Instead of the appointment being a heart-to-heart time of sharing relationship and vision, it's reduced to humoring the Christian worker while they proudly click through their mountain of prize-winning slides. Your goal is not to overwhelm them, but to hit the exciting, visionary highlights of your ministry. You could go into hours of detailed explanation, but the polite smile on most people's faces will give way after twenty to thirty minutes to their eyes starting to glaze over. Here are different parts of your presentation to work on:

Your Testimony and Calling

Write out a long version of your personal testimony and your calling into ministry. Condense each into three succinct sentences. If there is any correlation at all between how or when you came to Christ and the ministry to which God is calling you, highlight that in your presentation.

Your Ministry Vision

Whether you're a front-line missionary or a behind-the-scenes administrator, focus on hitting the big-picture parts of your overall vision. Lift your ministry partner's eyes up and give them a bird's-eye view of the eternal impact of the work God has called you to. Help them see how strategic it would be if they chose to direct some of their giving dollars toward this life-changing ministry. Always show how your ministry is part of touching the world for Christ. As biblical as leading people to the Lord and making disciples is, it's too small a vision. If your goals are not somehow tied to reaching the *whole* world for Jesus — expand them! We must embrace His command to make disciples of *all* the nations. (Matthew 28:18-20).

Story of a Transformed Life

Identify one person who has been impacted by you or your organization. Share their name and picture with your prospective donor. Q: What is the one thing the friend you are meeting with will remember as they walk away? A: The face and story of that one transformed life. What will be the primary reason they will choose to invest in you? They believe there will be more transformed lives through you. Return-on-investment to most people means changed lives, not just meeting numerical ministry goals. One idea is to record on your phone a one-minute video testimony of a person impacted by you or your ministry. Show it at your appointment. Simple, but very effective. The story of that changed life is a good place to transition to the ask. You've powerfully demonstrated your ministry is all about redeeming lives. Now, you want to invite your prospective supporter to partner with you.

The Ask

As you set up your appointments, you need to decide in advance whether you are going to ask each person you meet with to *join* your team or to just *pray* about joining your team. There is a big difference. As you might guess, I recommend you ask them, *during* the appointment, to come onto your team. Then let them answer. They've been asked many questions in their lives. They can handle yours! You've worked hard to get this appointment. You've traded four to five calls, rescheduled once, and now you get a precious forty minutes sitting across from this busy person. Don't waste it. And certainly don't assume you'll easily get another opportunity. Use those forty minutes for all they are worth! Your prospective donors know why you're there. You haven't hidden anything from them. Go ahead — invite them to join your team. Be quiet, and let them answer. You can trust the Lord that your God Ask has been heard, and that He is fully capable of directing that person's response. After you make the invitation to them to invest and become a ministry partner, it is between them and the Lord.

But let's admit it. The toughest part of the appointment is that face-to-face ask. I know it can feel a little intimidating sometimes. If there was only a "third party" present it might take a little of the pressure off. There is — God Himself! But, I am also referring to the Ministry Portfolio you bring with you. It allows you and your appointment to look back and forth between you and your documents. When I get to *the ask*, I point them to the Levels of Giving (or LOG) chart. Here are the different kinds:

Monthly LOG Chart

Almost without exception, my ask is composed of only *one* thing — a monthly commitment. Showing this chart and asking for a specific amount or range is not a hard-core ultimatum. No. In a loving, relational, sensitive way I am just opening up a dialogue with

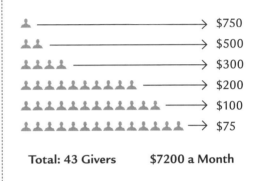

them. It serves as a place to *begin* the conversation. The person is able to see from the chart they can give more or less than the amount I suggested.

Annual LOG Chart

Maybe the person you are meeting with receives their income sporadically and isn't able to make a monthly commitment. If so, have an Annual LOG chart available. Suggest a particular annual amount or two and ask if they would be willing to

commit each year. I always ask what time of the year is best to approach them for this gift. I mark it down on my calendar to contact them every year on that date.

Church LOG Chart

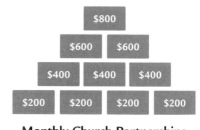

Monthly Church Partnerships

You should have a few churches you want to approach. They, too, have no idea what it is you are wanting of them, unless you tell them. Put a LOG chart together to present to the pastor or chairman of the missions committee. It can be a monthly and/or annual Church LOG Chart.

Work hard on these charts. Think through the various levels and make them challenging, but realistic. If you're only raising $3,000 per month, the highest gift level should be $250 a month. If you're raising $6,000 per month have one or two $500 a month slots. If you're raising $10,000 a month or more, include at least one $1,000 a month opportunity. Depending on the amount you are raising, I recommend at least thirty giving slots on your LOG Chart, but no more than fifty. People do appreciate you laying one of these LOG charts in front of them during an appointment. Two reasons:

1. *They want to join a team* — They don't just want to be Account #29078. They want to be part of a team — *your* team. They observe you have thought and prayed and customized your ask for them. You have showed them specifically what role they can play and how they strategically fit in.

2. *They want to do their part* — The chart helps people gauge what portion of the total they should take. As they look over your LOG chart they are privately running the percentages in their mind. They will determine what part of the whole is *their* responsibility. Regardless of their resources, a $500 a month commitment would seem too great a portion for someone only raising $3,000 monthly. Maybe they don't want you to have an unhealthy dependence upon them. But that same donor might justify a $500 or more monthly commitment for someone raising $6,000–$10,000 monthly. Why? They want to help you, they want to be on your team, they want to get you to 100%, but they also are trying to appropriately discern what is "their part" to play. The LOG charts help them do that.

The Close

The last part of putting your ministry presentation together is the close. How will you finish up your appointment? You must be super specific as to what the *exact* next steps are for you and them. Build yourself a flow chart, and script out where you will take the conversation based upon what their response is. For instance, if they say:

"Yes, we want to join your team."
- Establish the amount each month or year they want to commit to.
- Establish when they want their giving to start.
- Establish how they are going to begin their giving: Check, Electronic Fund Transfer,[74] or Credit Card. (Ask if you can set that up for them right then or if/when you need to come back.)
- Determine whether you should also ask them to contribute to your Ministry Launching Fund.
- Ask for referrals if needed.
- Give newsletter, get contact information, thank them.

"No, I cannot join your monthly support team."
- Determine if lowering the monthly commitment ask would be appropriate.
- Ask if they would be open to looking at your Annual LOG Chart and consider a yearly investment.
- Ask if they would be open, instead, to making a single gift to your Ministry Launching Fund.
- Ask for referrals if needed.
- Give them a newsletter and thank them.
- Ask if they are open to receiving your newsletter and meeting again in a year about the ministry and possible support.

"Maybe. Let me think about it and talk to my spouse."
- Affirm them and get a specific day and time in the next two to three days that you can call them back for a decision.
- Give them a newsletter, get their contact information, thank them.

If you've had people who said they would come on your team for $100 a month during your appointment, and three months later they have not started giving yet, don't get angry at them. Start with evaluating yourself as to whether you took enough initiative, in person or on the phone, to be very specific about what, when, where, and how they were to get started giving.

TOOL #3: YOUR PHONE SCRIPT FOR A FOLLOW-UP CALL

If you did ask them to join your team in the appointment, and they did request more time for a decision, *you* need to initiate the follow-up call. During the conversation you can thank them for the meeting and continue to build a relationship. But the main two purposes for a well-prepared follow-up call to someone who needs more time to make their decision are:

To Secure the Giving Decision

About half will give you their answer right there in the appointment. The other half will say they need to pray more, to talk to their spouse, or look at their budget.

To Determine Exact Next Steps to Begin Giving

If you hang up from this call having left things nebulous, you will regret it. After rejoicing they want to partner with you, make it very clear how much, when to start, method of giving, and *how* to actually secure that first gift. I encourage you to drop back by their house or office to pick up that first check. You may want to pull out your laptop or smartphone, log on to the giving page, turn the computer toward them, let them type in their info, and push submit. Now, they are officially on the team!

I know all these details may seem confusing or feel overwhelming to you. I understand. If you will dedicate yourself to asking the Holy Spirit to fill and empower you as you faithfully and consistently pray, plan, prepare, and practice, you will see God go before you. Remember, He wants your support raised even more than you do!

Note: *We will provide more practical details (in chapter 22-26) on the initial call, the appointments, and the follow-up.*

21

Crafting Your
SCHEDULE

When I first started raising support, I planned a road trip from Arkansas to Kansas City — a six-hour drive. I focused on other things that week and confirmed no appointments. I reasoned, "I know I don't have any meetings set up yet, but I *know* these guys. They're my friends. Certainly we'll be able to connect. Just trust God!" With that warm, fuzzy thought tucked into my brain I confidently set off for KC. When I arrived, I started calling. One person was out of town, another had family in, a third was sick, a fourth's number had been changed, and the debacle continued. After running through my entire list, I did not have one single appointment. I felt so foolish and cried out, "I will *never* do this again!" I got back in my car and drove home.

This is *not* a good example of how to manage your support raising schedule: Spend six hours driving to Kansas City. Make one hour of calls. Turn around and drive six hours back home. That glaring error in my foresight and planning cost me a lot of time and money.

"Whatever failures I have known, whatever errors I have committed, whatever follies I have witnessed in private and public life have been the consequences of action without thought."[75]

Bernard Baruch, American Businessman

I do not have the gift of administration, nor am I very organized. I struggle big time with details, and support raising is a myriad of daily "to do's." Even though managing ourselves efficiently may not come naturally, it's essential we shift ourselves into overdrive to pull it off.

YOUR LAUNCH AND FINISH DATES

Don't rush into raising support. Make sure you have all the training you could possibly attain. Some perceive themselves to be so *sharp* that subjecting themselves to thorough support raising training would be too humbling. Others perceive themselves so *smart* that getting additional training before they start is a waste of time. Please note: the breadth of your impact is usually determined by the depth of your preparation.

So carefully choose your launch and finish date. This means extensive time with God praying for yourself, your supporters, your presentation, and results. Take the time to get all your tools perfected. Engage in multiple role-plays, getting objective feedback. Get all your data and plans laid out in an organized manner. Put together a timeline for the entire process. If you pay the price in advance of launching, the people you meet with will see, hear, and sense your preparation, excellence, and professionalism. It will impress them and God will use it. They will conclude, "If this missionary has done such a great job in preparing for and raising their support, they're going to apply this same level of dedication to their ministry. I want to partner with this kind of worker."

People want to know finish dates. Artaxerxes asked when Nehemiah would complete his project, and he gave the king a "definite time" (Nehemiah 2:6). Others will not be impressed by our overly spiritual "whenever the Lord leads" type of answers to their specific questions. So, realistically determine when your completion date ought to be. Don't make it two weeks. Don't make it two years! I encourage workers to look at a three- to six-month time frame depending upon the amount they have to raise and if they are doing it full-or part-time. Don't *plan* for it to take this long, but if you end up finishing in twelve to eighteen months, don't feel like a failure. It may not mean you are lazy or disorganized. There may be extenuating circumstances beyond your control. The point is — do not give up until you are at least 100%, and be willing to do whatever is necessary to get there!

Tie your finish date to a ministry goal or event down the road. If your ministry is holding a huge pastors training event in Brazil, and you want to be there, tie your finish date to it. If the semester begins on August 25th and you want to be there to help students move in and start sharing Christ, make August 10th your finish date. If your potential ministry partner senses your burning passion is getting to those lost freshmen *more* than just getting to 100% budget, they are much more likely to invest *now* rather than later.

BUILD YOUR SUPPORT RAISING CALENDAR

Envision what a weekly schedule looks like. Prioritize your support raising trips. Planning them out in great detail will save you a lot of headaches.

Understand the Weekly Workload

Once you have established your launch and finish dates, you will know how many weeks you have to raise your support. Divide the total dollars needed by the number of weeks to determine the amount of new monthly support you must raise *each week*. For example, let's say you want to get to 100% in twenty weeks, you're required to raise $6,000 a month, and you're working on it full-time. This means you will need to average $300 of new monthly support each week.

It will depend on what you ask for, but let's say the average monthly commitment you receive will be $100. At this figure, it will require sixty new monthly partners to get you to $6,000 budget. My observation over the years is about every other person you meet with face-to-face will come on your team. Consequently, you will need to have at least 120 individual appointments to acquire sixty "yes" responses.

Sample Work Load
Raising $6,000 Monthly in 20 weeks

720 phone calls
240 requested appointments
120 face to face asks
60 commitments

For every appointment you're able to set up, you will normally have to ask at least two people to meet with you. In order to obtain those 120 face-to-face encounters, you will probably need to directly ask in person or over the phone at least 240 individuals. With the way our society and technology has evolved, with so many forms of communication options, it is harder than ever to connect with someone to even *have* the chance to ask for an appointment! You will average at least three attempts per person to get them on the line. That means those 240 requested appointments will require at least 720 phone calls.

We must face the reality of the daily, weekly, and monthly workload ahead of us. These figures are for the person who is serious and dedicated to the task. Some of you may need to *add* to the numbers listed.

Prioritize the Cities You'll Visit

As you build your support raising calendar, take the names from your namestorming and place them on a country map. Start with your high-priority names. Make a mark where each person lives. Do the same with medium- and low-priority names using a different color for each category. When you finish, you should have hundreds of names and a mixture of colored marks across your map. Take a pen and draw circles around the highest concentrations. Those are the cities you will visit.

Which city should you visit first, second, or third? I not only look for the quantity of my contacts in a city, but also the quality. If in one city I had thirty names, but most were medium- or low-priority people, I would prioritize it behind a city where I had only fifteen names, but most were high priority. Start with your launch date and finish date. Then plug in all the pertinent dates and trips. Try to rotate weeks between staying in your hometown to raise support and traveling to a different city to raise support.

PLANNING ROAD TRIPS

After my disastrous Kansas City trip, I determined whenever I took any kind of support raising trip, I would diligently work to pack out my schedule *before* I even backed out of my driveway. I formulated a plan that day which has served me, and many others, well. I like to go to a city, hit it hard, then come back. The ideal number of days in any particular city is three to four. If I am only coming for three to four days, I have noticed people are more willing, and work harder, to fit into my tight schedule. They know I am going to be in and out quickly. But if I tell them I am coming for seven or fourteen days, they see no pressing reason to set up an appointment in advance, replying, "Oh, just come on into town. We'll find a time to meet." I have found support raisers will average only one or two appointments a day if they camp out in cities for extended periods of time. This has a negative impact on you and the people you meet with.

Scenario #1:

You arrive at an 8:30 p.m. Starbucks appointment with James, an old high school friend, who now owns his own business. He says, "It's good to have you in town. Have you been able to shop at the new mall? Or play some golf? Or tour the new museum?"

You reply, "No, I haven't been able to."

"Why not?" James replies. "What have you been up to all day?"

"Well, let's see. I had a support breakfast at 6 a.m. with Terry Jones; a mid-morning coffee appointment with Pastor Strauss; lunch with a businessman who was referred to me by another supporter; and I just finished a dinner at Chili's with a couple who wanted to hear about our ministry vision. I didn't have much time to run around town today because, well, you're my fifth appointment for the day."

James is speechless. What do you think is going through his mind at this point? "This guy is serious!"

Scenario #2:

You meet Rachel, a key referral from a current supporter, at 8 p.m. for a coffee. Getting to know one another, Rachel says, "I understand you're in town to raise support for your ministry. Have you been able to have some good appointments today?"

You pause, look down, and stutter, "Well, yes, I have had a good day. I, umm, did not, technically, have any appointments yet today, though."

"Oh, well, what *did* you do with your day here in town?" she inquires.

"Today? Well, let's see. I got some good sleep. I had a great quiet time. Then I, uhh, exercised and did some reading. I also spent time at the library catching up on some work.

"So, I am your *only* appointment for the day?" she states bluntly.

"I guess that's right," you sheepishly admit.

Rachel is also speechless, but for a different reason than James. What do you think is going through her mind at this point? You need to go get a job!

If you had a salesperson who thought a successful day was one or two sales calls a day, how long would you keep them as an employee? I know some support raisers who just about break their arms patting themselves on the back, bragging they are averaging one to two appointments a day!

Even though I tenaciously work and pray to fill up each day of my support raising with six appointments, many times I have to settle for three or four meetings. Seldom do I have six appointments in one day, but it's not because of lack of initiative or effort. I was in Texas recently and had fourteen appointments in three days. One of my coworkers had sixteen appointments during a recent three-day trip to Little Rock. So please don't use other people's standard as your own. Don't compare other Christian workers' menial work ethic with yours. *You* set the pace.

SETTING UP MEETINGS

When planning your trips, lay out all the names of the high-, medium-, and low-priority people in that city. Pray for each of them and then rank them in order of importance as to how willing and able you think each is to invest in you and your ministry. Determine which higher-ranked person on your list will be the *most* difficult to get an appointment with based upon their busy schedule. Lock them in first. Then contact the second most difficult person to negotiate a slot on their calendar, then third. Build the trip schedule around those individuals. Leave your old friends who are willing to meet you *anytime* toward the end of your scheduling efforts. They love you enough to allow you to plug them into any opening you have. As you go down your list and call, email, or text each of them, working to build out your daily agenda, understand it is quite the challenge to juggle people, schedules, and travel. Be prepared for last-minute rearrangements of people and appointments every day in every city.

Yes, I want to pack out every day with meetings, but I like to leave a slot or two at the end of each trip for a "divine appointment." The reason? What if one afternoon I'm meeting with an old acquaintance and he gets excited and spouts, "I had no idea this is what you are doing. How long are you going to be in town? I want my business partner to hear *exactly* what you told me. Do you have any openings in your schedule before you leave?" Would you call that a divine appointment? Indeed!

In contrast, I have actually known people who embrace the divine-appointment concept *all* the time. In other words, they don't plan out their trips or appointments in advance. They show up in a city and walk around for three days, believing *God* will bring along just the right persons at the just right time. Obviously, I think we should listen to the Spirit when He directs or redirects us, but I don't think the Lord is going to bless our unwillingness to work hard. We can't justify our laziness. Our conscience always tells on us.

Planning and scheduling all these appointments takes a tremendous amount of time, energy, patience, and courage. No excuses allowed.

Some support raisers tell me the summer is bad for getting appointments because people are vacationing. They say the fall is not good because school is starting with all kinds of activities. Of course, November and December are out because of holidays. In fact, they can knock out the entire year if they want to! In reality, *every* day of the year is a great time to invite people to invest their resources to impact the world. It all depends on your perspective, doesn't it?

The
GOD ASK

Section V
IT'S GO TIME

*Step out of the stands, down on the track,
and run the race that God is calling you to.*

22

Entering
THE ZONE

The office door is shut. The coffee is poured. Chris is staring at the phone. He is planned and prayed up but is paralyzed with fear. His attention now seems to be redirected out the window somewhere. His stomach begins to churn. He rearranges his desk. His coffee is now cold. He should go exercise. Yes. "Why not start today?" he reasons. He puts on his jogging shoes and heads for the door. His wife sees him and is totally confused. She *thought* he was spending the morning making calls.

Maybe you can relate. It's that first afternoon when you're going into your office, locking the door, and determining not to come out until you have at least eight appointments lined up. You've sent a newsletter out, a batch of pre-call emails, and you are finally ready to make that first set of phone calls to set up appointments. But you are really nervous and begin to do every other task on your to-do list except the *most* important: Make calls.

This is where the battle begins. This is "go time!" You and I can be the most prayed-up and planned-up people anywhere, but now is the real test. Will we face the giants in our mind, walk *toward* our fears, and reject passivity and procrastination? Every time we pick up that phone to make a call, every time we knock on that door for a support appointment, every time we look deep into someone's eyes and ask the golden question, we are choosing to run toward the battle. As we get to the practical "how-to's" of support raising, let's commit, now, on the front end, to be men and women who are: prayerful and fully dependent upon God; personal and caring deeply about each life we intersect with; and finally, persistent, clinging to a "can-do," "never-give-up" attitude.

You ready?

I know *how* you secure the appointment is going to be somewhat generational. Younger support raisers may contact their peers for appointments via texting or social media. Some may use email. For many of you, you will be calling, especially if the person is older than you. Seek to discover and utilize the *most effective way* to connect with your potential supporters in order to set up an appointment. That is the determining factor as to the means of communication you choose — not simply because it is quickest or easiest or less scary.

HEART AND MIND PREPARATION

The phone is not your enemy! It can be your friend, if you let it. Pray before you begin. Ask God to give you enthusiasm, clarity, and courage. Ask Him to go before you, that people would answer their phones and that they would be receptive to you and your request to meet with them in person. Have your phone script in front of you. You may have been a smooth telemarketing rep, but don't rely on your eloquence, especially during those first twenty to thirty conversations as you perfect exactly what you want to say. How you go about handling that one- to five-minute phone call can make you or break you in your support raising success. Work hard at making it an enjoyable experience for every person.

You're calling dozens of people during each session. Choose a reliable method to record the information you're gathering during each conversation. During my call, I may discover *Weak ink is better than a strong memory.* we can't meet for lunch because my friend is taking his twelve-year-old son to his baseball playoff game, or maybe we can't do breakfast because he's taking his wife away for a twentieth wedding anniversary weekend. If so, when we finally do sit down and have a meal and support appointment together, the first thing I better *not* ask him is, "Say Joe. Did you tell me you had a family?" No! You ask how Bobby did in the playoff game. Did his wife enjoy the stay at the bed and breakfast he had chosen? You are trying to build a relationship with this person. Recording, storing, and reviewing that information before each appointment helps you establish strong rapport.

THE SUPPORT RAISING ZONE

Securing the right place to make your calls is essential. Find an office, a room, a quiet place where you can close the door and have uninterrupted stretches of time. I like to take two- to three-hour chunks to focus exclusively on calling. I need absolute focus. Getting started is half the battle. Once I make that first call, once I get that first appointment, I get in "the zone." Nothing can stop me. I am a man on a mission from God! I will not stop until I have *at least* those eight appointments I committed to line up. Yes, I was a little nervous and tentative when I started calling, but now there's no place I'd rather be than right here, lining up face-to-face appointments.

I am not afraid to call someone at their home, cell, office, *any* phone that I am able to get their number. I want to be sensitive and wise, but at the same time I refuse to let "paranoia tapes" play in the back of my mind, whispering, "You'll be bothering them," or "They're screening your calls."

I do try to use discernment as to *when* I call. To contact a middle age or older person before 8 a.m. or after 9 p.m. might be unwise. I usually call married couples with kids the earliest, then couples with no kids, and save the singles for the latest calls. When calling a prospective supporter at their place of work, I usually try to do so between 9-11:30 a.m. or 1:30-4:30 p.m. Friday mornings are a great time to contact them to get on their calendar for the next week.

LOCKING IN APPOINTMENTS

I like to have my schedule right in front of me so I will know exactly what slots I have open. Even if I have no appointments lined up, I don't say, "My whole week is clear. I'm free anytime. When can you meet?" Their first thought may be, "No appointments at all? What a loser!" A better approach would be to suggest a couple of specific times to meet, but express flexibility. I break my day into six possible appointments:

1. *Breakfast*: This can be for meeting people before work. If you treat and it's near where they're employed, it's usually a done deal.

2. *Mid-morning*: A great time to meet pastors, executives, business owners, or homemakers. Many of them have enough margin to meet for twenty to forty-five minutes at their office or home.

3. *Lunch*: Usually reserved for workers who have enough time and flexibility to go out for a meal. But, get them back to their work on time.

4. *Mid-afternoon*: Same as the mid-morning suggestions.

5. *Dinner*: Hang on to these slots for singles or couples you want to meet and have a more relaxed time with.

6. *Evening*: Meeting an old friend or younger acquaintance at 8:30 p.m. for coffee to catch up and share about your ministry can be the perfect time and place to have a support appointment.

And, of course, weekends can be a great time to plan appointments, as people have a lot more freedom with their schedules.

DETERMINE WHERE TO MEET

Before you make your phone call, think carefully where would be the best place to connect with this person. Ask yourself questions like: How well do I know them? Where would they feel most comfortable meeting? Do I want to try to meet with both husband and wife? How much time do I anticipate them being willing to give me? What is the age difference between this person and myself? These factors need to be considered as you suggest a place to meet. Here are three possible locations:

1. *Home:* I hate to invite myself over to someone's house for an appointment, much less a meal. I do however invite people over to our house to share about the ministry and partnering opportunities. Meeting at one or the other's home is usually reserved for people you know fairly well. A home visit usually is a little more open-ended too, and can last at least an hour, but should never surpass two.

2. *Office*: Most business owners, executives, or managers have enough freedom in their schedules to allow you to stop into their place of work for at least a twenty- to thirty-minute appointment. Be punctual and very respectful of their time limitations though, rarely staying more than forty-five minutes.

3. *Restaurant or coffee shop:* This is for someone willing to take the time *away* from home or office to meet. These are people who are comfortable enough with you to meet you in a more social setting

than their office. Always pay for the bill so as not to add to the perception we're nothing more than beggars looking for handouts!

If you're married or if the person you're meeting with is married, be careful with opposite gender appointments. Don't meet one-on-one behind closed doors or eat out together at a restaurant; not as much because of any temptation, but to guard against someone's accusation of impropriety.

WHAT TO SAY ON THE CALL

Don't embarrass yourself and risk losing the appointment by not being prepared for the call. Have a script in front of you. Here are the guidelines:

Build Rapport

"Is Mr. Smith there?"

"Mr. Smith, this is Steve Shadrach. How are you doing?"

"Have you got a minute to talk?"

"I have enjoyed getting to know your son and daughter at the youth group meetings. They are great kids. I know you must be proud of them."

Scheduling the Appointment

"Mr. Smith, I sent you a letter last week about our ministry. I'm wondering if you had a chance to read it. Did it make sense?"

"As I was thinking and praying about who I would love to sit down with and share a bit about our ministry vision and financial goals, you definitely came to mind."

"I'm going to be downtown later this week, on Thursday and Friday. Would there be a twenty to thirty minute slot I could squeeze into your schedule somewhere in your mid-morning or mid-afternoon one of those days? I could drop by your office."

Confirmation of Time and Place

"9:30 a.m. Thursday sounds great. You're in the Halter building, right?"

"Suite 206? Got it. Excellent! I know just where it is. I'll be knocking on your door a minute or two before 9:30 Thursday morning at your office."

"Thanks so much. See you then!"

WISDOM AND ATTITUDE

Don't say too *much* about money or they will try to answer you right there on the phone. Don't say too *little* about money so as to deceive them. Remember two key phrases to strike that balance: *ministry vision* and *financial goals*. To me, this is just enough to let them know we *are* going to discuss money and giving, but not say so much about it so as to frighten them off before we ever get together!

Notice I don't ask them *if* they would like to meet. Have confidence and assume they would like to meet and hear about your ministry vision. Simply ask *which* day and time could work for them. Your attitude is contagious. They can hear it in your voice and attitude whether or not you *believe* you are going to get the appointment. If we bring a downcast, discouraged, or defeated demeanor to that call, we may come across as a beggar with our hand out, expecting to be rejected. No wonder we don't get appointments.

Instead, smile during your call. Laugh if appropriate. Give them a taste of the vision and passion and joy in the Lord and your work you possess. Let them sense you are fired up to pass this excitement on to them during your appointment. Maybe you've never even met the person you're conversing with on the call. Why not start right then enjoying them and beginning to build a friendship? The actual appointment becomes simply a continuation of two people who have really connected.

Note: Here is an excellent alternative phone script The Navigators teach their staff to use: "My first ministry assignment is to put together a team of friends who will partner with me through their prayers and financial support. As I thought about who I'd like to have on my team, I naturally thought of you. Is there a time I could come by and visit you for 45 minutes to an hour in the next week or so, so I can fill you in on all the details?"[76] I like it.

START WITH FRIENDS AND FAMILY

Before you start firing real bullets, take some practice rounds. Grab your two best friends, two of your ministry coworkers, and two of your parents' good friends that watched you grow up. Ask them each to role-play with you. Make them promise they will be brutally honest with you as you call them up and practice going through this initial phone call to secure an appointment. Listen to their suggestions. Revise your script. Practice it again and again, and a few more times! After your first full day of *real* calls, start the role-play practice sessions again in order to do further refinement and confidence building.

The first appointments you seek to make should not be with strangers. They should not be with the ultra-busy millionaire who has three layers of secretaries to get to him. Start with the people who know you and love you. But, take *every* call seriously. Do it exactly like you would with anyone. Don't skip any of the steps. These initial calls will allow you to perfect your approach. They will give you tracks to run on when you start to make the tougher calls down the road.

In approaching family members for support, use wisdom. If you sense it might damage your relationship with them or hurt your chance to share Christ with them, you might hold off for the time being and just pray they would bring the subject up.

Occasionally you will get someone on the phone who absolutely will not meet with you. Maybe they're having a bad week. Maybe they have an aversion to meetings. More than likely they have *never* had a face-to-face meeting with a missionary raising support, and there is the fear of the unknown. If after several attempts, they will not agree to meet with you, kindly inquire if they would mind you telling them about your ministry right there on the phone. Turn a potentially negative experience into a positive one. Take five minutes to share your vision and financial goals. Ask them if it makes sense and if they have questions. Ask them if they would be open to partnering with you by coming onto your monthly support team for $75, $100, or even $150 a month. At some point, zip the lip, and let them answer. No telling what God might do!

WHEN TIMES GET TOUGH

What if your attitude turns sour and you get discouraged during your support raising? How do you "shake it off" and keep going? Mike, a fully-funded staffer with our mission mobilization ministry, shares some insights: "When my wife and I raised support, we were unstoppable at times, and God was bringing everything in at an incredible rate. Other times it felt like we hit a brick wall. Some days every call resulted in an appointment, but then we would have stretches with no meetings, no new support, no returned calls. All our efforts seemed for naught, with nowhere else to go. My wife helped me understand that although these were discouraging and draining times, they were not bad or wrong. They just come with the territory."

Mike continued, "Yes, most days we did just lock ourselves in a room and plow through the work we needed to do, but we discovered just toughing it out during the dry times wasn't always the answer. Sometimes we would go before God and humbly admit our weakness and disappointment. When we opened our hearts to Him, He was always quick to cheer us up through a new gift or simply telling us, 'My grace is sufficient for you. Trust Me that I will get this accomplished.' We learned to love these hard times because they forced us to crawl up into God's lap, allow Him to see our struggles, then watch in awe as He stepped into the gap and did what we could never do alone."

This is good stuff. When it's "Go Time" and we have a low motivation level, all we have to do is make the God Ask, buckle up, and push ahead. He will honor our decision to rely on faith, rather than our feelings.

23

Building BRIDGES

Maybe I shouldn't be so transparent, but there have been times I was on my way to a meeting, or attempting to initiate conversation at a support appointment, that I was totally paralyzed with fear. I remember one time driving ten times around the block before I had enough courage to get out of the car, walk up to the house, and knock on the door. Once, I was in the office of a wealthy, high-profile lawyer-politician I was going to ask for a large annual gift. I was using my portfolio to try to hide my hands and knees — both were shaking uncontrollably! I was sure he was going to expose me by saying, "Son, do you need to use the restroom? There's one right down the hall."

The key to meeting your fears head-on is to walk toward them and never forget to make the God Ask before you ever step into that appointment. Rely on the power of the Holy Spirit and His promises in the Word. Following through on these frightening scenarios will be some of the greatest preparation for ministry and life you will experience. Don't usurp what God wants to do in your life by bailing out on some of the tougher appointments. Forget the "it's out of my comfort zone" line. Hang in

"God never uses anyone greatly until He tests them deeply."[77]

A. W. Tozer,
Author and
Evangelist

there and develop a collection of war stories you can share with other new staffers who are starting their support raising and need encouragement and modeling from you. The following are some essentials:

KNOW THE GROUND RULES

Be on time. Get directions ahead of time. Map it out on your computer or phone. Allow time for traffic, getting lost, parking, and finding the right office or café. If you tell someone you will meet at the restaurant at 12:15 p.m., don't show up at 12:20 — for *any* reason. Your appointment *might* still be there, but if they are, you will have a strike against you already. Punctuality is huge in support raising. It reveals your level of faithfulness and maturity to the person you are meeting with.

Dress appropriately. Back on campus, in your student ministry, you might wear sloppy clothing, have a lip ring, show off the tattoo on your arm, and call everyone "dude." If you're on a support appointment with a sixty-year-old couple, you would be wise to put on your khakis and a long sleeve button down. Take off the hardware, and say "Yes, sir" and "Yes, ma'am."

You might retort, "I gotta be me. I ain't changin' who I am." Instead, take a 1 Corinthians 9:19-23 approach where Paul was willing to bend and adapt himself. He shares, "I have become all things to all men" in order to try to relate and woo them to Christ. In our appointments, we need to learn when to turn the volume up and when to turn the volume down. Let's seek to always be the mature one by our willingness to adjust *ourselves* to be most effective when reaching out to others — whether it's in evangelism or support raising. Know what I mean, dude?

Work on eye contact and smiling. As one proverb tells us, "the eyes are the window to the soul." In most cultures, people appreciate you looking them in *the eyes* when you — and they — talk. When someone comes to you to present something and they will not look you in the eyes, what's going through your mind? Either they're not telling the truth, or they are fearful or insecure in what they're saying. Author Richard Moss highlights this truth, "The greatest gift you can give to another is the purity of your attention."[78] So, whether you are talking or listening — look into their eyes!

Another subtle way we reveal our insecurities is to rely too heavily on our props. Some Christian workers flip page after page of their portfolio or computer slides until their potential supporter gets bored. Have a well prepared, but brief, notebook or computer presentation to show them, but do not let it dominate *all* your time with them. Support raising is about vision and relationship, and in the appointment, it primarily needs to be your eyes on their eyes. Your heart connecting to their heart. Your smile and warmth radiating the love of Christ to them.

MEAL TIMES

Use good manners. This may seem elementary, but the way you handle yourself during a meal says a lot. Where to sit, how to sit, which utensil to use, not talking with a full mouth are all important. Let them order first, and when it's your turn don't ask for the King Neptune's Seafood Deluxe Platter! You will be doing most of the speaking. You are not there to eat. So order something small.

Again, always pay for the meal. Breaching this longstanding custom is one of the worst forms of "poor talk." Isn't it a known fact that the person who extends the invitation to go out for a meal picks up the tab? So why is this basic practice violated so often by Christian workers and support raisers? When the check comes, we make a weak attempt to reach for it, saying, "No, let me." In reality, deep down, we *want* them to pay the bill. No wonder people treat us like beggars. We have trained them to do so!

Allowing them to pay generally works against you — big time. Why? Some think taking care of your $25 lunch tab is their way of supporting you. No! This is not about a little $25 bill. This is about whether they are going to become a long-term ministry partner with you, investing $75, $150, or $300 a month in you and your work. If I sense there might be a tussle over who pays the bill, I excuse myself during the meal to use the restroom. On the way back, I take care of the tab. That especially explodes the perception high-control executive types have of Christian workers as poor and needy. This puts us on an even plane with one another. It's not the wealthy businessman doling a few of his shekels out to the guy without a job. If I read Philippians 4:17 correctly, this mealtime is actually me doing *them* a favor by helping them redirect their earthly treasure toward eternal kingdom investments.

Note that there may be a rare exception to this ground rule. For example, if you are a twenty-three-year-old girl who asked an elderly couple out for dinner to present your ministry to them, don't bust the man in the nose, fighting over the bill. That may be one of the occasions where one custom should trump another one.

RELATIONAL BRIDGES

When I sit down with someone, I don't immediately launch into my ministry presentation. I like to spend time getting to know them. Some will allow me to do that more than others, but I am going to make every attempt to begin to cultivate a relationship with this person. Here's what I do:

Look for Entry Points Into Their Lives

Upon arriving at their office or home, my antenna immediately goes up, on the look out for any pictures, trophies, pets, books, diplomas, awards, anything at all that gives me an introduction into their interests, activities, and especially their family. People love to talk about themselves. If we take a genuine interest, and know how to get the conversation going, we will be friends in no time.

Initiate Conversation Through Questions

Jesus was a master at question asking. I spent a month of quiet times in the Gospels, studying every place Jesus asked a question. Sometimes He would even answer a question with a question. We, too, must become skilled question askers. It aids us in support raising, in ministry, and in life!

Start With Closed-Ended Questions

Getting the conversation going through light, fact-oriented, closed-ended questions is where I begin. "Is this a picture of your family?" or "I see your diploma. What years were you at the University?" or "You must be a soccer coach. Do you coach some of your kids?" or "What are the names and ages of your children?" Small talk leads to big talk. Shallow questions can pave the way for deeper ones.

Move to Open-Ended Questions

You've won the right to gradually shift to more substantial, feeling-oriented, open-ended questions: "What hopes and dreams do you have for your kids?" "What dangers do they face as they grow up?" "What do you see as some of the greatest needs and problems in our world today?"

Connect Their Interests and Concerns With Your Ministry

You've asked lots of good questions. You have listened closely with your eyes, ears, and heart. You have learned all kinds of things about this person and their world. You now have enough information to gently transition to the sharing of your life and ministry. Attempt to find the common denominators between what they have revealed and you and your work. This listen first, speak second principle is from Proverbs 18:13, "He who gives an answer before he hears, it is folly and shame to him."

After asking questions, doing a lot of listening, and building rapport, it is now your turn to do most of the sharing. It will include:

- Your Personal Testimony
- Your Calling Into Ministry
- Your Ministry Vision
- The Story of a Transformed Life
- Asking for a Giving Commitment
- Closing of Appointment with Specific Next Steps

We'll cover the first two now and the others in the next two chapters.

YOUR PERSONAL TESTIMONY

"Mr. Smith, one reason I identify with the fears you mentioned for your children is because I grew up with all kinds of fear myself. Fear of dying, what others thought of me, and of being rejected. At age seventeen a man led me to faith in Jesus Christ. I realized I did not need to fear anymore because God loved me completely. He helped me conquer my fears. I get to spend my days passing those blessings on by helping other troubled teenagers overcome their fears through the love of Christ."

As you share your testimony, include three ingredients: Share what your life was like before you became a Christian. Next, the circumstances surrounding your decision to trust Christ as your Savior and Lord. Finally, include some of the changes He has wrought in your life since. I like to actually recite the brief prayer I offered up to the Lord the day I invited Him into my life. This way the person can walk away at least knowing how to receive Christ if they choose to. You never know when a support appointment may turn into an evangelistic one!

Make it short, but powerful. One young man who approached me for support went through his entire presentation with me, then asked for some feedback. Everything was great, except he spent twenty minutes on his personal testimony. He could have condensed it to two to three minutes. If I had questions or wanted him to elaborate, he could have gone deeper. With your testimony, and all of your presentation, just hit the exciting, visionary high points of your life and ministry. You could talk for hours, sharing every tiny detail, but again, once you get past twenty minutes, certainly thirty at most, you need to be winding down, transitioning to the ask, and letting them get back to their life.

YOUR CALLING INTO MINISTRY

After you have listened to portions of their life and briefly shared your personal testimony, it's now time to tie it back in to your calling into this ministry. "I praise God He led me into this ministry. Now I've come full circle. Just as my life was impacted by an inner city-worker who knocked on my door one day and led me to Christ, I get to help struggling young people start a relationship with Christ the same way."

If the person you are meeting with shared something about their life or children, you can relate it back to them. "And the hopes and dreams you shared for your own children, Mr. Smith, are the same ones God wants for these thousands of young men walking the streets of Thailand every night. They are so lost and in need of forgiveness and hope. I believe the Lord would love to use you and me to touch their lives in a powerful way."

Share when and how God stirred your heart to pursue this work, and if applicable, tie your calling into this ministry back into your testimony. This can help your supporter connect all the dots in their mind as to what and *why* you are doing what you're doing.

OTHER TIPS

Make it a dialogue, not a monologue. Make it so packed with goodies they can't help but ask a question or two along the way. It's ideal if they ask questions, but even if they don't, you still need to create a few spaces in your appointment to try to draw them out. Attempt to get the conversation going in both directions. A lazy, and sometimes condescending, question like "Does that make sense?" can be replaced by a more honoring and stimulating question like "What do *you* feel like are some of the personal problems our young people struggle with today?"

Gear your story to your audience. Know whom you are talking to. Are they a mature, long-time elder or missions' committee member? Or are they a business associate of your aunt who has never attended church? Don't assume you can use religious terminology with people. To share "We want to contextualize the gospel by planting multiplying churches among unengaged unreached people groups within the 10/40 Window" may not register with someone who doesn't have a degree in missiology! You will have to put things right down on the bottom shelf in many of your appointments. Use common language so they can grasp the basic concept of what you are about, like: "We want to help young people become whole and complete, the way God designed them to be. We want to prepare them personally, morally, and spiritually, so they can have great marriages and families, and positively affect the next generation."

It's preferred to have both husband and wife present in the appointment, but not always possible. When Nehemiah appeared before the king, he deftly observed "the queen [was] sitting beside him" (Nehemiah 2:6). Just as Nehemiah was sharing his vision and request with both husband and wife, we would be wise to try to have both spouses present. In our culture we might assume the husband is the primary decision maker. I've discovered many of the giving choices are made by the wife. Practically speaking, though, if you are trying to fill up your days and weeks with appointments, it is unrealistic to expect you can synchronize both the husband and wife's schedules for every appointment.

If you are married, sit down with your spouse and talk through what the support raising roles and expectations are for each of you *before* you get started. This will save you from some tough conversations down the road. It won't work if one spouse's attitude is, "Honey, raising support is *your* job." No, both must own it. As much as possible, team up and work together with all your heart and soul. Your supporters will observe your unity and collaboration and be impressed.

Don't ever use the phrase "one-time gift" in your presentation or materials. I know it's universally used among support raisers everywhere, but it is one of the worst things you can communicate. The phrase implies it's a once and for all, never to be repeated, contribution. Instead, use phrases like: special gift, first-time gift, single gift, launching gift… *anything* but one-time gift! Why? I believe that first gift is the beginning of a long-term, ministry partnership together.

Keep in mind support raising is not about money. It's not about you or your needs. It is about vision and relationships. The thing that means most to your prospective supporter is not your mission statement or five-year goals. It is the heart-to-heart connection you make with them as they observe your vision, passion, and authenticity. Ask good questions, listen, and seek to link their interests and concerns with your ministry. They truly would like to partner with you. Build a bridge and give them a chance to do so.

24

Sharing Your
VISION

Carol and I were maxed out. We could not financially partner with any other Christian workers. Then Marshall called. He was on his way to India to reach students for Christ and wanted to meet with me. I am impressed with *anyone* who takes the time and effort to contact and personally meet with a potential donor. It shows courage, excellence, and makes me think what they have to share must be really important.

Even though Marshall was only twenty-two, he pulled his chair up close to mine on the porch and took me through his portfolio presentation. It was filled with pictures about how he came to Christ, his campus ministry, and his burden for India. He explained how strategic it is for him to focus on winning the ten million Hindu collegians to Jesus.

As he transitioned to the ask, he leaned forward, looked into my eyes, and quietly stated, "Mr. Shadrach, it would be such an incredible honor to have you and your family partnering with me as I give myself to helping these Hindu students know the love of Christ. I wonder if you would be willing to invest $100 a month, or even $150 a month, to launch me into this ministry?" His face now less than a foot from mine, he zipped his lip. I was looking at him and he was looking at me — and waiting. It was obvious it was *my* turn to talk. He was confident and polite enough to let me answer. I was so captivated I could barely speak. I babbled out something about needing to talk to my wife first.

As soon as I got back in the house, I immediately went straight to Carol and proclaimed, "I know we can't take on any more monthly commitments, but we *must* support Marshall!" The combination of his willingness to approach an intimidating older man, his grasp of the overwhelming spiritual needs in India, and finally his up-close-and-personal invitation to join him was downright irresistible. I'm in!

Even though some might say my wife and I had reached our limit regarding the giving percentage of our income, just this past month, we joined two new support teams. We also doubled the amount we give to another missionary. We were not planning to increase our giving at all, so why did we? One simple reason. Each of these three individuals personally contacted us, persisted in getting an appointment, met with us face-to-face, and then... asked. Whether it is asking someone to receive Christ, asking them to marry you, or asking them to become a ministry partner, I believe there is always power that resides in the ask.

Yes, it can be scary to single someone out to pursue for a support appointment. It risks the relationship, and rejection is possible. To lay everything out on the table for them and then ask has a mesmerizing effect on the listener. It creates a bond of trust and respect between the "asker" and the "askee." None of this really happens by a phone call, email, letter, or group presentation. Now, in a more comprehensive way, let's break down each part of presenting the ministry vision and making the ask.

MINISTRY VISION

After building a relational bridge, and sharing your testimony and calling, transition into the sharing of your vision. It's always good to offer some context to help the listener understand the purpose and breadth of the agency you work with. Include a simple visual showing the founding, the leader, the target audience, the geographic area the organization focuses on, and a few stats of the track record of impact. This is the broader macro look at the work that will help your potential supporter understand the big picture. They will be able to see how you and your role fit in.

Major on the vision of your ministry. This is the heart and soul of your entire appointment. Pray over it, work on it, revise it, role-play it, let it sink deep into your mind and heart. Here are the six basic questions you need to address with your potential supporter. I include sample responses to these questions, using a hypothetical campus staffer as my ministry support raiser.

Why?

What is the biblical and practical rationale behind your vision?

"Second Peter 3:9 expresses the heart of God in that He doesn't wish for 'any to perish but for all to come to repentance.' Seeking and saving the lost is why Christ came. It's why we minister. Most of the almost seventeen million college students on America's 3,500 campuses are in spiritual darkness, not knowing or experiencing the love and forgiveness Jesus wants them to have. John 14:6 confirms the only way to the Father is through Jesus, and I am compelled to share the life-changing gospel message with these students, who so profoundly need truth and hope in their lives."

Who?

Who will be impacted and changed by this ministry?

"College students make up just a tiny percentage of the world's population, but in many ways, they are the most powerful slice of humanity on earth. They are and will be the leaders of every facet of society. Reaching the campus today is a key to reaching the world tomorrow. Eighteen- to twenty-five-year-olds are making the most important decisions of their life. If we can help them embrace Jesus Christ and mentor them in the right direction, it could set the course of their entire lives."

Where?

Where do they live or work?

"My assignment will be to the University of Arkansas (UA) in Fayetteville. It's a campus of 25,000 students made up of athletes, fraternity and sorority members, dorm students, internationals, and others. The one common denominator they have is they are all in desperate need of a personal relationship with Christ. That's why I'm saying no to other career options and giving myself completely to this. I want to help these students know the Lord and become sold-out disciples of Christ."

What?

What is the strategy to accomplish the vision?

"I will be spending all day, every day, in the dorms, Greek houses, Student Center, and athletic fields, meeting students. I will be building relationships, sharing the gospel, starting small-group Bible studies, and hopefully leading them to Christ. Then we will establish them in their faith and equip them to be leaders and laborers for Christ. As you know, Jesus commanded us to make disciples in Matthew 28. I want to fulfill what is on His heart right there on the UA campus."

How?

What is your goal and how will you measure success?

"We want to start a movement of students on campus and ultimately have an impactful large-group meeting in place. The real measure of success for us is how many lost students we can win to Christ, how many new Christians we can help become mature followers of Jesus, and then how many of these students we can train to start laboring themselves. If we can graduate at least ten world-changers each year who are going to spend a lifetime making disciples, we believe it makes a real difference in eternity."

You?

What is your specific role in fulfilling this vision?

"My role is as a campus staffer. I am part of a team who has made at least a three-year commitment to reaching UA. I will live near the college with a group of young fraternity guys who are involved in the ministry. My specific targets will be the Sig Ep and Lambda Chi fraternities. All together they represent about 325 of the most influential students on campus. If we can see some of these key leaders come to know Christ in a radical way, it could completely change the direction of the student body. I have to be honest, though. Sometimes it's a little scary walking into those big fraternity houses. Pray for me."

Note: I love how our Via mission mobilizers present their ministry vision in their support appointments. After taking a person through their brochure explaining the ministry, they flip it over to a blank section. The staffer then draws out a diagram showing where the unreached are in the world, and how believers can be mobilized to reach them. The potential supporter's eyes are glued to this personalized, customized presentation the staff person is crafting. Try it.

STORY OF A TRANSFORMED LIFE

As you transition to the ask, now is a great time to drop a brief anchor and insert the testimony of a person whose life has been changed by God. "May I share one story of a transformed life? Rory was one of the biggest partiers on campus. He was on the verge of becoming an alcoholic. When he finally hit bottom, he came to one of our meetings and committed his life to Christ. The turnaround was immediate and dramatic as he started sharing his testimony with everyone. He is devouring his Bible in preparation for our small group, and is even dating a Christian girl. Now many of his fraternity brothers want to know how they can experience the same new life in Christ. Will you take just a moment to watch this sixty-second video clip on my phone? It's Rory himself sharing how Jesus changed his life."

ASKING FOR A GIVING COMMITMENT

If needed, you may want to draw out the God Ask triangle, showing them your role, their role, and God's role in this appointment, giving decision, and ministry partnership. Don't wait too long, though, to make the transition to *the ask*. It is difficult for some, but it doesn't have to be. You can seamlessly move from the third person (telling about a Rory) to the first person: "Mr. Smith, there will be 3,000 freshmen, many of them lost like Rory was, who will be moving onto that UA campus on August 25th. I want to be there to reach them for Christ. But I'm not allowed to even move to my assignment until I'm at 100% support. That means I only have fifty-three days left and $1,950 more monthly support to get me to those 3,000 freshmen. Here's a chart that shows some of the various levels I'm asking our ministry partners to support. I've thought and prayed about what figure to present to you. This may be high or low, but I wanted to ask you to consider investing in me and my ministry at this $100 a month level, or possibly even at this $150 a month level. What do you think? Could one of those work for you?"

At this stage of *the ask*, they seem to always appreciate two things: 1) Giving them an idea of *what* it is I am asking them for, and 2) Zipping my lip and extending enough honor and dignity to them to allow them to answer my question. Though I may include the words "consider" or "suggest" in my ask, it's always clear, by my silence and eye contact, that I am looking for a *decision* with my question. In other words, it is obvious to all — it is *their* turn to talk!

John Maisel, Founder of East-West Ministries, shares, "Just as Satan never wants you to ask a person if they would like to pray to receive Christ, so the 'father of lies' never wants you to ask people to support you in your work of sharing the love of Christ. When we understand this, we are less likely to cut and run. God is at work and delights to use our circumstances to prove His power. We must stand against our enemy and resist the temptation to flee."[79] Yes, your throat may get dry. Your heart may start racing. Your eyes will be tempted to divert from theirs. But don't bail out. That "golden question" must be asked!

I work hard at not allowing the ask to be awkward or abrupt, making sure I have properly prepared them for my request. Thus, I like to make the person feel very comfortable in my presence, but you still must kindly, tenderly, passionately *invite* them to join your team with a specific monthly amount or a range. Then wait. They may be looking at you or your Levels of Giving Chart. Either way, they need to be given the freedom to answer without us being so insecure about a second or two of silence that we jump in to rephrase, review, or recalibrate our ask.

DEALING WITH OBJECTIONS

Be prepared for all kinds of responses to your golden question. Some of them will be easy to answer, others tougher. Here are typical ones:

"I can't give that much."

"I understand, Mr. Smith. Some of our supporters are on our team for $50 or $75 a month. Would one of those be a more comfortable fit for you right now?"

"I need to pray/talk with my spouse and/or look at my budget."

"I understand, Mr. Smith. That's very wise. Let me just take responsibility to call you back. I know you are busy, and as you can tell, I'm really focused on this. Let's see, it's Tuesday morning at 10 a.m. What if I were to call you back Thursday morning at this same time to find out how God has led you in this decision? Would that be a good time?"

"I can't make a monthly commitment."

"I understand, Mr. Smith. That's no problem. We have a number of our ministry partners who are *yearly* investors. Here's an *Annual* Levels of Giving Chart I have with me. Again, I don't know if this is high or low, but it would put so much strength into us if you would consider supporting us, possibly at this $1,000 a year figure, or maybe even this $1,500 amount. What do you think? Could one of those work for you?

"I already give to my church."

"That's great, Mr. Smith. I, too, give to my church and encourage all believers to do so. I am in no way asking you to divert any giving *away* from your church, but it would be an incredible honor to have you on our personal support team. On top of our church giving, my wife and I invest in a number of missionaries each month. I know we all have a limit as to how much we can give, and we want our funds to go to strategic ministries. I wonder if you would consider a $50 or $75 a month commitment to allow us to get to those freshmen by August 25th and reach them for Christ?"

An objection is like a yellow light. Take note, but don't let it frighten or stop you. Most people, even Christians, have never had an appointment like the one we're describing. Your appointment may make them nervous, producing all kinds of responses! You will have to calmly discern whether they are giving you a red light — meaning stop, don't go any further. Or are they simply flashing a yellow light — meaning you sensitively continue to present your vision and giving opportunity, until you get a definite "no"? Don't let fear or paranoia grip you.

WHEN YOU GET A "NO"

"I understand, Mr. Smith. I'm wondering if there are any issues or questions you have for me or about our ministry?"

"If you can't join our monthly team right now, would you be open to making a special gift to our 'Ministry Launching Fund'? We need to raise $7,500 by August 1st to move us to the campus, help us set up the office, and get our work started. Would you consider a $200, $300, or some other amount to help us launch?"

"You've been so gracious to give me thirty minutes of your time, Mr. Smith. I wonder if you would allow me to put you on my mailing list to receive our periodic newsletters? We would be honored for you to read it and pray for us."

"After you get a feel for our ministry over the next year or so, I wonder if you would give me permission to come back this time next year and visit with you again about the ministry and possible support?"

They will probably say yes to your request of putting them on your newsletter list as well as coming back in a year. Why? Because they believe once you walk out that door they will *never* hear from you again. That's probably been their experience with other Christian workers. If you actually do follow through with what you say, start sending them newsletters, writing them occasional notes, asking for periodic prayer requests, etc… guess what? By this time next year, you may have moved right to the top of their list to support if they happen to get a raise or someone drops out they've been giving to. I know of one person that responds like this to a "no": I understand you can't partner with me right now, but would you be open to possibly allowing me the privilege of being the next person you support?" Maybe I'm an eternal optimist, but I believe around the corner from almost every "no"… is a "yes!"

WHEN YOU GET A "YES"

"That's fantastic, Mr. Smith. Thank you so much. Your investment of $150 per month will make a tremendous difference. You have put us $150 closer to those freshmen coming August 15th! Please let your wife and children know how excited we are to have you as ministry partners."

"Mr. Smith, I'm wondering if you would be open to go ahead and get started so I could count your gift toward reaching my goal? I would really appreciate it. Could I show you what the giving options are and let you pick the one which most fits you?"

After welcoming them to the team and getting their giving commitment, you want to focus on the specifics. Have a graphic of some sort showing the various giving options, from writing a check right then to automatic withdrawals to online credit card options. You can pull out your laptop or smartphone, type in their information, and get them set up right then.

How you finish up the appointment is crucial. If they want to support you, but you just say, "Praise the Lord. Great to have you on the team. See you later!" you will be sorry. You must be the one who takes the initiative by confirming the exact next steps. Don't leave their home or office until you have made it extremely clear in your mind *and* theirs!

OTHER TIPS

Go back to the basics if you get confused. During appointments people will come up with crazy comments or questions. Whether intentional or not, their remarks can spin you around and cause you to lose track of what you're trying to communicate. Keep these three basics in mind as you weave your way through your ministry presentation:

- *Who you are* (This is your testimony and calling.)
- *What you do* (This is your ministry vision.)
- *What you want* (This is your ask and close.)

Make only one request at a time. This is not a multiple-choice request. Step into each appointment with the main objective of asking them to come onto your *monthly* team. If they cannot, suggest your annual team. If they cannot, suggest your ministry-launching fund. If they cannot, ask if you can come back in a year and approach them again. But only one request, one decision at a time. You never know what they are willing to do — until you ask!

There are pros and cons to using pledge or response cards. I know some support trainers encourage support raisers to use these as a "leave behind" to act as a silent reminder to the prospective donor. It will set on their desk as they ponder and pray whether they should come on your team or not. I can see their point, but it is not convincing enough to me to endorse the using of pledge cards.

My principle is simple. I don't want *anything* to do the asking for me. No substitutes. No mediators. I want to meet with them. I want to do the asking. I want to get the decision. I want to get them started on their first gift. In other words, I don't need anything to be a silent reminder. *I* want to be their *non*-silent reminder! Do I mind a Christian worker carrying an information card with them to fill out the basic data on a new donor? Of course not. That's different from a pledge card. Some organizations require their staff to include that info with the donor's first gift.

A THIRTY-MINUTE APPOINTMENT

If you have half an hour in a support appointment, how should you space your time out? Here's a suggested breakdown:

- *Connect with the heart* (12 minutes)
  Establish rapport (6 minutes)
  Bridge to their world (4 minutes)

Share your calling and testimony (2 minutes)

- *Cast the vision* (18 minutes)
Who we are — History of organization and growth of movement (3 minutes)
- *What I do* — My ministry strategy and goals, my specific role, story of a transformed life (6 minutes)
- *What I want* — Share opportunity to invest, ask for decision of amount or range (4 minutes)
- *Wrap it up* — Ask for referrals, thank them for their time (5 minutes)

（25）

Finishing
STRONG

Sarah came bouncing into my office. She was so excited. She was at 80% in only three months of support raising. I congratulated her. I even used her as an example in a training session. Then something strange happened. A few months later I received a printout from our financial supervisor. I scrolled down the monthly accounts of all our staff. Sarah received only $750 that month. A far cry from the 80% she said she was at. I called her into my office to chat. Turns out she had gotten a number of "yes" responses in her appointments, but very few of her new supporters actually began their giving. Unfortunately, Sarah's story will be your story if you think it's too pushy to ask your new donor to get started with their first gift right there in the appointment.

Don't think it's weird to come by their office or home a *second* time to pick up the first check or get them set up to give online. Otherwise, how *do* you go about getting them started giving? Praying, waiting, hoping they will send in the gift? And if they don't start after one, two, three months, what then? Here's the voice mail that an exasperated Sarah left for the supporter who had not yet begun: "Ummm, I'm sorry

The worst form of communication is assumption, followed closely by email!

to be bugging you, but you *said* you would come on my team. Why haven't you started giving yet?" Awkward! She resorted to email instead. No response.

Remember, if we find ourselves frustrated at someone because they haven't started their giving yet, don't get angry at them. Nine times out of ten it is not their fault. It is ours! *We* were the ones who were not clear enough at the end of each appointment or phone call as to what the specific next steps, including timelines, are for them to begin giving.

MAKING THE CALL

For those who need more time to give you their decision, give a certain day and time you will definitely call back. They may not be accustomed to Christian workers working hard, getting specific, following through with their commitments. Why don't you surprise them and break the stereotype in their mind? At the *exact* day and time you said you would call back, call back! Whether you "feel led" to or not, follow through faithfully. Repeat the day and specific time you will be calling back, helping them understand it is a "phone appointment," and you will be calling to get their decision. That will help them not to take your ask, your call, or their response lightly.

Brad, a new staff person who just reached 100% in four months, shared this observation: "I don't want to wait too long to call back for a decision. The more time I give them, the less sense of urgency they will have, and it becomes harder to get them back on the phone. So, call back the exact day and time you said you would!" I agree. The chances they commit to your team start nosediving if you wait beyond two to three days to call back or if you don't follow through and call when you said you would. View it as a "phone appointment" you have set up with this person. If their voice mail clicks on at the agreed upon time, keep calling back that day until you talk with them. Why? Because you both have mutually committed to a phone appointment on that day and time. And you *always* fulfill your commitments!

PERSEVERANCE TO RECONNECT

More times than not, it seems we get answering machines and people's voice mails. This is frustrating. I always continue to call until I reach them to find out their decision. Why? Because I *promised* I would. It may take two, four, six, eight calls to get hold of them. That's okay. I don't let insecurities take over my mind that they are avoiding me or screening my calls. That's why I don't mind calling back at different times of the day or night at any number I might have for them. If I can't get hold of them via phone, I don't mind stopping back by their office, home, or catching them at church, if appropriate. Why? Because I promised I would. I *always* keep my promises!

LEAVING MESSAGES

I do leave messages at times, but I never ask them to call me back. I always assume the best as to why they may not have been able to be available to take my call. I must take responsibility to call them back again — every time. There have been a couple of times over the years when, after months of calling back, I finally just said, "Mr. Smith, I'm not sure why we have not been able to connect on the phone. I promised I would call you back and wanted to be faithful. I would be honored to have you on our team. If you are able to call back and give me an indication of what you would like to do, I would appreciate it. Thanks so much." Don't be surprised if you don't hear back, though. That's okay. You did all you could do.

SCRIPT OF THE CALL

When I get them on the phone, here is what I say:
"Mr. Smith, this is Steve Shadrach. How are you doing today?
"I sure enjoyed the time with you on Thursday. Thanks again for spending it with me.
"As you remember, I promised I would call back this morning to see if you had further questions about our ministry and to find out how God has led you regarding investing in us and our ministry. Have you been able to make a decision yet?"

PURPOSE OF THE FOLLOW-UP APPOINTMENT

When a person expresses a desire to come on your team, that's when the hard part begins — *actually* getting them started! You can attempt to do this over the phone, but doing it in person is so much more effective. There are three main reasons to stop back by.

1) Secure First Gift

When I call back and get a yes, I say, "That is great, Mr. Smith. Thank you so much. Coming on our team for $100 a month will make a huge difference! Praise God."

"Mr. Smith, I'm wondering if you would be open to go ahead and get started this month so I could count your gift toward reaching my goal? I would really appreciate it. Could I come by your office or home for just five to ten minutes to show you what the giving options are? You can pick the one that works best for you. While there, I can show you how the receipting process works. When would be a good time in the next two to three days I could slip by for a few moments? How about Thursday mid-morning or Friday afternoon? Would one of those work for you? It will be brief!"

2) Show Them Receipting Process

This can be a second reason to drop by. Take a hard copy or email version of a receipt by to explain it and answer any questions.

3) Asking for referrals

If you are going to ask for referrals, the *end* of this follow-up visit is the best time to do so.

REFERRAL STRATEGY

Utilizing this approach may prepare you to become a master networker. In Nehemiah 2 the king's cupbearer wasn't exactly sure how much Artaxerxes wanted to be of help. But he was going to find out! Shrewdly, Nehemiah implemented the "domino effect" in that he first approached and secured the commitment of the most influential person, the king. He then asked Artaxerxes for endorsements and referrals. Nehemiah took those referral letters and gave them to the second most influential — the governors in the provinces. After getting yeses from first the king and the governors, it was almost a sure thing the third most influential, the manager of the lumber company, would give him all he asked.

Here's how Olga, a twenty-four-year-old Ukrainian ministry staffer, used referrals. She came to America needing to raise $2,700 in new monthly support to cover her budget, as well as two other staff. She knew no one here and had only a twenty-one-day visa. A fellow U.S. staffer gave her forty of his referrals to provide a starting point. Olga was so motivated she raised the entire $2,700 in new monthly support using *only* referrals — and referrals of referrals. True to her word, as she was exiting the U.S., she gave that staff guy forty new referrals. Let's talk about referrals:

Will You Need to Ask for Referrals?

For some support raisers, asking for referrals is unnecessary because they have hundreds of people from different stages of life who they can invite on their team. But, some will *have* to pursue a strategy of asking for referrals to get to 100%. Maybe they met with all their high-, medium-, and low-priority contacts and are still not at full funding. Asking for referrals becomes this person's only option.

Some ministries feel so strongly about referrals they ask *all* their staff to ask for referrals *every* time. Mike Hearon, a regional director for Campus Outreach, trains his staff to first ask the "golden question" in their appointments, seeking to secure a monthly commitment. But then, at the end of each meeting, he has them ask the "platinum question," the one seeking to secure a batch of referrals.

The Right Timing in Asking

If you ask for referrals, *when* you do the ask makes all the difference. When I go into an appointment, I am normally focused on asking them to become *monthly* team members. I am committed to present one request at a time and get one decision at a time. Don't say, "Yes, I'd love for you to come on my monthly team, and possibly give me names of people to contact too." No. That muddies the water. They will usually choose the least painful option if you give them multiple choices. The time to ask for referrals is *after* they have made their final giving decision, *after* they have decided on an amount. Then, and only then, do you ask about one final way they can be of help — to brainstorm for referrals.

The Right Attitude

You can really mess up when asking for referrals if you do it the wrong way or with the wrong person. Here are some tips: Expand your thinking — before you start contacting people you don't know, have you been diligent

*"The lazy let it
happen. The wise
make it happen."[80]*

*Rick Warren,
Pastor and Author*

to contact every person you *do* know? Have
you really worked hard at namestorming every
person you've ever known or even met and put
them down on your list? You will need a sense
of urgency to have a successful referral strategy.
Like Olga, are you willing to go anywhere and
talk to anyone about your ministry and coming
on your support team? Some are too proud or too lazy to do whatever it
takes to get to their ministry assignment. Asking for referrals is the key to
expanding your list and multiplying contacts exponentially.

Be positive and thankful. *Expect* to get a good response when asking
for referrals. Believe in God and that you and your ministry are worth a
significant investment. Be thankful to the Lord and to each person who
trusts you enough to give referrals to you. Treat each one with great care.
If you sense a strong negative reaction when you mention referrals, use
wisdom and sensitivity and be willing to back away.

The Right Approach

Don't just wing it when asking for referrals. Craft a script and role-play.
Get feedback and practice again. Make your first ten appointments with
people who will be favorable toward your request for referrals after they
have made their giving decisions. Whether you ask the person in the initial
appointment or whether you ask them in the shorter follow-up visit, here
is what I say.

"Mr. Smith, before I go, there may be one more very important way
you can help me. I want to quickly get to full support and my ministry
assignment, but I'm limited in the number of people I know personally in
this area. Would you take a moment to think about all the people you and
your family know? If you are open to it, I'd like to write down a few names
of people you think might share our mutual concern for the lost. I would
love to have the opportunity to sit down and share the ministry with them
as I have with you."

Help Them Think of Names

If your contact doesn't give you names, it may be they're not stonewalling
you, they just need their memory jogged. If possible, do a little advance
homework. If they are part of a church, small group, or club, you might

mention them one at a time to see if names come to their mind. For example, if they are an attorney in town, you might bring a list of other attorneys in the city to let them peruse the names. This will help uncover others in their profession they think might be open to meeting with you. If they give you names, ask if they have phone numbers and addresses available.

Enlist the Person to Advocate for You

You never know how much the individual or couple you meet is willing to do for you until you ask. As a follow-up request, Nehemiah gave the king specifics of what to include in his reference letters. Then Nehemiah held on to those letters, and *he* was the one who decided when and how they should be sent. If a person you meet with is willing to give you names, use discernment as to the most effective way to contact them. Craft an email or letter for your advocate to *individually* send out to their friends. They will obviously want to look at it, tweak it, and approve it. At the right time, when *you* are ready to follow up on those referrals, ask your advocate to send out those emails or letters to their contacts. Coordinate the timing so you can begin the follow-up calling a few days later to initiate appointments.

Triangles of Trust

Make a list of some of your close friends and associates. *After* you have met with and secured giving commitments from these individuals, make a follow-up request. Ask: "*Who* do you know well enough that they would meet with me, simply because *you* asked them to?" Those names and appointments will probably be good ones, because a triangle of trust is created whereby your friend's credibility and that relationship is now extended to you.

If you have divided your contacts into high-, medium-, and low-priority, a referral from your high category will normally be a better referral than one from your medium category. A medium will probably be more favorable than low. Prioritize them accordingly.

MAKING ASKS FROM A DISTANCE

What if someone lives so far away you can't meet with them face-to-face? Don't be the guy who reasons: "I live all the way up here in Dallas, and it's four hours of heavy traffic to Houston. I'm just going to call or email him instead." There may be an occasional isolated contact with limited resources that it may *not* be good stewardship of your time and money to go see. If so, send a personal letter or email, greeting them and sharing about your life and ministry. Give them details of your support goal and desire to invite them onto your monthly team for a certain amount or range. Include a simple brochure explaining your work. Give them a certain day you will contact them.

Once they get your information, call and catch up. Be sure they got the letter or email. Ask if they have questions. See if they have been able to pray and make a decision about joining your team. If yes, make sure you're very specific about the *exact* next steps to get them started. Ask if they can go ahead and get started that month. Inform them of the various giving options. I say something like, "Today is the 15th and you mentioned you could get started this month. That's great! I am putting a self-addressed stamped envelope in the mail tomorrow. If you can fill out your check (or other option) and put it back in the mail by the 25th, it should get to me by the 1st. If I haven't received it by the 10th of next month, something happened to it in the mail. I will call you. Thanks so much!"

NO NINE-TO-FIVE SCHEDULE

You don't clock in and clock out during this season of support raising. There may be days you start out meeting someone at 6 a.m. and don't get home that evening until 11 p.m., having had a full day of appointments. It can be a crazy schedule that has to be very flexible. Self-discipline during the support raising time is essential. Spare moments between meetings could be used to write letters or emails, setting up appointments, thank you or reminder texts, prayer, phone calls, even reading or exercise. Don't get idle for any reason. It can be a killer. Your donors will not sense that you are a man or woman on a mission. Don't neglect to insert periodic days of Sabbath rest during your support raising journey. Time to get alone with God, refocus, and refresh will be essential.

26

You Need
THE CHURCH

Lance came to the Lord in college. He began sharing his faith, making disciples, and gaining a heart for the world. Upon graduation, he got married, applied to a mission agency, and began raising his support. In addition to asking his family and friends to join his team, he also approached the church he was raised in. This was on old-fashioned church with a world map in the foyer. On it were placed the pictures of the one hundred missionaries they were supporting — each for $200 a month. They were so proud of the number of workers who had come out from their body. They were also proud of the *amount* they were giving to each.

Then, in walks Lance. He went to the missions' committee meeting held every Sunday afternoon. It was full of older men wanting to quickly wrap up the meeting so they could get to their pro football-game watching. They were all supportive of Lance and obviously going to get behind the young man who grew up there. Lance went through his presentation, but noticed the men were yawning and anxious for him to finish up. He moved rapidly to his ask by saying, "I am required to raise $4,600 of monthly support to get me to China. I want to ask you, as my home church, to come on my team for $2,300 a month — 50% of my total budget."

The moment "$2,300 a month" came out of Lance's mouth, each man's head instantly jerked up. Their eyes bulged open. They started stammering and stuttering all at once: "Well, well, yes, Lance, we, we, want to support you, but, but you know that *all* anyone ever receives is $200 a month. That, that's what we *always* give." Finally Lance was able to quiet them down and responded, "I understand, but will you *at least* pray about it?" Oops. That incited a whole new chorus of chaotic jabbering — these old guys attempting to blunt Lance's request with a bundle of reasons why it was an impossibility. At last, Lance exited the meeting. A friend on the committee later told him, "Wow, did *we* have a missions' committee meeting when you left! You rearranged the circuits of the 'we've always done it this way crowd!'"

When Lance came back the following Sunday to get their decision, the men unanimously proclaimed; "Let's do it! 50% of your budget. We'll provide $2,300 a month." Right now, you may be thinking your church would never ever be willing or able to support you at that level. Well, if Lance's "stuck in a rut" church was willing to reconsider their ancient policies, maybe yours will too. Many times, we have not because we ask not.

I challenge you to ask your home church for 20 to 50% of your total budget. What's the worst they could say? "I'm so sorry we can't do 20 to 50%, but would 15% help?" Absolutely! They will never forget the boldness you demonstrated. They will respect you for asking what no one else has ever dared to ask for. They will be open to future increases to your team, surmising you must really believe you and your ministry are a strategic investment. God may very well surprise you if you are willing to lay it all on the line by asking big. A disclaimer: Having one church take such a huge portion of your support has potential negatives. If the pastor or finances of the church change, or they decide to attach unreasonable demands to their support, it can put your team in jeopardy. So, use discernment — and keep working on increasing the number of individuals who are giving monthly.

HOW *NOT* TO RAISE SUPPORT FROM CHURCHES

The apostle Paul had local congregations investing in his work. Why shouldn't we? There's a right way and a wrong way to approach this. I have observed all kinds of desperate things Christian workers do to get to full funding. Some are unwilling to set up face-to-face appointments with individuals to ask for support. Instead they decide to try a mass appeal to churches across the country.

Missionaries spend tons of time and money preparing bulging packets filled with a cover letter, brochures, video, pledge card, and return envelope.

They confidently mail them to hundreds of churches at a time, fully believing every pastor will eagerly open, read, and immediately respond with a large gift from their missions' budget.

Not a good plan.

Some finally discover this older and more expensive form of spamming doesn't yield results and decide to take to the road instead. Believing they have the gift of public persuasion, they pile their family into a car and go from town-to-town, church-to-church,

> *Going to people you do know will almost always bear more fruit than approaching churches you don't know.*

delivering impassioned speeches about their ministry. They hope the congregations will give them large love offerings. After a year or two, those offerings have barely covered the hotel, food, gas, and car repair bills. Worst of all, they're no closer to having a solid monthly support team! What they are left with is a worn-out vehicle and a worn-out family in the process. I understand why some denominations want their workers to travel like this to spread vision to their local churches, but the wear and tear on the missionaries can be substantial.

HOW *TO* RAISE SUPPORT FROM CHURCHES

Work smarter, not harder. Let's develop a strategy for church partnerships, but don't go overboard. I know of one man who bragged to me about having one hundred churches on his team. Problem was, they were all giving only $25 a month. Some even had "strings attached" to their $25! He was expected to fly back at his own expense to their missions' conference. Another worker was required to send in extensive reports each year justifying the support he received. Still others are asked to plan and host short-term trips the church was sending to them.

Besides, how could anyone stay connected and caring for that many congregations and their leadership? Impossible. We should have a few churches on our team, but we need to be more wise and strategic as to *which* churches we ask and *how* we invite them to partner with us. Here are some ideas:

Start With Your Home Church

The place to begin is with your home church. If you don't have one, get one! But choose wisely. Yes, select one who will embrace your ministry and support requests. By the way, where's the verse that says you can only have one home church? Along with the church in which you're currently involved, what about the church you grew up in? Why can't that also be your home church? And what about the one you attended while in college, or the one you served in for ten years before you moved to your current city? These congregations are going to most likely feel the strongest about partnering with you. Please let them join you.

Share With the Pastor

Begin here. You don't want your pastor to hear secondhand about you going into ministry or raising support from his church. It's far better that he hear it directly from you — early on in the process. He may not be familiar with your organization or the concept of personal support raising. He may be one of the few people who ask to see your budget. Have it available.

Ask him what the steps are for applying to the church for support. Seek to honor him by getting his advice and guidance. If you want to get his buy-in, you'd better let him weigh in. Listen to what he tells you. Try to follow it. Coming to him first, and in a personal way, may prompt him to give you some insider information on how to approach the missions' committee for support.

Ask him which people in the church he would recommend you approach. These are going to be good names. Being able to call someone and say, "The pastor recommended I talk to you," carries a lot of weight. Years ago, my pastor responded to this request by giving me only one name — a prominent businessman I didn't know personally. As I met with him, his skepticism turned to extreme generosity when he understood the *pastor* had given me his name. Bingo!

Ask him *personally* to come on your team. This is going to be fun. Call up your pastor and request an appointment to share your ministry vision and financial goals. He is obligated to meet with you because you are one of his parishioners. Right? As you lay out your ministry vision, ask him to come on your team. He'll be confused. "You're asking to be supported by the church, right?" he will inquire with a puzzled look. "Yes, Pastor," you say. "I certainly want to approach the missions' committee to be supported by the church. Today, though, I am just talking to *you*. It would be an incredible honor, and put such an incredible strength into us, if you and your family would personally come on our monthly support team." He won't know where to take the conversation. He's been approached a hundred times by Christian workers requesting support from the church, but this is the very first time he has *ever* been asked personally like this!

It's a win-win regardless of how he responds. If he says yes and comes onto your monthly team, think how much credibility that will give you as you approach others. Even if he says he cannot, he will probably feel compelled to be an advocate for you, offering to give you names, speak to the church, and write a reference letter on your behalf.

I can't tell you how many leaders I have talked to over the years who have been local church pastors for decades and have never *once* been asked to come on a worker's personal support team. What a tragedy. Start with the senior pastor, then call up the assistant pastor, then the next one in line. Meet with each of the staff. Word will get out, "She's a comin'!" That's okay. Just do it anyway. Each of them deserves a once-in-a-lifetime experience to have this kind of appointment and opportunity to invest in a real Great Commission worker. It might just change the course of their lives.

SPEAKING TO GROUPS

Exercise self-control when asked to speak or make appeals in group settings. No doubt you'll be invited to address Sunday school classes, worship services, home groups, and evening desserts. I'm not saying turn these down, just use discernment as to *which* ones you accept and *how* you present yourself and ministry. Just because you're invited to share your support presentation with the wealthiest Sunday school class in the whole city, don't get too excited. Ellis Goldstein doesn't think asking in large groups is near as effective as one-on-one. He likes to share that often-quoted principle, "Every man's challenge is no man's challenge."[81] So, when asked to speak to groups, apply this overriding principle in all your decision-making: Don't do anything in a group that would in any way hamper you getting *individual* appointments. Cases in point:

Scenario #1: Small Group Invite

This is a Sunday school class, home group, or dessert sponsored by friends. If you choose to accept, get there early and stay late, meeting and greeting, remembering names and building rapport. When it comes time to make your presentation, don't take the whole hour and pour out your entire ministry vision. Just take five minutes to thank them, introduce yourself, the name of your ministry, and finish off with a key verse and a brief story of a transformed life who has been impacted through your ministry. All in five to ten minutes!

Then transition to, "There is so much more about our ministry vision, organization, and financial goals I would love to share. I am committed to doing that on a more personal, individual basis. I know you're busy. It would be a tremendous honor for me to be able to squeeze into your schedule for a short twenty or thirty minutes sometime soon to go more in-depth into the work the Lord has led us into."

After this you can follow up with one of two options:

1. *Pass out contact cards* — "If you don't mind, I'd like to pass out this little card to everyone. If you'd be willing to simply write your name and phone number down, I will do my very best to get back with each of you and find out when a convenient time might be to get together. I would be grateful for the opportunity." Collecting those cards, you will get back about fifteen or so from a group of thirty. Out of those fifteen you'll secure about six to seven appointments. Out of those appointments you'll gain around two to three monthly supporters and two to three special gifts. Those could turn into monthly or annual gifts in the future if you follow up correctly with them.

2. *Just contact everyone* — "I would like to do my best to get back with as many of you as possible to try to set up an appointment with you. If you don't mind I will be in touch with you this next week or the following. Thanks again." You will need to coordinate with a friend in that class or the director to get all the names and numbers of the attendees that day. Then pray, plan, and start calling!

The twenty hours you put into planning a big fundraising dessert could be used much more wisely and produce far superior amounts of faithful, ongoing support by simply having twenty one-hour appointments. There's no comparison. If your ministry does plan some kind of annual banquet, don't use it as a fundraiser as much as to meet, greet, and get their contact information. Now those one hundred banquet attendees don't just chip in their $100 to cover the meal. No, they are now going to each get an individual visit from a staff member inviting them to come on to their support team for $100 *a month*! In other words, use any group gathering you organize as a *means* to an end, not an end itself. The end?

Individual appointments. Individual asks.

Scenario #2: Church Service Invite

Resist the temptation to accept the pastor's offer to use an upfront speaking opportunity before the congregation to unveil your ministry plans and goals. Take the five-minute teaser route I previously described, then sit down. Or take the whole session, but use it to share a message from the Bible highlighting key passages revealing the heart of God for the lost. (Likewise, you could use the *whole* class time at one of the small groups previously described to give a visionary message from the Word.)

If you elect to use the small or large group invite to go ahead and present your *full* ministry vision or make an appeal, it will automatically undermine your ability to secure *individual* appointments with the majority of the people present. If afterwards you do attempt to call and meet with them personally, they'll naturally ask, "Why do we need to meet? I heard the details of your work. What else could we possibly talk about?"

Make sure every-thing you do or say in a group setting helps, not hinders, getting individual appointments.

Also, if you give the traditional announcement: "If anyone wants to know more about our ministry, we have a sign-up sheet at the back table," you will regret it. If only four people out of the 500 present sign your sheet, ethically how can you approach the other 496? And if you do, they will think, "Why are you calling me? I didn't sign your sheet!"

UNIQUE CHURCH CHALLENGES

As a former pastor, I still remember all the demands put on me by so many. Over the years I've had the privilege of interacting with thousands of different pastors from almost every denomination. My respect for them is immense. I have observed that the pressures of keeping the church and building budgets fully funded can have an effect on how a pastor interprets certain passages. That constant financial stress can influence the attitudes and approaches they develop toward parachurch ministries and support raisers.[82] Here are three challenges you may face when approaching churches:

1) Denominational Churches

Having been a pastor of a denominational church, I know the limitations that are placed on church leadership to *only* fund programs and people who are officially associated with them. I am haunted by the look of utter despair — and even betrayal — I have seen on the faces of zealous young missionaries who were going to their own home church for support only to be turned away due to their calling to a *non*denominational work. All you can do is go to the church leadership and make your case for support. If they are unable to provide funds from their budget, this may make them more willing to allow you to meet with individuals in the church.

2) Highly Structured Funding Formulas

It's encouraging many churches are specifically thinking through how they want to more strategically disperse their giving dollars. However, God does not always fit into those well-intentioned categories and percentages! As you approach your church, you may try to do research in advance to understand the breakdowns and ministries they do and don't support. When you make your presentation, seek to highlight the aspects of your ministry that fit into the kinds of work the committee is committed to funding.

3) High-Control Leadership

Some pastors seem to think it is "my church" and "my people" and "my budget." It can feel like he is building his own church, rather than Christ's. I'm sure they have good motives, but you may want to be prepared to present creative alternatives. For example, if they make you choose between accepting support from the church *or* approaching individual members, which should you choose? Always choose individuals, but I don't think you'll have to. Here's what I would say to that church leader:

"Sir, I *must* have my home church on my team. How can I possibly go to other churches or individuals and ask for support if my *own* church is not behind me? It cuts the slats right out from underneath me! But, I have another dilemma. I have all these personal relationships in the church, and they're waiting for me to come to them and include them in my support team. They'll be angry if I don't! I understand the reasoning behind your policy in that you don't want outsiders to come and use our church directory for solicitation. May I present a plan to you to see if it might be acceptable? Here is a list of the thirty-two couples in our church I am close to and that are expecting me to contact them. I promise not to approach any of our members for support outside of this list before I gain your permission first. Will that work?"

FINAL TIPS

Create and present a customized version of a Levels of Giving chart to present to churches in your time with the missions' committee. Showing them how they might fit into your "Church Anchor Donor Team" on a monthly or annual basis will vividly show them what their part to play is.

Find key advocates in various churches. You can scatter full-color ministry packets out to churches across the country, but you'll be sorely disappointed in the results. Instead, get your entire list of contacts out, pray and peruse over them, determine which of those individuals have some significant involvement and influence in their own local church. Write them a note, asking them to advocate on your behalf to key decision makers in their congregation. Take their cues as to what the steps are for partnering with them to make a request to the church. Your odds of success just went up!

Whether you realize it or not, you are one or two contacts away from hundreds of key churches across the nation. Don't base your entire support raising strategy on going from church-to-church, but having several key congregations behind you can make a real difference. The Lord has already prepared a few churches to partner with you. Your job now is to discover them!

The
GOD ASK

Section VI
NURTURE YOUR FLOCK

Life is grounded in relationships.
We must be intentional to be relational.

27

Three Laws of
GIVING

Gavin gave me the news. He was leaving our staff. It was hard to see him go. Over the last five years, he had taken a ministry from nothing to hundreds. Students converted, disciples made, laborers launched. Now he was leaving us. Did his calling change? Was the Lord transitioning him? I asked a few questions, but I was not prepared for what I was about to hear. Gavin, who had raised his support in record time, told me something that surprised me. He had lost half his original supporters over the previous few years. He won them, but he did not know how to keep or lift them.

Don't let Gavin's story become your story. Yes, pray and work hard to get to full support. Pack up all your stuff and report to your assigned city. Your relationship with your donors is strong. You're excited. They're excited. You've pumped them up about your incredible ministry, and them being a strategic member of your support team. You've promised you would be a committed ministry "partner" — praying for them, keeping them informed and involved. Yes, the expectations we create during this honeymoon period are sky high, and sometimes we fall very short in meeting them.

In the book *Raving Fans* by Blanchard and Bowles, they describe how businesses can create such satisfied customers they become raving fans of that company. The abiding loyalty produced in their clientele is so strong and lasting they would never even think about going to a competitor.[83] I began to ask the same question regarding my supporters. How can I treat them in such a way they would never want to leave my team? And when others inquired, they would always give a good report of me, my ministry, and the way I have cared for them.

What if you resolved in your heart you were going to actually *over-deliver* what you had promised to your supporters? Determine how you will honor and cherish your ministry partners in such a way they would never want to redirect their giving dollars anywhere else. Sound intriguing? Let's find out how to create "raving fans" of our supporters.

TRUE SECURITY

My uncle just shakes his head in disbelief. He is unable to grasp why I choose a seemingly small and fixed level of income to live on. He is also unable to grasp I have the most secure job on the planet! Most people believe their college degree, hard work, and the supposedly unbreakable U.S. economy will guarantee a good job and long-term stability. I've been offered several jobs during my years of living and ministering on support, many of which paid more. A lot more.

We know all security and stability comes from God, and God alone. We also know that esteemed executive position with a corner office, silver nameplate, and six-digit salary is like the fescue seed I scattered in my yard yesterday. It can vanish at the first wisp of a wind. But, I feel totally different about my support team. Do you know people who hesitate to make the jump from their secure secular job and monthly paycheck to go into full-time ministry and raise their unsecured support? Help them rethink their perspective. Taking that step may be the most stable, steady, *secure* thing they've ever done!

As for Carol and me, God has given us monthly and annual supporters who live in different parts of the country and work in various industry sectors. Similar to a stockbroker's advice, it's wise to try to develop a diversified "portfolio" team of givers, if possible. If the economy is hammering my supporters in the Northeast, my West coast givers probably are doing better and want to share. If my donors in banking need to cut back for a year or two, my partners in the energy industry may be able to pour extra funds into our account.

We have around fifty monthly partners, and about thirty or so annual or special gift donors. We have three churches on our monthly team, but they don't give a huge amount. Why do we like our team to be about this size? Well, we can get our arms around a group like that and care for them properly. Praise God, we've won them, but now we need to be faithful to keep them and lift them. Here are some principles to keep in mind.

MAINTAIN AND CULTIVATE YOUR TEAM

Once you get to 100% support, what are you supposed to do? Well, some people stagger over to their sofa, plop down, wipe the sweat from their brow and exclaim, "I'm glad *that's* over with!" No, it's just the beginning. You have simply completed the first one hundred yards of your marathon. That all-out sprint over the last two, four, six, eight, or ten months now turns into a steady long-distance race, and you need to pace yourself to stay on course.

Our focus now becomes maintaining and cultivating. "The upkeep of property or equipment" is how Webster defines maintenance. Not too exciting. But applying the concept to our donor teams, it is the "process of regularly communicating and appreciating our supporters." Webster's defines cultivation: "to prepare or loosen the soil for the raising up of crops; to foster the growth of; to improve by labor, care, and study." For our purposes, let's use the word to mean "the process of involving and building lifelong relationships with your current supporters as well as preparing others to become new ones."

Every great sports team has a good defense as well as offense. Maintenance is our *defense*. God has given us these supporters. We need to hang on to them and try to develop actual relationships with these precious partners. Don't be praying for new supporters if you haven't taken care of the ones He's given you. Cultivation is our *offense*. We need to continually be growing the quantity and quality of our flock. Our goal should be a healthier and stronger team month-by-month and year-by-year. In addition, John Patton, operations director at Via, seeks to "influence and minister to my supporters, helping them see how their investment is making an eternal impact. I like to challenge them to get personally involved, and to pray and give more."

THREE LAWS OF GIVING

Veteran fund-raiser consultant William McConkey came up with a short overview of the entire support process. He calls it winning, keeping, and lifting.[84]

- *Winning* — Up to this point we have majored on getting people on your support team. You started out asking for $100–$200–$300 per month. It's possible you had to come down a few notches to fit into a few budgets. Even if that new supporter is only able to come on for $25 or $50 a month, that's okay. At least you've got them on your team. That's a start!

- *Keeping* — Winning them to your team is just first base. Now maintaining their commitment to you and your ministry is the next stage of a healthy support team.

- *Lifting* — This is the regular cultivating of your current supporters to, at periodic intervals, increase their investment.

Let's touch on winning here, then keeping and lifting in the next two chapters.

WINNING

What are the primary motives why people joined your team? We are all different, and they invest for a variety of reasons. For some it is:

- *To be a partner in something worthwhile* — They've given to good causes, and maybe not so good ones, but see your mission and passion and realize this could be an eternal investment.

- *To participate vicariously* — They would love to be there themselves doing ministry, but feel led to stay and give and see the work accomplished *through* you.

- *To accomplish a purpose they want accomplished* — They want to see an orphanage built in Zambia or a youth ministry started at their children's high school, so they give.

- *To achieve or maintain a sense of self-worth* — This is why people give large gifts to universities or hospitals. They will leave behind a tangible legacy.

- *Because they love Christ* — They obey Him by giving to you.

- *Because they love you* — They have watched you grow up, or you have touched their child's life for Christ. These are the people closest to you.

- *To receive a blessing* — Some donors are motivated by the return. Realize this doesn't always mean a financial return, but whatever God gives back will be in abundance.

- *For financial security* — Sometimes individuals, especially those with significant resources, may make a gift to you in order to reduce their taxable income that year. They would rather give to you than the IRS.

- *A need to give* — It's an innate, built-in characteristic of human beings. Whether Christian or not, people derive joy and fulfillment in giving to others.

- *Because they were asked* — From all the studies I have seen, this is always the number-one reason people give. In so many areas of life, support raising included, we simply have not received — because we have not asked.

YOUR SUPPORTER'S GIVING PASSIONS

Spend time getting to know each of your ministry partners. Pray, think, and discern what kind of a giver they are. You will notice some unique characteristics. They will fall into one of these groups:

- *Some are starters* — They love to launch people or projects. They want to provide seed money for a new ministry or initiative. They like to get in on the ground floor of a new initiative. Approach them first. They will appreciate it — and give!

- *Some are finishers* — They enjoy the satisfaction of putting you over the top. Let them know when you get to 90% of your funding, or if you lack a final $2,500 to finish off the cost of a conference. They will jump on the opportunity to push you over the goal line.

- *Some are project oriented* — They don't care about coming on your monthly team or committing to an annual amount. They want you to lay a ministry project in front of them. Specifically pray and seek to customize it to fit their interests and giving ability. Whether it's buying Bibles for servicemen on a base or drilling a water well in Africa, these givers like to see the what, why, and how much of a particular opportunity. They give to meet the need, and move on —

waiting, of course, for the next exciting and visionary project to be handed to them!

- *Some are impulsive* — When presented with an urgent challenge, and their hearts are moved, they like to be the "go-to" guy in a pinch. They want to know about last-minute needs or emergencies you may have. If you're careful not to overuse these valued givers, they can be your "safety-valve" supporters over the long haul.

- *Some are programmed donors* — Approach them before January 1st. Once they have an amount, they are locked in for twelve straight months. I have a supporter who has not missed a month in nineteen years. He started out at $41.53 every month; increased to $76.17; later raised to $132.91. Now, after numerous increases he's at $462.52 a month. Ask them to increase *before* their fiscal year begins, and it's a done deal.

- *Some are primarily annual donors* — They like to make a once-a-year gift to your ministry. Almost always it's in December. There are definitely people you know who make extra (and sometimes significant) gifts at this time each year. For some support raisers, 30 to 40% of their total support comes in during December. This is why you must have a solid end-of-the-year asking strategy. Beginning November 1st each year, start to think and pray about whom you will be approaching in late November or early December for more substantial end-of-the-year gifts.[85]

- *Some want to use their business to bless you* — Think through individuals who own a company or practice. They may want to use their profits, products, or expertise to expand the kingdom. Ask them to partner with you and your ministry. Christian business owners around the country are sleeping giants, waiting to be awakened!

- *Some may want to be your key man or woman* — Pray over your giving list, looking for individuals who care about you and your cause. Create a clear job description how they can be of practical help to get you to full support and stay there. Set up an appointment with them and present the vision for your ministry, the need for a key man, and a job description for them. Make sure they have a good reputation in the community. Choose someone who is well-networked. It will be a huge boost to your support raising efforts.

Besides giving themselves, some of their duties can include: going on appointments with you, as well as setting up appointments and meetings for you.

ANCHOR DONOR TEAMS

Scott Morton, in his book *Funding Your Ministry,* uses the word "anchor" to describe a larger gift you would seek for a monthly or annual commitment.[86] I wanted to give it a try with my own support team. I asked my wife to run a report for me on our giving over the last thirty-six months. I wanted to see who had given a gift of $500 or more during that time. It was a broad mixture of regular, annual, and sporadic givers. These individuals would be my candidates to potentially join a new "$2,500 Annual Anchor Donor Team" my wife and I were launching.

I identified those who gave a $500 to $2,000 gift over the previous three years. I prayed over which five the Lord wanted us to ask to join this team of investors who would commit at least $2,500 a year. I contacted each of them and all five were excited, even honored, to join. I asked them which month they would like for me to contact them each year to remind them of their gift. Some of the best candidates for annual anchor donors are those who have been regular investors to your monthly team, but who also have the ability to send in a substantial annual gift too.

That was such a positive experience for us, we decided to bump it up and identify supporters who gave $2,500 to $5,000 gifts over the previous thirty-six months. I again prayed and picked out five to invite to join an even newer "$5,000 Annual Anchor Donor Team." Most said yes. They felt privileged to play such a significant role in our ministry. Prayerfully and personally going to each individual and extending an invitation to join one of these annual anchor donor teams makes all the difference. It will for you as well. Many of you may be making smaller annual asks than the levels I have listed here, some of you much larger.

Matt Burns, a missions mobilizer for us in Southeast Asia, uses this approach extensively. Functioning as his "Levels of Giving" chart, he draws out an aircraft carrier in his appointments, asking the potential donor to climb aboard with him as they together launch mission mobilization movements all over the world. He shows the role of "copilot" for one individual who is willing to invest $20,000 a year. He presents four spots for "Wing Men" who will each commit at least $10,000–15,000 annually. He shows the ten "Deck Crew" slots where supporters can join him at

$3,000–5,000 each year; and the twenty spots completing the "Fuel Team." He understands monthly commitments are a more sustainable way to put a healthy team together, but he combines the monthly asks with these substantial annual asks. Matt feels so deeply about the power of face-to-face appointments he has even flown to London and Dubai to meet with top anchor donors.

The question is, how deeply do *you* feel about it?

28

The
LOVE BANK

He met her at a wedding. She caught his eye right away. He approached her, but she was leaving for college the next week, 1,000 miles away. He got her number from her friend and called to ask her out. She said no. He continued to get to know her and asked her out again. Still no. After two years she finally said yes to a date. He planned it all out. It was perfect. Not only the first date, but many of the others. He proposed, and the two were married. Now, after a decade of marriage he still brings her flowers. He still plans and prepares all their dates. My friend's motto in marriage? Don't overpromise and *under*deliver. A great motto in marriage. A great motto in support raising!

When a new supporter comes on our team, our love bank is full of "love points." We can do no wrong. But if year-after-year all we do is make withdrawals rather than deposits in that account, at some point, it will become bankrupt. No wonder they leave our team. There is nothing left in the relationship! We've taken their money month-after-month-after-month, but have not invested anything back into their lives, families, or walk with Christ.

A disastrous ending to a bright beginning can take place, not only in marriage, but with our support team. We'll pay the consequences if we fail to exercise wisdom and foresight and spend the time to maintain and cultivate our supporters. What is it we are trying to maintain and cultivate? Relationships. Like a marriage, we need to remember it's for life. If you simply appreciate and communicate with your supporters over the long haul, they will stick with you through thick and thin, whether you are with the same organization or move to another. About 85% or more of our original supporters are still with us today.

The key is to continue making deposits in the lives of our support team. Just this past Sunday afternoon I spent two hours writing personal notes in a book I purchased for each of the husbands on our team about living radically for Christ. At the same time Carol ordered every wife a copy of Elizabeth Elliott's classic *Through Gates of Splendor*, wrote a note in each, and mailed them out. It costs time and money but it lets them know we care about them for more than just *their* money.

WHY PEOPLE QUIT GIVING

I'm referring to "lapsed donors," those who were giving regularly, but for some reason, stopped. From my informal surveys over the years, I have made some ballpark estimates. Out of every one hundred donors who dropped off:

- *Four moved away or died* — Sometimes we are unaware of a supporter who moves and quits giving. As they transition banks and finances, we need to track them down and make the necessary arrangements to keep their giving going too.

- *Fifteen decided a different organization could serve them better* — They're not unhappy with you, they just decided to give somewhere else. Personally, I don't want to give up on those people. I will continue to appreciate and involve them, and hopefully see them rejoin my team in the future. I believe once a team member, *always* a team member! This affects how I view them and treat them.

- *Fifteen are unhappy with your organization* — Out of those one hundred lapsed donors, fifteen are disgruntled for some reason. Maybe they *thought* they were coming on *your* support team, but every month they received a high-pressure appeal from the president of your organization pressing them to give to various projects. They are tired of it and want out.

- *Sixty-Six think you don't care about them anymore* — The majority, sixty-six out of those one hundred donors, quit giving because they think you have lost interest in them. And the truth is, they might be right. Ouch! Many times they stop because they haven't heard from you in months and months. On the front end, you created some expectations in their mind about this being an exciting, ongoing "partnership" with lots of communication. It really didn't turn out to be quite like you described. Overpromising, but underdelivering can ultimately ravage your team.

WHEN A DONOR LAPSES

Can you guess what most Christian workers on support do when a regular donor has missed for two, three, four months, or more? It's hard to fathom, but most do: *Absolutely nothing.* They may not be keeping good records and don't know the person has missed. Or, if they do know, they are unwilling to do anything about it. The silent treatment of just hoping or praying they will someday, somehow restore their giving is the worst way to handle it.

What do you think is going through someone's mind who has been a regular monthly giver for years, and for some reason they stopped giving, but have not heard from you for two, three, four months or more? They assume you either don't know or don't care. They begin to think their gift is insignificant or not needed. So if you have a lapsed donor, don't avoid it or go into denial, prayerfully and carefully be proactive. Take the initiative to find out why. What do you have to lose?

When one of our monthly donors misses two months in a row, I give them a phone call at the beginning of that third month, certainly no later than the fourth. When they pick up, I say, "Hi, Doug. I'm glad I got you on the line. I wanted to check on you guys. I happen to be looking over our monthly printout this morning and you had been giving like clockwork for so long, and for some reason you have missed the last two months. I got concerned about you. Is everything okay with you all?"

90% of the time they respond, "Oh, I'm sorry. We just moved." or "We just changed banks." I say, "No problem at all. Just glad you all are doing okay. Do you think you might be able to catch up? Would you be open to moving to an EFT? Most of my supporters have gone to that. It seems a lot easier for everyone." A couple of times over the years, after I've asked if everything is okay, there's a long pause and they say something like, "I really didn't want to tell you this, but Brooke and I are separated." Wow. At this point, the call is no longer about a dinky $100 monthly gift. No. This is about helping a friend salvage his marriage! My call to a lapsed donor is truly because I am more concerned about them than their money.

WRONG ATTITUDES TOWARD YOUR SUPPORTERS

What is the lens you have affixed toward your ministry partners? Are you making excuses as to why you are not able to invest yourself in staying connected and nurturing them? As you look at these four excuses, maybe you need to ask the Lord to give you an "attitude adjustment."

- *I don't have enough time* — You're busy and have major responsibilities. You have commitments to family, church, and community. How are you supposed to juggle everything with this incredible amount of support raising logistics? You may feel burned out from constantly negotiating a variety of pressure-filled obligations. I understand. But, there are some things in life we can't afford *not* to do. If the Lord has called you to this ministry, and to support raising, then it must be a priority. We will always have conflicts with time. Days will always seem short. It's a challenge to balance all these areas of life with support raising, but please learn to do it, and do it well.

- *I don't have the money* — Wrong answer. Remember what pulls the train: vision, not budget. Determine what is God's will for your life and ministry. Go raise the funds to fulfill that. Create an initial, then ongoing support raising budget to cover all travel, meals, and calling to get to 100%… and stay there! That gives you the freedom to continue to maintain and cultivate your ministry partners month-after-month, year-after-year. Build it into your budget. Don't let money *ever* be the determining factor.

- *I'm not good at keeping in touch* — "That's not my spiritual gift," one person told me. I had to laugh. I didn't know it was a spiritual gift. I thought it was just a *decision* we made. If I truly care for someone, I'll continue to take the initiative to keep in touch. Right? Apply the Golden Rule in support raising — doing to others what you would like done to you. I have to be honest. My wife and I are on a number of monthly support teams. If we treated our donors the way some of the people we support treat us, we would have lost our team long ago.

- *If they're really committed, they'll keep giving* — This is the most naïve excuse of all. You and I cannot forget about people and expect them to continue to support us. Did you know your donors were contacted this week by three different nonprofits, out of the one million in the U.S.? If *we* don't care for our supporters, someone else will! They are lining up to woo our donors away from us, *hoping* we will neglect them, so *they* can be the beneficiary of our reckless and woeful "ministry partner abandonment."

PRAY FOR YOUR SUPPORTERS

What greater form of love could you show your ministry partners than to lift them and their needs up to the Lord? This communicates to them you really do care. God will use your prayers to work in their lives, but also to spiritually bond you with them. Most likely, you are the *only* person who is interceding for them on a regular basis. As you pray,

- *Get specific requests from them* — My wife and I are experimenting with something. We are setting aside one hour a week to make calls to our supporters. We are working down a list, she to the wives and me to the husbands. We communicate three things, sometimes just leaving a voice mail: we were just thinking about you; we are so grateful for your friendship and ministry partnership; give us a couple of specifics we can pray for you about this upcoming month. All of our staff are given a half day each month to do nothing but pray. We are interceding for our families, staff, ministries, and our supporters as well. As Carol and I are prepping for our half-day of prayer together, we amass the prayer requests we have gathered via our phone calls. We sometimes send an email or text to our supporters in advance of our prayer times to collect specific requests. We pray out loud for our supporters by name, then text them telling them we lifted up their request right then! We are feeling such a deeper connection to the supporters we are praying for like this. I think the feeling is mutual.

- *Pray for passion, vision, and generous giving* — Paul prays in Ephesians that the "eyes of their heart" would be enlightened. Ask God to open their minds and change their perspective so they can clearly see and feel how God is working in and through your ministry. Ask the Lord to give each of your supporters a burden to get involved in personal ministry in *practical* ways. Ask the Lord to prosper your supporters' companies so they can give more to God's work. Ministry partners often ask me to pray for a particular meeting or potential deal that could significantly advance their company and profits. I do add them to my prayer list and specifically lift those up.

KEEPING YOUR TEAM HEALTHY AND VIBRANT

How do you keep your team stable and growing over the long haul? How do you create *raving fans* of your support team? Two tips — the first from the mind, the second from the heart.

1. *Keep accurate records* — I use a software program to track all my supporters so I can know exactly which individuals are giving annually, monthly, sporadically, or when asked. Each year I list the stakeholders in our ministry, from top to bottom. I learned the hard way not to treat everyone the same. Sometimes the greater the investment, the greater the need is to communicate. The person giving $400 a month may want to know how their investment is paying off more than the person giving $25. In order to get complete info on our new supporters, we email a "Getting to Know You" form to fill out and send back. It includes birthdays, anniversary, children's names, contact info, church, activities, and prayer requests. We put them in a notebook and intercede for them during our half days of prayer.

2. *Cultivate a heart of thankfulness* — Luke 17 describes ten lepers who were made clean by Jesus. Do you remember how many returned to offer a thank you to their Healer? One! Amazing. I'd like to *think* I would come back and express my gratitude, but it's hard to know our hearts. We must learn to consistently say "thank you." We've had staff lose their support teams and drop out of ministry because they could not bring themselves to genuinely thank their donors for their generous support.

All of us possess a basic need to be appreciated — including our supporters! Author John Maxwell concurs, "Encouragement is like oxygen to the soul."[87] A little appreciation goes a long way, and that's why I exhort all support raisers to "Thank before you bank." When you get a special gift or an increase, make it a discipline to contact your donor within forty-eight hours. In fact, I sometimes do it within thirty seconds of seeing the gift so as to capitalize on my flash of gratitude! Those are fun calls to make to my supporters.

May I tell you what most Christian workers do when they receive a new or special gift or increase? *Nothing.* Unbelievable! To do nothing is the worst thing you can do. What do you think goes through the mind of a person who sent in a new or special gift, then doesn't hear back from you after two, four, six weeks? About a year ago we sent $500 to a worker we had never given to before and whom we knew was at low support. Although we talk to him

If we are not grateful to our supporters, it's probably because we are not thankful to God.

fairly often, he has never even acknowledged the gift. Did he get it? Does he care? I don't know, but I thought, "no wonder he's at low support," if he can't even take a moment to express appreciation. He will continue to struggle because these first-time gifts really do turn out to be just that: *one-time* gifts!

If you choose this less-traveled path of truly caring for the precious people the Lord has gifted to you, you might find they will also make a choice — to walk alongside you for a lifetime. God is raising up partners to invest in you. We must thank Him. And them.

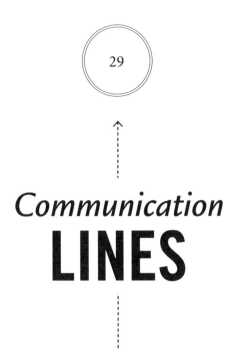

29

Communication LINES

I got it. Twice a week it came. Every week. Every month. We were supporting them as church planters, but I began to wonder if they were doing any actual ministry. Their constant emails were packed with news and pictures about their kid's activities, their weekend sightseeing trips, and the emotional ups and downs of adopting a local child. It was draining on us. I wanted to let them know we were interested and praying for them, but didn't have the heart to say, "Send fewer emails, and let us hear more about your ministry." It is important to communicate. It is more important to communicate well!

COMMIT TO COMMUNICATE REGULARLY

If we truly care about those who are sacrificing to allow us to minister, we will do what is necessary to reach out to them. Some ministries require their workers to communicate in *some* form to their supporters on a monthly basis. Whether it is a newsletter, call, card, or some other medium I would encourage you to connect with them *at least* every other month. These are the benefits:

Stronger Accountability and Loyalty

You're less likely to sleep in on Monday mornings and check out what is on the afternoon talk shows if you're required to report the fruit of your ministry to your supporters on a regular basis. Know that many of them are up at 6 a.m. every morning and working forty, fifty, sixty hours a week to earn enough to send their monthly gift to you. This has a way of creating a strong work ethic in us! Every contact you make with your supporters bonds them to you more closely. Where your treasure is, there is your heart also, and every time you make the effort to communicate with your donors, it connects your hearts more, builds loyalty, and creates a long-term allegiance.

Enjoying Your Supporters

Resolve right now you are going to *like* your ministry partners. We are commanded to *love* one another, but not like! Make up your mind not to view them as necessary evils. No, you are going to embrace your supporters, not just tolerate them, and choose to enjoy them. This is the greatest compliment you can pay anyone — that you simply *enjoy* being with them. You're not reaching out to your ministry partners because you have to, but because you *want* to. Ask the Lord to change your heart if hanging out with your supporters is not something you naturally gravitate toward.

> *"We Christians need to be into giving and receiving a lot more than buying and selling!"[88]*
>
> *Betty Barnett and Earl Pitts, Trainers with YWAM*

We've always lived right next to campus so we can minister to students and have them live with us. We currently live around the corner from the stadium. On game day we turn our yard into a parking lot. On our street, Razorback fans pay between $30 and $125 per parking spot! If we parked sixty cars we could probably clear $2,000+ per game. We decided it was worth giving up some parking revenue to rub shoulders, eat a burger, and enjoy tailgating with our supporters. We are trying to look at the big picture instead, believing God will honor placing our friendship and hospitality over short-term financial gains.

As much as you would like it, not every supporter is going to want to be your best friend or take family vacations together. As hard as you might try to bond with them, they may *just* want to give their money to you and your cause, and not get personally involved. That hurts some, but we must let the donor define the relationship. Continue to reach out and appreciate them, but you can't force it.

Welcoming Them to the Team

When someone joins your team, what do you do? Have a plan. Go through all the necessary steps to show your new supporter what the giving options are, how to get started, how the receipting works, answering any and all of their questions. You want to get all of their contact info so you can get started communicating with them. As mentioned, you can do that through a Get to Know You sheet of some kind. Send an immediate thank-you note. Why not do something special for them to communicate how excited and grateful you are to have them on the team? If there is a favorite book or CD you think will encourage your new supporter, send it with a handwritten card. Brainstorm and think of creative ways to make them feel a part.

COMMIT TO COMMUNICATE WELL

As you begin to evaluate how you are going to regularly communicate with your supporters, don't drift back to a budget-driven approach. Don't ask how *much* will it cost to send that newsletter or this gift. No, determine you will be *vision*-driven, asking what can you do that will be the most effective way to reach out to your ministry partners. Use all these avenues:

In Person

Any opportunity you have to get face-to-face with your supporters on an individual basis, take advantage of it. Schedule at least one meal or coffee per week to meet one-on-one with a different donor. No agenda beyond catching up. At the end of a year, you will have connected with fifty-two different partners. You do that enough, and I promise your supporters will begin to view themselves as not just your donor, but your friend. When you travel, make sure to give your ministry partners in those cities a call so you can meet. Most of them have *never* had a Christian worker they support ask them to get together. Don't be surprised if they are stunned by your invitation! Note: if you are overseas or have supporters who live far away, why not schedule fifteen-minute Internet-based video conversations with a different donor each week to share and catch up?

In Small Group Settings

We have traveled to cities and planned a small drop-in reception at one of our supporter's homes. We do the necessary contact work ahead of time to make sure who is coming. We've hosted a weekend "snacks and play" gathering at a local park where the adults can talk while the children play. Some host other kinds of events with success, like small desserts, or even banquets where a more formal presentation of their ministry can be shared. Some of the settings may be a perfect venue for a current donor to bring a friend, introduce them to you and the ministry, and thus provide a natural lead-in for you to follow up with a call and support appointment.

Handwritten Note

I was thinking about a particular businessman in Dallas and wrote him a postcard. I let him know I was praying for him. A few days later I received a check from him for $5,000. I, of course, immediately called to thank him. He said, "I put your card on my mirror to remind me each morning that *someone* is praying for me." A simple postcard meant that much to a prominent businessman, who has all the trappings of a successful life? We *do* live in a lonely world. I urge you to connect with people on your support team. You will be so glad you did.

Phone Call, Email, Text

With so many other things pressing, it takes commitment to communicate with your supporters regularly. When I'm on a road trip, instead of listening to the radio, I will spend the time in the car calling through the list of my supporters. During that time, I can have thirty short conversations or leave voice mails. How easy it is to simply say, "Greg! Just driving along here thinking about you and your family, and how grateful we are for your friendship, and for being a ministry partner with us. It means a lot, and puts so much strength into us. As I hang up, I will lift you all up to the Lord. Thanks again!" That took thirty seconds. It is probably the only time they've ever received a message like that from one of the Christian workers they support. How encouraged they will be.

Utilize an email service and create a template where you can send out personalized newsletters that include links, pictures, and videos. Find one that allows you to see who has opened your newsletters. Every six months, I print a list of everyone who's been opening my newsletter and circle the people who I've never approached for support. I always have a handful of new names to call for appointments!

I find myself regularly texting with my supporters, asking them to pray about a gospel appointment I am about to have with a student, or a meeting I am scheduled to speak at, or asking them for prayer requests, or a follow-up to a conversation we had about their sick teenager. The list goes on. It is quick and easy and many times they are more likely to respond to a text than a phone call.

SOCIAL MEDIA

Where does it end? Where are we going with all this technology? How can we possibly keep up? It can seem like a runaway freight train overloaded with complex technology. If you are having a hard time keeping up with all the new social media options constantly popping up, you're not alone. Netpop Research's surveys claim eighteen to thirty-four-year-olds make up 82% of all the social media users.[89] How about you? Have you embraced the social media "tsunami"? Here's a few do's and don'ts of using it for support.

> *"If you're not engaging in social media today, you're not a communicator; every individual has an online brand."[90]*
>
> Marcus Messner,
> Journalism Professor
> at VCU

- *Do* explore the different options. Ask lots of questions, experiment with a few things. See what works for you.

- *Don't* think social media is the secret to full support. It's great to initially contact someone or to keep them informed of your life and ministry along the way, but for those who are building a long-term support team, nothing substitutes the face-to-face ask. In this high-tech age, there are some times we must still insist on being high *touch*. Take the personal approach.

- *Do* utilize social media for short-term projects. There is a place for putting a Donate Here link on a web page. Quick and easy, you may get a burst of small gifts that put you over the $3,250 figure you need to get you to those Haitian orphans this summer.

- *Don't* abuse your supporters by *over*communicating. You can overwhelm your ministry partners if they constantly get messages, emails, links, videos, and blog posts from you. Get started developing a social media *strategy*, but don't let it morph into a social media *circus*!

- *Do* use social media in your individual support appointments. Instead of spending ten minutes droning on about how great your ministry is, *show* them a short testimony of a video interview of a changed life. Or click to your ministry's social media page. Let them see posts left by various couples whose marriages are being restored. We live in a very visual, storytelling world. If you can show them rather than just *tell* them what kind of eternal return on investment they'll be receiving, you will see people jump on your support team!

- *Don't* be foolish about what you post to your social media sites. If you use them to complain to the world, make political commentary, post vacation pics, just know that all your donors who are following you will see them too. Don't ever put something up that will be a stumbling block or hurt your credibility with them.

SPECIAL DAYS AND GIFTS

Remember birthdays and anniversaries. The older you grow, the fewer people remember your special days. I carry my "Important Dates" list with me everywhere I go. A week does not go by I am not calling, texting, emailing, or postcarding happy birthday or anniversary to multiple supporters. Care enough to remember your supporters' birthdays and anniversaries. Don't overlook their children, either. You take an interest in someone's child, and they will never forget you.

My wife has perfected the art of making toffee. It's delicious! Years ago we started sending some to our supporters each Christmas. Now, one hundred fifty boxes go out each December 1st. Carol will be at the stove stirring and giving directions, while the rest of us are chopping, boxing, including little notes and pictures, and rushing off to the post office. It requires a lot of time, energy, and money to pull it off, but it is well worth it. There's a man who sends in $1000 each year. He told me, "You *know* why I send in that $1,000 each year, don't you?" I said, "No. Why?" "Because of the toffee!" he spouted. I laughed and replied, "We'd still send the candy even if you didn't send the gift." "Yeah, I know," he said, "but I just wanna make sure!" He was joking, of course, but just sending that small gift was

COMMUNICATION LINES

a tangible display of our love and appreciation for him and his wife. Yes, it costs money for the ingredients and postage to send all the toffee, but his single $1,000 gift almost covers it.

NEWSLETTERS

Your supporters really do want to hear from you. If you establish healthy communication patterns with them, it will be "like cold water to a weary soul, so is good news from a distant land," according to Proverbs 25:25. Some of your ministry partners will save every single one of your newsletters. Whether you are producing hard-copy newsletters or email versions, look at what others have produced and borrow the best of the best. Let's look at the bad, then the good of newsletters. Include any of the elements below, and it will be your demise.

- *Distress signal* — Inserting a "We're going under unless *you* give!" message in your newsletter may work once, but doing it again raises huge questions about your ability to raise and manage funds. *Never do it.*

- *Hint-hint support raising* — Instead of asking others face-to-face to join your team, you slip in subtle hints in the prayer requests, hoping it will act as a subliminal message producing an instant craving to send you money! Even worse, is if you include envelopes to do "the ask" for you. The ultimate manipulation? Putting a stamp on it to guilt them into giving.

- *All family news* — As excited as you are about your son's baseball team or your daughter's ballet class, your supporters are not investing in you to find out about your kid's activities. Have a small family section periodically, but always focus on the ministry's progress and changed lives.

- *Sea of words* — A newsletter that's all text overwhelms your supporters. If it has no pictures, captions, graphics, or white space, it won't have many readers either.

- *Poor talk* — Publishing pics of the old van with 250,000 miles on it, or sharing about how neighbors gave clothes to your kids, or explaining that health insurance has gone up makes you look like beggars. It diminishes the honor and calling of your ministry role.

These bad ones normally go straight to my file folder on how *not* to do newsletters. But, if you want to create "raving fans" of your supporters, here's how:

- *Get permission* — Ask if they would like to receive a newsletter. Then they won't view it as junk mail. If they are not supporters yet, this can open the door for future appointments.

- *Insist on a standard of excellence* — A well-written, well-designed newsletter says everything about us and our ministry. This is one reason to have a very sharp person proofread it. Don't skimp on cost. A full-color newsletter increases readership 60%. It's worth it.

- *Make it all about vision* — Make sure the headlines, pictures, stories, and prayer requests stay focused on the vision of the ministry. Even in my family news section, we try to highlight my kid's ministries, not their school awards. I want my supporters to understand it's a family affair and they're getting seven for the price of one with their monthly investment!

- *Focus on changed lives* — Each newsletter should include a picture and story of a transformed life. It doesn't always have to be someone *you* led to Christ. It can be a person impacted by your organization in some way. Your supporters are making spiritual investments, and they want to see the dividends. When I receive a newsletter like this, I show it to my family to help build vision and passion in our children's hearts.

- *Keep it simple* — Put everything on the bottom shelf. Assume your supporters don't know *anything* about your ministry and it's the first time they have ever read your stuff. Don't confuse or try to impress them by using religious jargon, acronyms, or insider-speak that your staff understands — but no one else!

OTHER NEWSLETTER ESSENTIALS

- *Decide on the frequency* — Your supporters need to hear from you at least every other month. Many support raisers *only* send out email newsletters, but this is a mistake. Your emails may be caught by spam filters. Email addresses change all the time. And think about how full your own email box is. Much of the stuff you get is never opened, much less read. Commit to doing at least three to four printed newsletters each year, and fill in the rest with email versions. Social media updates can be on top of that, not replacements. Keeping us on our supporters radar means they will be more likely to continue to pray and invest.

- *Map out the themes* — Why not plan a year in advance and come up with a schedule of themes you can follow? That way, you won't be wondering at the end of each month what you should write about when it's due in three days! This past year, I interviewed a different person each month that has been impacted by our ministry. I included their story and picture in a monthly email entitled *One Life to Give*. We got some great feedback as supporters clearly saw what the return on investment was for their giving.

- *Mix in quality ingredients* — Don't start off with "We have three great Bible studies in the dorm this fall." Hook them in with excitement and suspense instead: "As I was walking through Pomfret Dorm third floor, the smell of pepperoni pizza was wafting out of the cracked door of room 338. As I poked my nose in I was astonished to see…" Whoa! Where are you going with this? Make it interesting. Write so they look forward to receiving and reading it each time. Make it a story, not just stale information.

- *Special note for admin or "behind the scenes" staff* — The fruit God raises up through your organization is also *your* fruit. Never succumb to the lie that you don't have great news to share with your supporters. Yes, it may have been one of the field staff out there who actually did the rescuing of a group of orphans in Zambia. But it was you who prayed. It was you who did all the paperwork to bring them on staff and orient them. It was you who helped design their support raising materials and helped plan their travel to Africa. It's you who provides the week-by-week communication and tools they need to stay on the field and continue to rescue orphans. You are just as essential to the overall work in Zambia as the staff on the ground.

So gather stories of changed lives from your field staff and use them in your own newsletters. Don't focus on the office news or the specifics of your job. Instead, publish the pictures and testimonies of how Christ is impacting lives. Show your supporters how their investments in you and

The purpose of newsletters is to share vision and changed lives. your organization are being incredibly multiplied, the kingdom is being expanded, and God is glorified.

Will you make a commitment now to truly care for your supporters? You've *won* them to your team, now *keep* them by communicating regularly and communicating well. You will strengthen the bond you have with each of them. If you do, they may well stick with you and your ministry team — for a lifetime!

THRIVE!

I remember the day my perspective changed. It was Scott. He had joined my support team for $100 a month. Things were going great until he lost his job with one brokerage firm and had to start over with another. During this time he wanted to meet. As I was driving to the appointment I braced myself for the news that he needed to drop off my team.

Just as we sat down he said, "I've been on your team for over two years now, and you've never asked me to increase. Not *one* single time. How come?" I was stunned. I didn't know what to say. I started stammering and muttering all kinds of *ummms* and *uhhhs*, trying to come up with some response.

Finally he broke in and emphatically said, "Well, ask me!"

I nervously replied, "OK, how about possibly, increasing, what you, um, are currently giving?"

"Well *how much* do you want me to increase?" he bellowed.

"Oh, yes, well, uh," I stalled, then timidly added, "how about maybe, uh, moving it, from say, $100 to $200 a month?"

"Well, *when* do you want me to start?" he shot back.

"Could you possibly, um, get started, this month?" I inquired.

Thinking my grilling was finished, he continued, "Well, over this past year, how many of your *other* supporters have you asked to increase?"

"Pa-past ye-year?" stretching each word out to buy me some time. "Lemme think. I've been *real* busy this year. Uhhh." It was obvious I couldn't think of *anyone*. He made me promise I would contact at least two supporters a month over the next six months and ask them to increase.

I began calling up various ministry partners who had been giving the same amount for years, whom I had never asked to increase. After catching up, I said, "You know, you guys have been on our team forever — faithfully giving $75 a month like clockwork. But in all these years I've never asked you to increase, not once. I was just wondering if you would consider giving us a raise?"

You miss 100% of the shots you never take. Translation: the answer is always no... unless you ask!

Each and every one of them burst into laughter. "Well, *of course,* we'll increase" each one affirmed. "We just thought you didn't need more support, because you *never* asked!" During each of those conversations the Lord was attempting to drill into my mind and heart again: "We *have* not... because we *ask* not." I seem to keep relearning the same lesson!

BENEFITS OF ASKING FOR INCREASES

Besides adding funds to your account, there are other benefits of periodically asking your supporters to increase. We don't ask for increases because we feel like we're being unappreciative or presumptuous by asking. If you think that, then you will project those negative feelings onto your donors. Donna Wilson with InterVarsity concurs, "Our worst fear when asking for an increase is we'll be accused of being ungrateful, but I truly believe an upgrade or increase ask is a no-lose proposition."[91] We all need to improve in this critical area. Consider these benefits:[92]

- *You have a contact with them* — Any contact you have with your supporters can enhance your relationship and connection with them.

- *You thank them* — You are visiting with them in order to ask for an increase. You will want to saturate the before, during, and after with thanking them for their current support. Creating one more opportunity to express an attitude of gratitude can't be anything but good, right?

- *You educate them* — Asking them for additional support serves to inform them that your support needs increase over time. This is logical and makes sense to them, but that fact has never crossed their minds! Many of them get cost-of-living increases in their paycheck. If they're tithing, they will increase their current giving or find new places to give. It makes sense to donors your budget also grows with the increase in cost of living, as well as expansion of your ministry plans.

- *You prepare them for future giving* — A request to increase can be a positive transaction even if the donor declines. It's usually not an issue of whether they would like to increase. Almost all of them *would* increase if they felt they had the resources. Now that you have met with them and your request for additional support is shared, it moves onto their mental list of future needs to fund. I have had ministry partners decline to increase only to do so at a later date, without being asked. Since I had previously taken the time to share the opportunity, they increased when they could. From observations over the years, most donors will not increase unless they are *asked*. Their lives are just too busy, and it never occurs to them until we enter their world and bring it to their attention!

GOOD MAINTENANCE IS THE KEY TO INCREASES

There may be supporters you can ask to increase after twelve to eighteen months of giving, but I normally like to wait closer to twenty-four months before I approach them. A lot of it has to do with your relationship with them or how well you have been communicating and thanking them. Keeping them informed and appreciated is the key to getting good responses when you ask for increases.

If you will just do the simple basics of a regular newsletter and periodic thank-you notes or calls, you will be doing more than 80% of what other support raisers do for their donors. But most organizations and individual workers thank donors impersonally, or not at all. Thank-you notes communicate you are a grateful person who values their partnership. Each year evaluate each of your current supporters. As you do, ask three questions:

1. *Who could increase this year?* If they have been giving faithfully for twelve to twenty-four months or longer and have never been asked, they are candidates. If your relationship has deepened, or they have expressed a greater interest in you or your ministry, they

are candidates for an ask even more so. If they were able to attend an event and see your ministry up close, or their income increased, these are indicators it may be time to "lift" them.

2. *How much could they increase?* Normally I ask for at least a 50 to 100% increase from what they are giving — occasionally more, occasionally less — depending upon the situation and the discernment the Lord may give me at the time.

3. *What is the best way to approach them?* Obviously, a face-to-face ask is optimum. A phone ask is next best, with or without a prior email or letter. *Only* sending an email or letter with no phone call does more harm than good. It will feel unappreciative and presumptuous to your supporter.

Over and above what they are already giving, asking for a gift to a special project can also be a way to move donors into deeper involvement. Sometimes supporters who don't feel comfortable increasing their monthly gift may be willing to give a special gift for a unique project or need.

MOTIVES ARE VITAL

Like the initial ask, the lifting ask should not be driven primarily by *need* but by *vision.* Carol and I are on many monthly support teams. When a worker asks me for an increase, I'm looking for two things:[93]

1. *Ministry fruit* — Is God's hand on this person's ministry? Is this person effective? Can he show me a track record of fruit? In other words, why should I invest further in this person's ministry if he hasn't proven faithful with the initial investment? If the person is ministering on unreached "hard soil," I will of course take this into account.

2. *Vision-driven ask* — To warrant an increase, I am looking for some new vision or a recast of the original great vision. The opposite of vision-driven asking is *need*-driven asking.

SETTING UP THE "LIFTING ASK"

Here is a sample script of what I would say in a phone call or email to set up an appointment with a current donor to ask for an increase:

"The last couple days Carol and I have been taking stock of what God has done through our church-planting ministry the past three years. It's amazing to see all the lives God has touched for His glory. As I was thinking and praying about whom I wanted to personally connect with, the Lord brought you to mind.

"I would love to be able to take you to lunch and share two things. First, I want to thank you in person and update you on the tremendous impact your generous gifts have made here. These past three years have been incredible, and I want to share with you a few of the stories. You have been so consistent to give every single month for three years, and it's been a tremendous blessing for Carol and me. Thank you for your faithfulness and investment in us!

"Second, to build upon our ministry from the last three years, we are gearing up for more expansion and impact these next three. This summer, I am raising a significant amount of new resources to fund this growing movement. I would be honored to treat you to a meal and share about our ministry vision and financial goals, and to see how the Lord might lead you. Would a Thursday or Friday lunch this week work for you? I can be flexible on the time and place."

Asking a church to increase would be very similar. You would seek to take out the pastor or missions' committee chairman — whoever the decision maker is. Share with them the ministry fruit from the *past*, and the exciting plans for the *future*… and make your ask!

ANNUAL FOCUS ON GROWING YOUR TEAM

Ask your supervisor if you could have one, two, or three weeks each year to do nothing but work on keeping your support team healthy and developing. This is not vacation time. It is hard work time! Do it during a "down time" when your ministry is not as busy. Pray and think, well in advance, in order to effectively use this annual time for three main tasks:

Maintain Current Supporters

Along with making a plethora of calls to your supporters to catch up with each other, try to schedule road trips to those areas where you have a

"100% matters because there is no comparison between 'thriving in ministry' and 'just getting by.'"[95]

Joe Michie, Creative Director at Via

concentration of ministry partners. Don't just leave messages. Get them on the phone. *Meet with them.* Pack your schedule with meals and get-togethers on an individual and small-group basis. Appreciate them. Encourage them. Fill them in on your life and ministry. In order to do that effectively, your support team can't be too big. I remember one guy bragging to me about having a team of 300 donors. That's nothing to brag about! How can you really care for a team that large?[94]

Lift Certain Current Supporters

Plan ahead. Discern which donors you are going to ask to lift, and how much of an increase you will request. Never wing it. Let them know you have prayed and thought about it. You might share, "We are asking God to provide another $1,000 in monthly support this summer before we launch our work again this August. We've been praying the Lord would give us ten of our current ministry partners who might be willing to increase their giving an average of $100 a month. Some will be able to do more, others less. We would be honored if you would consider being one of those ten. Would you be open to increasing your monthly investment in us and our work?"

Ask New Friends to Come on Your Team

Once you get to full support, some of the pressure is off. Now, when you meet someone, you can just spend time getting to know them rather than immediately feeling the need to set up a support appointment. During the twelve months after you get to full support, meet as many people as you can, build as many friendships as you can, and simply ask them if they would like to receive your newsletter. Make no requests of them beyond this. Keep an ongoing list of your new contacts. When it comes time to invite new people on your team, you might call and say, "Shelby, I am taking a break from our inner-city work next week to invite some new friends onto our support team. I have enjoyed getting to know you so much this past year. I was wondering if you would let me treat you to lunch, lay out what our ministry vision and financial goals are for this next year, and see if the Lord would want you to join in with us in some way?"

So, this annual support raising time is simply the culmination of your yearlong maintenance and cultivation efforts. You have been praying, informing, encouraging, calling, visiting, and writing your current and potential supporters for the previous twelve months. Now this one- to three-week period becomes the best and most natural time to ask your friends to come on your team for the first time or increase their current monthly or annual giving. You can do it. Set goals. Work hard. Trust God.

At this point, you may realize that support raising is an ongoing commitment and takes consistent investment of time each week. Why not consider tithing your time to your supporters? Your ministry partners work hard to give a percentage of their income to you and your work, so why don't you reciprocate by seeking to tithe your time back to them? In other words, at the end of each year, after all the dust clears, what if you had given 90% of your time to your immediate ministry, but 10% of your total time to pray for, communicate with, and encourage your support team?[96] Is that too much to ask? Not if you recognize you now have two flocks. You obviously need to shepherd your personal ministry, but don't forget about the equally needy and important group — your supporters. View them as lifelong team members and friends.

FINAL TIPS

- *Find your advocates* — Continue to evaluate all your contacts to pick out any individuals who would really want to shoulder up with you and help with your support team. There are definitely donors who are staff or lay leaders within their churches who would advocate for you if you asked them. You give them all the information they need about you and your ministry, and they would take it to the right people or committees and represent you and your support requests. Think broadly and find out if any of your ministry partners sit on a foundation board or work for a company with a charitable giving program where everything they give to you will be matched.

- *First look within to finish the job* — The additional support you need may be resident with your current team. If you are not at full support or your ministry budget has grown, consider this: When you get to the 85, 90, 95% range of completing your budget, there are individuals or churches that would be willing to increase their monthly or annual commitment. They just need to know how close you are to the finish line. In other words, you may not need to even go out and approach *new* people. Instead, focus first on identifying and asking certain *current* supporters to bump up their investment to help you get to your assignment — quickly and fully funded! At one of our seminars, Sean Vollendorf, a regional director for Student Mobilization, got excited about asking his supporters to lift. He immediately went home and began calling and meeting with various current supporters, asking them to increase. The result? $1200 in new monthly support in just one week!

- *Ask high on the front end* — During your initial support raising efforts, try to stay focused on asking for higher figures in your appointments. If the person joins your team at that amount, praise the Lord. But, even if they are not able to match your request they will always remember the amount you asked for. Many times they will increase at a later point, whether of their own initiative or because of your lifting ask. In light of your initial request, this ask for an increase will not be offensive or shocking. In many ways, it will be expected.

If you have done a good job praying for, informing, and appreciating your partners, the majority of them will be glad you came and asked for a raise. You have invested more and more in them. Now they have the privilege to reciprocate. *Winning* and *keeping* your supporters is critical. As your life, ministry, and expenses grow over the years, you'll be grateful you had a consistent, annual *lifting* strategy in place. Remember big visions require big dollars. Ask and believe God for both!

D-DAY

The date was June 6, 1944, and Hitler and his Nazi regime were threatening to take over all of Europe. The only hope to stop them appeared to be the American and British soldiers gathered in England the night before, waiting for the go-ahead to cross the English Channel for France. The jails were full of AWOL soldiers who had refused to fight or had attempted suicide. The reason? Everyone knew full well the Nazis had spent the previous two years fortifying the Normandy beaches with machine-gun bunkers, mines, and barbwire. There would be massive casualties.

At dawn, when U.S. barges carrying the soldiers got near the shore, the large loading ramps dropped open for the men to swim and run to the battle. Instead, they were instantly mowed down by the Germans. For hours virtually all of our soldiers either lay dead or paralyzed on the beaches, afraid to move into the line of constant Nazi gunfire. Some men were so frozen with fear they hid, laid down in the fetal position, and cried out for their mothers.

Finally, one shell-shocked officer mustered the courage to rally his terrified men. Colonel George Taylor stood up in the blood-red water next to Normandy Beach and yelled to his ravaged unit, "Men, there are only two kinds of soldiers on this beach; those who are dead and those who will die. Now let's move into the beach!"[97] His vision and resolve galvanized his men, and for the next five hours they made their way up the hill, climbing over dead bodies all the way, at last creating a break, through which the Allies could enter to win the battle, and ultimately the war. It was a "now-or-never" decision Taylor made. Either he aggressively took the offensive or waited for his enemies to annihilate them.

It may have been the decisive hour in all of World War II.

Just like those soldiers on that bloody June morning generations ago, we have a "now-or-never" question to ask ourselves, "Am I going to *stay* in the water, lay paralyzed on the beach, or am I going to risk everything to get up and *run* to where the battle is?" God grants us a brief window of opportunity to make our lives count. Will we waste it? Will we make excuses why we can't pursue and accomplish His plan for us? Will fear or distraction or apathy rob us of victory?

You must wrestle with and answer these questions if you are going to truly fulfill the Lord's calling in your life. Don't turn back. You will never ever regret staying the course.

Today is your D-Day — the most decisive hour of *your* life.

RUN TO THE BATTLE

You and I have an invisible enemy bent on our destruction. He's a million times more diabolical than Hitler. Satan will do *anything* to distract, disrupt, or point-blank destroy us. You are a Christ follower and full-time officer in God's army. Your current assignment is gathering the necessary resources to enter the war. You will have all kinds of obstacles. Satan will catch wind of your intentions. Your objective is to build up the kingdom of God. Because you are determined to mobilize people, prayer, and resources, all hell will break loose. The Enemy will come against you like never before. In fact, right now, "Your adversary, the devil, prowls around like a roaring lion, seeking someone to devour" (1 Peter 5:8).

As you proceed in your day-to-day support raising activities, God's will isn't always the easy, smooth route. In fact it may be just the opposite. If a door is closed, don't politely shuffle off, quietly assuming "the Lord" has shut it. No, in the name of Jesus you may need to press on, busting through obstacles, knowing we have an enemy opposing us at every turn!

REMEMBER THE GOD ASK

Get the diagram and the various roles fixed in your mind. Review and embrace the biblical truths it communicates. When in doubt, remind yourself that you are *not* just asking man to give you money. No, you are asking God Himself to go before you and direct the mind, heart, and finances of your prospective supporter. Your face-to-face appeal is not a horizontal ask, but a vertical one. When you do open your mouth to speak, understand you are simply inviting the person you are meeting with to invest in the work of God, through you. At the same time you're looking up to

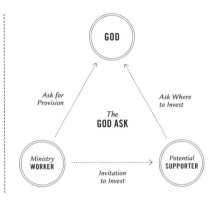

the Lord for your provision, you are encouraging your friend to ask God what their giving goals should be. The God Ask, if properly understood and applied, is a powerful experience for all three persons involved. It can truly be a beautiful triangle of trust.

THE POWER OF CHOOSING

Support raising requires you to constantly be operating in your "*dis*comfort zone." That's good for you. Unless you actually *choose* to raise support, you will never experience the full joy and blessings of having a support team. You must move from the "ought to" to the "want to" in order to discover God's *real* purpose in living and ministering from support. We learned from 1 Corinthians 9:14 it is the Lord's command that we do so. Then why are we reluctant, unwilling, or approach support raising with negative attitudes? Let's be transformed and cheerfully embrace God's will for our lives.

Has the Lord worked so deeply in your heart that you now view support raising not as an obligation, but an opportunity? Not as a problem, but a privilege? No longer a drudgery, but a delight? Know that if you are raising support because you are *required* to, you will struggle, and may not be in ministry for long. My hope is your perspective has shifted. That you have come to the point where you *choose* to go out, from scratch, and raise your entire support.

I have one final question: If you could push a magic button, and have a guaranteed monthly salary check the rest of your life, and not have to fool with all the scary, time-consuming tasks we've outlined in this book, would you push it?

Neither would I!

ENDNOTES

1. I got this from Scott Morton and The Navigators 4:10 Solution Support Raising Training Sessions in Colorado Springs, March 2000. He called it the "Fundraising Acceptance Barometer." Aptly named!
2. From an email I exchanged with Tom Stickney, Nov. 12, 2012.
3. These two stats were taken from a quote from Dr. Ralph Winter in 1985. As I give seminars around the country, I have taken the liberty of slightly increasing the number of inquirers to 20,000 because of the substantial increase in population, Christian organizations, and opportunities available.
4. From an email I exchanged with George Verwer in 2009.
5. Scott Morton, Funding Your Ministry (Colorado Springs, CO: NavPress, 2007), 5.
6. Charles Swindoll, Great Days with the Great Lives: Daily Insight from Great Lives of the Bible (Nashville, TN: Thomas Nelson Inc, 2006).
7. Edward McKendree and Harold Chadwick, E M Bounds: The Classic Collection on Prayer (Alachua, FL: Bridge Logos Foundation, 2002).
8. coSTART Manual for Support Raising by Andrew Knight, 8.
9. At the 2003, 2006, 2009 Urbana student mission conferences hosted by InterVarsity Christian Fellowship, we had BodyBuilders staffers go from booth-to-booth asking the senior leader who was present there this question. We may have made some progress because of the earlier Urbana's the average was closer to twenty-three months, while the 2009 survey revealed it was closer to eighteen months!
10. For info on how to transition from part-time to full-time support raising — and still pay all your bills — read chapter 22 of the book: ViewPoints: Fresh Perspectives on Personal Support Raising by Steve Shadrach. The chapter is entitled: Full or Part-time Support Raising: Which Approach Is Right for You?
11. Steven Furtick, Sun Stand Still: What Happens When You Dare to Ask God for the Impossible (Random House Digital Inc., 2010), 7.
12. Some support raising coaches will set up "Encourager Schedules" whereby they can affirm the support raiser for reaching different milestones. For instance, if eight months was the projected length of time to raise support:
    - If after two months, they were at 25%, they were "off to a good start."
    - If after four months, they were at 50%, they should be encouraged because it "looks like they will make it!"
    - If after six months, they were at 75% they would share with the support raiser that God has brought them this far, now it's a matter of "finishing it off." Not *if* they get to full support, only *when*!
    - If after eight months, they make it to the 100% figure, they get taken out for a steak dinner and celebration! Of course, you want to celebrate with them whenever they get to full support, whether it is ahead of (or behind!) schedule.
13. Rick Warren, Tweet, 12 August 2012, https://twitter.com/RickWarren/status/234817891684470785.
14. In February of 2006, Dr. Campolo spoke at the National Pastors' Convention in San Diego, CA. He formed his talk around a sociological study conducted with people over the age of ninety-five and shared the results. He asked the survey group: "If you

could do life over again, what would you do differently?" Most responses fell into three categories: 1) Reflect more, 2) Risk more, and 3) Do more that will live on after I'm gone.

15. John Eldredge, Dare to Desire: An Invitation to Fulfill Your Deepest Dreams (Nashville, TN: Thomas Nelson Inc, 2002).

16. Ibid.

17. Howard Hendricks — From notes of his "Christian Home" class lecture I took in fall of 1982 at Dallas Theological Seminary.

18. Ralph Blum, The Book of Runes (New York: Macmillan, 2008), 135.

19. For more extensive help on this read chapter 24 in ViewPoints.

20. Rick Warren, 10 Key Points to Remember in 2012, http://pastors.com/10-key-points-to-remember-in-2012/.

21. From a 12/05/2012 email exchange with Mark Stephens, FCA Maryland State Director.

22. Mick Ukleja and Robert Lorber, Who Are You? What Do You Want?: Four Questions That Will Change Your Life (New York: Penguin, 2009).

23. From conversations with Tim Howington, former campus staff person with Student Mobilization, now Christian businessman and disciple in Northwest Arkansas.

24. From the "Have You Made the Wonderful Discovery of the Spirit-Filled Life" booklet at www.cru.org.

25. Quote from Todd Ahrend, content editor for this book, who wrote this in his commentary on the early manuscript.

26. Scott Morton, — From lecture notes of Scott teaching at the 4:10 Solution School support raising training at Glen Eyrie, Navigators headquarters in October, 2000.

27. John C Maxwell, Tweet, 19 February 2012, https://twitter.com/JohnCMaxwell/status/171217696627761152.

28. From lecture notes of Ellis Goldstein teaching at the Campus Crusade MPD staff training in Daytona Beach, FL in February, 2000.

29. Steve Shadrach, "Asking Non-Believers for Support: Is It Wrong?" Via Generosity Newsletter (September 2007): https://viagenerosity.org/asking-non-believers-for-support-is-it-wrong/

30. Steve Shadrach, The Fuel and the Flame (Via, 2012), 102.

31. Annual studies show about 75% of giving that goes on each year in the United States is done by individuals. The other 25% is from corporations, foundations, and bequests. I would encourage you to follow that rule of thumb — make at least 75% of your team from individuals. The rest can come from churches, foundations, corporate matching funds, etc. Source is from Giving USA Foundation. More information at www.givingUSAreports.org

32. Scott Morton, Funding Your Ministry (Colorado Springs, CO: NavPress, 2007), 40.

33. Ellis Goldstein, from a personal email from Ellis in response to reading and evaluating this manuscript.

34. For more info, go to page 383 in the New International Commentary on the New Testament, Second Epistles to the Corinthians by Philip E. Hughes from Eerdmans Publishing.

35. Taken from the preaching notes of Ken Wilson, Pastor of Conway's Fellowship Bible Church. Teaching through Romans in 2004 and 2012, he included this statement as the purpose of the book on his book chart of Romans.

36. Steve Rentz, from lecture notes of Steve teaching at the Campus Crusade MPD staff training in Daytona Beach, Florida, in February, 2000.

37. From Andrew Knight's excellent coSTART support raising manual for Campus Outreach staff, page 31.

38. From a 2/27/2013 email exchange with Mike Congrove, staff member with Empower Sudan (www.empowersudan.org) who had been through one of our Bootcamps in 2005 and has been at full support since.

39. For further reading on this controversial, but important subject, get a copy of Randy Alcorn's book Money, Possessions, and Eternity. Especially note pages 181–183 on "Grace, Law, and Tithing." He believes that some people use this concept of "grace giving" I describe as an excuse to not give generously or consistently — or not at all!

40. David Platt, Radical: Taking Back Your Faith from the American Dream (New York: Random House Digital, Inc., 2010).

41. William P. Dillon, People Raising (Chicago: Moody Publishers, 1993), 60.

42. Part of the endorsement quote Ellis Goldstein provided for this book via email on 2/20/2013.

43. Andy Stanley, Visioneering: God's Blueprint for Developing and Maintaining Personal Vision (New York: Random House Digital, Inc., 2012).

44. A.W. Tozer, The Knowledge of the Holy (Fig, 1961).

45. David J. Scott, The Pebble and the Tower (Xulon Press, 2007), 201.

46. Steve Shadrach "Asking Big: Does It Offend or Affirm?" Via Generosity Newsletter (March 2006): https://viagenerosity.org/asking-big-does-it-offend-or-affirm/

47. Ron Dunn, Don't Just Stand There, Pray Something (Grand Rapids, MI: Zondervan, 2001), 38.

48. At least one of the times Jesus did this with the Twelve was just one chapter earlier in Mark 9:30-32.

49. Dan and Dave Davidson and George Verwer, God's Great Ambition (Downers Grove, IL: InterVarsity Press, 2004).

50. From www.thetravelingteam.org website of "World Christian" quotes.

51. Cleophus Jackson, Reprogram Your Mind for Success and Happiness (iUniverse, 2011), 152.

52. Some of Anderson's books: The Bondage Breaker, Victory Over the Darkness, Steps to Freedom in Christ, Who I Am in Christ, and others.

53. Neil Anderson and David Park, Ultimate Love (Eugene, OR: Harvest House, 2006), 214.

54. Albert Mehrabian, research scientist in Human Resource Development, has studied the comparative impact of our words, voice, and nonverbal communication. Words alone account for only 7% of the total communication effort. Voice inflection is 38%; nonverbal communication, like gestures, facial expressions, body language, etc. account for 55%.

55. Actually, the ten unbelieving spies were struck down in the very next chapter: Numbers 14:36.

56. Marilee Zdenek, Inventing the Future (New York: McGraw-Hill, 1988).

57. Dr. Larry Crabb and Dr. Dan Allender, Encouragement; The Key to Caring (Grand Rapids, MI: Zondervan, 1990).

58. Bill Hybels, Honest to God?: Becoming an Authentic Christian (Grand Rapids, MI: Zondervan, 1992), 140.

59. From a talk Robert Lewis gave at Little Rock's Fellowship Bible Church to lay and ministry leaders, approximately fall of 2006.

60. From Andrew Knight's excellent coSTART support raising manual for Campus Outreach staff, page 15.

61. USA Giving Foundation annual statistics of Americans' giving can be found at www.givingUSAreports.org.

62. Rick Warren, Tweet, 6 August 2012, https://twitter.com/RickWarren/

status/232675836090785793.

63. Alan was a Crown Financial Ministry staff person when he went through one of our Bootcamps. This quote is from the evaluation sheet he filled out.

64. From a 7-16-2012 email from Donna where she reviewed and commented on the manuscript of this book.

65. A recent government report found that a middle-income family will spend about $235,000 in child-related expenses from birth to age seventeen. Implication? If you are going to have a family, you better raise lots of support!

66. Scott Morton, Funding Your Ministry (Colorado Springs, CO: NavPress, 2007), 68.

67. For more information on what it means to "maximize the fruitfulness" for your family or ministry go to ViewPoints, chapter 25 entitled: "Standard of Living: What Should It Be for Christian Workers?"

68. These figures were taken from Campus Consultants President Kal Chany who wrote the book Paying for College Without Going Broke (Published by Princeton Review, 2011). I plugged my own figures in and found that if I had a newborn (in 2012) and wanted to someday fully fund my child for four years at a public university (including room and board) I would have to be setting aside $450 a month, every month, for the next eighteen years. These figures assume a 6% annual inflation rate for college costs and an 8% annual return on my investments. More info at www.campusconsultants.com.

69. According to George Barna's book Revolution published by Tyndale House Publishers in February 2006. Especially read chapter 2 about the new breed of revolutionaries attempting to become the Church Christ commissioned us to be.

70. To see various BAM models, and lay people, companies, pastors, etc. discussing and promoting BAM, go to: businessasmissionnetwork.com.

71. I recommend TntMPD, the free software program developed to aid all the Campus Crusade staff who raise their support. www.tntware.com. Download and install this fantastic tool to help you record and track all of your contact and giving information.

72. For more help on this — and the reconnecting with friends from your past, go to ViewPoints chapter 18: "How Old Friends Can Become New Supporters."

73. Support of this concept comes from various texts, including the expression "in the beginning of the gospel" (Philippians 4:15-16). It's clearly referring to Paul's first preaching of the gospel in Macedonia, about ten years before the composition of that letter. These Philippian believers were long-term supporters of Paul and his ministry as he traveled around planting churches in other regions. 2 Corinthians 11:9 describes how Silas and Timothy had come from Macedonia to Corinth to bring Paul funds provided by the Philippian church so he could transition out of part-time ministry to full-time work among the Corinthians (Acts 17:14–15). More info on pages 114-15 in Philippians: Triumph in Christ by John F. Walvoord.

74. My estimate is that well over half of the givers in America are not doing so via paper check. They are giving via Electronic Fund Transfer (EFT) which is the same as a bank draft, or going online to make their donations via credit card or debit card.

75. Stewart Levine, The Book of Agreement: 10 Essential Elements for Getting the Results You Want (San Francisco: Berrett-Koehler Publishers, 2002), 213.

76. From the Nav 4:10 Solution School training I attended in March, 2000.

77. A.W. Tozer, Root of the Righteous (Wilder Publications, Limited, 2010), Chapter 39.

78. From a May 4, 2012 tweet by author and leadership expert John Maxwell. Moss is an author and speaker (RichardMoss.com).

79. Steve Shadrach, "Front Door-Back Door: Why Do People Leave Your Organization?" Via Generosity Newsletter (April 2006), https://viagenerosity.org/front-door-back-

door-why-do-people-leave-your-organization/.

80. Rick Warren, Tweet, July 2012, https://twitter.com/rickwarren.

81. Ellis got this initally from his support raising training mentor, Steve Rentz, but is a quote that has been all over the internet for years.

82. I grew up in a denominational church, came to Christ through a parachurch ministry, was involved with both church and parachurch throughout college, attended a denominational and later a nondenominational seminary, became a college and missions pastor for years at a denominational church, then started a parachurch ministry, was an elder in planting a nondenominational church, served in all kinds of church leadership roles along the way, started and led several parachurch organizations, have consulted with hundreds of groups from both churches and parachurches, and even starting and finishing a (seven-year long!) Doctorate of Ministry track at Denver Seminary on "Church and Parachurch Executive Leadership." My conclusion is that so many of the divisions that exist between believers are man-made. My ecclesiology is fairly broad: In the eyes of God, I believe there are only two groups on the planet: those who are part of God's family, and those who are not. The Holy Spirit is seeking to mobilize one group to reach out and win the other group! For more information on this subject you might read my article: "Church and Parachurch: Friend or Foe?" at www.thetravelingteam.org/articles/church-and-para-church-friend-or-foe. Also, Dr. Ralph Winter's article on sodalities and modalities ("The Two Structures of God's Redemptive Mission" by Dr. Ralph Winter, in Perspectives on the World Christian Movement, published by William Carey Library, 2010) will shed some light on the subject. I (and the Lord!) have a great love for all believers, in all kinds of groups/identities. God yearns that we work together, show the world what unity in Christ looks like, and be openhanded, sharing all the resources He has entrusted to us.

83. Ken Blanchard and Sheldon Bowles, Raving Fans: A Revolutionary Approach to Customer Service (New York: HarperCollins, 1993).

84. Steve Shadrach, "Successful Support Raising in a Suffering Economy" Via Generosity Newsletter (December 2008), https://viagenerosity.org/successful-support-raising-in-a-suffering-economy/.

85. On average, charities receive 41% of their annual conbtributions between Thanksgiving and New Years, according to a 2011 study by Charity Navigators Holiday Giving Guide.

86. Scott Morton, Funding Your Ministry (NavPress, 2007).

87. John Maxwell, Failing Forward (Nashville: Thomas Nelson, 2007), 1.

88. Betty Barnett, Friend Raising, (YWAM Publishing, 2002).

89. Go to NetPopResearch.com reports for more info.

90. Steve Shadrach "Do's and Don'ts of Using Social Media in Support Raising" Via Generosity Newsletter (June 2011): https://viagenerosity.org/dos-and-donts-of-using-social-media-in-support-raising/

91. Donna Wilson, assistant director of development for InterVarsity, was quoting Shannon Marion, a National Field Director for IVCF.

92. This list of benefits is primarily taken from Donna Wilson and the IVCF training material she takes staff through. She is an excellent trainer and has two articles at TheGodAsk.org/Resources — "Support Raising and Your Emotions" and "Support Raising in an Increasingly Diverse World"

93. This pair of questions as well as the script to ask for an increase comes primarily from Sean Vollendorf, the regional director for Student Mobilization who got excited after one of our Personal Support Raising Bootcamps and immediately started calling his supporters for appointments in order to ask for increases. A week later he had over $1200 in new monthly support!

94. Some churches will require you to fill out extensive annual reports to continue to receive support, or travel from your field of service to their annual missions conference, or sometimes act as an adjunct staff person, taking on church responsibilities. Use discernment!

95. Taken from staff discussions within the Via organization.

96. Over the course of a year or month, when all the dust clears, you will have spent roughly 10% of your time focused on your supporters... i.e. praying for them, visiting, calling, newsletters, etc. For example, if you put in a fifty-hour week this week, then approximately five hours could be dedicated to your ministry partners in some form or fashion.

97. Steve Shadrach, "Evangelism: The Cutting Edge of Your Ministry" Campus Ministry Blog (February 2012), http://www.campusministrytoolbox.org/campus-ministry-blog/evangelism-the-cutting-edge-of-your-ministry/.

98. Grateful to Rachel Thompson and Kyle Mathews with Via for putting together this list. Excellent job!

99. Grateful to Scott Morton with The Navigators for permission to adapt some of his materials from the 2010 version of "Biblically Funding the Work of God" Navigator staff training manual.

100. Some concepts here adapted from The Navigator's Scott Morton and 4:10 Solution School support training for staff.

101. Have seen versions of this over the years from Campus Crusade and The Navigators.

102. With permission, adapted from Andrew Knight's coSTART support raising training manual.

103. Adapted from The Navigators iNFO School support raising manual, Section 7, p 33.

104. Adapted from John Patton, Operations Director at Via.

105. Some ideas here are borrowed from the MPD Accountability Covenant used by Ellis Goldstein and Campus Crusade for Christ.

ABOUT THE AUTHOR

Dr. Steve Shadrach and his family have lived and ministered on support for more than 30 years — and love it! Founder and Global Ambassador of Via (formerly the Center for Mission Mobilization), Steve is passionate about mobilizing the body of Christ to fulfill the Great Commission. As a mobilizer, Steve saw the need to empower laborers to overcome the financial hurdles keeping them from the ministry field, which led to the development of Via Generosity (formerly Support Raising Solutions) and ultimately *The God Ask*. Using Support Raising Bootcamps and resources, Steve and his team have trained over 20,000 Christian workers from more than 1,500 organizations around the world to raise their personl support.

Born and raised in Dallas, Texas, Steve received Christ at age eighteen through the ministries of Athletes in Action and Fellowship of Christian Athletes. He enrolled in the University of Arkansas in the fall of 1973, and was involved with Cru, The Navigators, and University Baptist Church during college. After graduation he attended Southwestern Baptist Theological Seminary before transferring to Dallas Theological Seminary. That spring he married Carol Vahey, also from Dallas. They moved back to Fayetteville, Arkansas in 1983, where Steve became a collegiate pastor. He and Carol had five children while living and ministering next to the University of Arkansas campus. They also began the Kaleo Summer Training Projects and brought Perspectives on the World Christian Movement to Arkansas.

In 1986, Steve transitioned off the church staff to start Student Mobilization (StuMo), a non-denominational collegiate ministry, raising financial support for the first time and serving as Executive Director. Steve and Carol and the founding staff started ministries on campuses across Arkansas, Oklahoma, Mississippi, and in Kharkov, Ukraine. In 1995, the Shadrachs spent a year in Ukraine helping establish a long-term campus ministry there, then brought home a baby girl from an orphanage to join their family. In the late 90s, Steve helped launch The Traveling Team, a collegiate missions mobilization ministry. Turning the StuMo leadership over to the next generation in 2000, Steve started Via (formerly called the Center for Mission Mobilization) to offer practical training and resources to Christian ministries, agencies, and churches around the world.

During this time, Via formed a partnership with Frontier Ventures from 2004 to 2012, which allowed Steve to continue as Executive Director of Via while also leading the Mobilization Division of Frontier Ventures, which included the Perspectives on the World Christian Movement programs globally. In 2018, Steve transitioned executive leadership of Via to Dave Rofkahr, while continuing on as Via Global Ambassador to continue writing, teaching, and advocating for Via's global efforts. Since 1986, Steve and Carol have relied upon the Lord and the faithful friends who have joined as ministry partners for their financial support, never taking a subsidy from the ministries he led. Via continues to mobilize the global church to send missionaries to the unreached.

Steve has a Masters in Biblical Studies from Dallas Theological Seminary and a Doctorate in Church and Para-Church Executive Leadership from Denver Seminary. He and Carol have five grown children, many grandchildren, and still reside near the University of Arkansas campus, where they continue to minister to college students.

Via Generosity champions biblical and relational fundraising training to Christians worldwide. We provide articles, resources, podcasts, trainings and conferences at ViaGenerosity.org. We invite you to visit us online!

Via is an international ministry helping mobilize the global church to send missionaries to the unreached. We believe equipping Great Commission workers and ministries in the area of personal support raising is a crucial component to see more laborers mobilized and sent. Visit us online at vianations.org.

Ministry Links

- ViaNations.org
- ViaGenerosity.org
- ViaChurches.org
- ViaFamilies.org
- ViaStudents.org

Other Ministry Links

- stumo.org
- thetravelingteam.org
- perspectives.org

ACKNOWLEDGMENTS

I have nowhere else to go to and no one else to go to but Jesus Christ Himself. I acknowledge Him as the centerpiece and sustainer of my life and future. I am one of the most blessed men on the planet to have my wife, Carol, and our family at my side. My wealth far surpasses any monetary value. Thanks for your patience with me as I struggled through writing this book the last five years. All the staff of the Center for Mission Mobilization are a pure joy to work with. God is at work through each of you, and all of you. I am simply hanging on for dear life! I acknowledge Scott Morton with The Navigators and Ellis Goldstein with Cru as two of my support raising training mentors. They shoot straight with me and that is my definition of friendship. A big thank you to Tim Howington, who held my feet to the fire each week to finish this book. I am so grateful for Todd Ahrend who carved this manuscript up like a Thanksgiving turkey. I call him "the Slasher" and I love him for it! Other volunteer editors who gave great input were John Patton, Christina Jerrett, Kyle Mathews, Andrew Knight, Micah May, and a host of other readers whose suggested changes were taken. I acknowledge my friend and Kenyan missionary Tom Stickney as the one who came up with the *God Ask* name for this book. At first it sounded strange, then fascinating, and finally … profound. Thanks to my trusted assistants Laura McDowell and Rachel Turner for their tireless serving. I am grateful to Joe Michie and Ian Fraiser for their ideation and creativity in crafting this book's identity. May God multiply your hard work and excellence. Appreciation goes out to Karen Pickering with BookVillages for her patient shepherding of this book through various stages. To those who publicly endorsed this book, thank you. I respect each of you immensely. To the thousands of "Bootcampers" we've had the privilege of training from ministries all over the world: I have learned more from you than you ever did from me! Lastly, to our own personal-support team: You are truly lifelong ministry partners to Carol and me. You have stuck with us, sacrificed, prayed, and made it possible to do all that we do. When we launched out to raise support in 1986, we, too, made the "The God Ask," that He would give us a team like you that would last clear into eternity. The Lord answered our prayers — big time! We are going to have one huge party together in heaven celebrating all the fruit that Jesus bore in and through us all. You will receive just as much a reward as anyone. Thank you!

Find additional resources to help kick-start your support raising journey

TheGodAsk.org/Resources

We place the essentials at your fingertips:

- Support Raising Bible Studies
- Checklist for Your First 30 Days
- Worksheets, sample scripts, tools, and resources
- Articles on support raising in communities of color and other cultures
- 5 keys to raising organizational funds from major donors
- Social media tips
- Current resources for raising personal support

For more support raising resources, visit ViaGenerosity.org